Date Due

23 '58			
NOV 1 4 1961			

Library Bureau Cat. No. 1137

A MAN
SENT FROM GOD

BY W. REGINALD WHEELER

A Book of Verse of the Great War   Editor

China and the World War

Modern Missions in Mexico

Modern Missions on the Spanish Main
  (with W. E. Browning)

The Foreign Student in America   Editor

Modern Missions in Chile and Brazil   Co-author

The Words of God in an African Forest

John E. Williams of Nanking

Jimmy: The Biography of a Brother

Mike Sweeney of The Hill   Editor

The Road to Victory (2 vols.)   Editor

Flight to Cathay

The Crisis Decade   Editor

A Man Sent from God:
  A Biography of Robert E. Speer

A MAN
SENT FROM GOD

A BIOGRAPHY OF
ROBERT E. SPEER

BY

W. REGINALD WHEELER

INTRODUCTION BY
JOHN A. MACKAY

Illustrated

FLEMING H. REVELL COMPANY

LIBRARY OF CONGRESS CATALOG CARD NUMBER: 56-5242

Westwood, N. J.—316 Third Avenue
London E. C. 4—29 Ludgate Hill
Glasgow C. 2—229 Bothwell Street

CONTENTS

CONTENTS

INTRODUCTION

John A. Mackay

I first saw Robert E. Speer in 1910. It was the year of the World Missionary Conference in Edinburgh. He came from Edinburgh to Aberdeen, where I was a student in Arts, to deliver the Duff Lectures on Missions. He was the first American that I had ever looked on in the flesh. I thought as I listened to him speak that he was the greatest man I had ever seen. After nearly forty years, during which circumstances brought me into the most intimate relationship with the man who, under God, was destined to shape my life more than any other human being, I have had no occasion to alter my youthful judgment. Robert E. Speer was the greatest personality I have ever known.

He was incomparably great as a man. To hear him open up a basic theme with his penetrating analytical mind, his structural power, his limitless illustrative resources, his impressive voice, was a liberal education. No public speaker of his generation was better read than he. Nor could any hold an audience more in thrall with riches garnered from vast fields of knowledge and made tributary to the driving passion of his life. During his years as a Board Secretary it was a usual thing for him to read some seventy-five books a year. In the freer years of his retirement he read annually at least one hundred and fifty.

His will was as strong as his intellect was clear. With buoyant zest and unruffled determination, he took in his stride difficulties that would sour or dismay most other men. A year before his death, when in his seventy-ninth year, he

9

left Princeton late one evening. He had stayed until the end of a meeting at which he presided, declining, though urged to do so, to accept hospitality for the night. He took a chance on securing hotel accommodation in New York. Failing to find lodging, he sat quietly all night reading in the Grand Central Station, enjoying the human panorama of life all about him, and taking the early morning train for his home in Lakeville, Connecticut. Only quite casually did one come to learn later what had happened.

Robert E. Speer was a great Christian missionary statesman. Speer, the Christian, was a Pauline figure among his contemporaries, a man who loved Jesus Christ with a glowing, radiant passion. Myers' "St. Paul" was one of his favorite poems through life. Christ was the center of his virile faith, the Saviour and Lord of his life, the companion of his way, the pattern of his behavior, the goal of his ardent longing. Many of his most impressive public prayers would begin with the simple words, "Lord Jesus." The new life in Christ was the ultimate reality in which he believed. Christ's missionary cause was the supreme loyalty to which he dedicated his days and years. Christ's followers were his friends, whatever their name or denominational label.

At home his ardent zeal for missions, communicated to youth with subjugating eloquence, enlisted more men and women for Christ's service than any voice in the last hundred years. He will be remembered as one of the greatest advocates for foreign missions of all time in the history of the Church Universal. Abroad, his statesmanlike vision and administrative gifts laid the foundations of churches in many parts of the world that have since come of age. With his friend, Guy Inman, he organized in 1916 the Panama Conference on Christian Work. That Conference marked the beginning of a new era in Christian missions. The Latin American world was officially brought within the purview of evangelical concern. Today, largely because of Dr. Speer's statesmanship, the evangelical Churches of Latin America constitute a growing Christian community and an ever more vital force in the Church Universal.

Life is lonelier because Robert E. Speer is gone. But our heritage of faith is richer because he dwells in memory. And on the dust of the King's Highway are fresh prints of crusading feet that summon us lesser people to follow in their trail.

"He being dead yet speaketh," and he will continue to speak "until the kingdoms of this world have become the kingdoms of our God and of his Christ."

PREFACE

W. Reginald Wheeler

Some years ago I had the privilege of accompanying Robert E. Speer on a deputation visit to the Chile Mission of the Presbyterian Church of South America. We met with the members of the Mission in Santiago. Dr. Speer had been asked to lead the devotional services of the Mission, and one day he chose for his reading the beautiful words of the first chapter of John's Gospel: "In him (the Word) was life; and the life was the light of men. The light shineth in the darkness; and the darkness overcame it not. There came a man sent from God, whose name was John."

Robert Speer spoke of the original Latin root for the English word "missions" and "missionaries," pointing out that the words meant "sent" and that missionaries were not only those who were "sent" but were truly men and women who were "sent from God." He spoke of the duty and privilege which were ours in carrying out this high mission. He closed his talk with reading John's words quoted above, translating from the Greek: "There came a man sent from God: his name John"; and then making the application, he repeated the words softly: "There came a man sent from God; his name; your name? my name?"

Robert E. Speer was in truth a man sent from God and it is as such that I would describe him in this book.

In his Introduction to this biography, John A. Mackay has written that he thought Robert E. Speer was the greatest man he had ever known.

Many of those who knew Robert E. Speer in this country

and overseas would endorse that appraisal, and would affirm that from the standpoint of nobility of spirit, dedication to high purpose, breadth of sympathy, ability with the written and spoken word, financial judgment, and administrative capacity, he was the greatest man they, too, had ever known. Shakespeare's words in "Hamlet" are true of him: "He was a man, take him for all in all; I shall not look upon his like again."

For forty-six years, Robert E. Speer was Secretary of the Board of Foreign Missions of the Presbyterian Church in the United States of America. But his career transcended that channel of denominational service. He served as President of the Foreign Missions Conference of North America, the association of the representatives of over fifty foreign mission boards in the United States and Canada; as Chairman of the Committee on Co-operation in Latin America from its organization in 1916 until his retirement in 1937; as President for a four-year term of the Federal Council of Churches in North America, the body that brings together the representatives of nearly all the Protestant churches on this continent; as Moderator of the General Assembly of the Presbyterian Church of the United States of America, 1927-1928, and as a member of the Moderatorial Council in succeeding years. He was author and editor of sixty-seven books. He was also one of the most eloquent and influential preachers and speakers of his generation. In fact and indeed, he was a Christian world statesman.

A number of futile attempts were made to persuade Robert Speer to write his autobiography or to permit someone else to write his life story. He was reminded that he himself had written and edited a dozen biographies or collections of biographical sketches of others, and that all the reasons that had led him to expend spirit and time and effort in writing and editing these books applied even more forcefully to his own career and to the need of a permanent record of his service as one of the spokesmen of his Church and the foreign mission cause throughout the world. Repeatedly the writer of this biography approached him about such a book. His reply to each request revealed both his humility and his sense of humor. "Nix on the biography," he wrote, "merely say the cuss lived; he worked; he died; there are others coming along." And in a letter written after his birthday, September 10, 1946, a little more than a year before his death he wrote:

It was a great pleasure to get your birthday greeting and to receive your letter with its affectionate but erroneous estimate of my importance. No biography for me! Living or dead! . . . "This rock shall fly from its firm base as soon as I"!!! . . . You are good to want to do such a job. Only God has some far better work for you."

This decision was maintained after Robert Speer's death, November 23, 1947, until May, 1952. Mrs. Speer has written of the developments that led to the undertaking of the writing of this book:

"Robert Speer did not want a biography. A shy person, extremely reserved, he felt as did Herbert Butterfield, the Cambridge historian, that no man could know the inside of another man's mind. While he appreciated the kindness that prompted praise, his true humility made him keenly conscious of being unworthy of it. He agreed with Kipling:

'Where there is good in that I wrought,
Thy hand compelled it, Master, Thine.
Where I have failed to meet Thy thought
I know, through Thee, the blame is mine.'

And so he repeatedly said that he did not want a biography. It was this explicit direction, both by the spoken and written word, that seemed to his family to be a final answer to the requests that came after his death for a record of his life and work.

"He read many biographies and wrote several with great care, as well as a number of biographical sketches of good men whose memory he thought should be preserved in print, but he shrank from having such a record of his own life and thought, and his family respected his wish.

"In May, 1952, however, at the meeting of the General Assembly of the Presbyterian Church, in New York, the retiring Moderator, Harrison Ray Anderson, offered the following resolution which the Assembly passed:

'That serious consideration be given to the matter of the preparation and publication of a life of Dr. Robert E. Speer in which, for the sake of present and future generations, his saintly character, exalted position and outstanding career as Christ's Servant should be sympathetically and comprehensively set forth.'

"This seemed to the family sufficient reason to reconsider the whole matter. When Reginald Wheeler, a devoted friend, a close associate in the work of the Board of Foreign Missions, and formerly a missionary in China, offered to give up all other work and devote himself to the writing of such a biography, the Assembly's resolution appeared to be a mandate to be obeyed. Therefore, the family has put at Mr. Wheeler's disposal the papers which my husband had accumulated over sixty years: diaries, notebooks, letters, records, and clippings which he had kept for his own use and for his children.

"This book, based on these sources, is sent out with the hope and prayer that it may meet a present-day need to show forth the reality of Jesus Christ as Master, Lord and Saviour, and so may 'Worthily magnify His Holy Name.' "

ACKNOWLEDGMENTS

GRATEFUL ACKNOWLEDGMENT IS MADE TO THE FOLLOWING friends of Robert Speer who have described for this book characteristic incidents in his life and service: John Alison, William R. Barbour, Eugene E. Barnett, Howard Bement, Eugene Carson Blake, John Sutherland Bonnell, Arthur J. Brown, William Adams Brown, Emile Cailliet, E. Fay Campbell, Samuel M. Cavert, Henry Sloane Coffin, Mrs. Horace C. Coleman, Edward M. Dodd, M.D., Sherwood Eddy, Boyd Edwards, Peter K. Emmons, Charles R. Erdman, Frederick L. Fagley, Galen M. Fisher, William H. Foulkes, Stanley K. Gambell, Austin Philip Guiles, William Harris, Hermann Hagedorn, W. E. Hervey, M.D., John D. Hayes, Allan V. Heely, James B. Hodgson, Stanley A. Hunter, Stuart Nye Hutchison, Samuel Guy Inman, Ernest Johnson, Adolph Keller, Fred G. Klerekoper, Kenneth S. Latourette, Charles T. Leber, John A. Lester, Henry Smith Leiper, Janet Mabie, Clarence E. Macartney, John A. Mackay, John G. Magee, William Arnot Mather, Francis J. McConnell, Margaret C. McCord, Arthur Y. Meeker, Willard C. Mellin, William Pierson Merrill, E. W. Mersereau, William M. Miller, John R. Mott, James H. Nicol, Morgan P. Noyes, Glenn Ogden, Daniel A. Poling, Walton W. Rankin, John H. Reisner, Howard L. Rubendall, T. H. P. Sailer, William P. Schell, Mabel V. Schluter, Charles Ernest Scott, George T. Scott, Thomas Sharp, William A. Shedd, Henry Knox Sherrill, T. F. Smiley, H. Alexander Smith, Emma Bailey Speer, Margaret Bailey Speer, T. Guthrie Speers, Amos Alonzo

Stagg, Clarence A. Steele, George Stewart, Anson Phelps Stokes, John Timothy Stone, John Henry Strong, J. Leighton Stuart, Frederick J. Tooker, M.D., George H. Trull, H. W. Uffelin, R. E. Vale, George Van Santvoord, Alice M. White, Mrs. John E. Williams, J. Christy Wilson, William N. Wysham.

Warm thanks are expressed to the friends who have contributed to the expense of preparing the manuscript and to the Presbyterian Department of History, to the Presbyterian Board of Foreign Missions and the office of the General Assembly for their financial aid in its publication.

Acknowledgment is made of permission to use in this volume material copyrighted by the following publishers: Fleming H. Revell Company, for quotations from books written by Robert E. Speer and listed in the text; Westminster Press, "Prayers of Robert E. Speer and Emma Bailey Speer," contained in *Five Minutes a Day*; the Board of Foreign Missions for selections from Chapter 33 by Robert E. Speer in *The Crisis Decade*.

Gratitude is due to Eugene Carson Blake, William N. Wysham, and Charles A. Anderson for their interest and influential aid; to Margaret Bailey Speer for her editorial suggestions and for the chapter on "Marriage and Family"; to my wife, Constance H. Wheeler, for her invaluable cooperation; to Louise Benesch, Margaret H. Normington, Augustine Schafer, and others, for their help in preparing the manuscript; and to Ruth Reifel for her aid in distributing the book.

The Church in this land and overseas and all friends of Robert Speer are grateful to Mrs. Speer for her assent to the request of the General Assembly that this book be prepared for publication, for writing a portion of the Preface and the chapters and sections of the book which bear her name, and for making available the rich treasures of Robert Speer's personal records and of his library for this biography.

January 1, 1956   W. REGINALD WHEELER

A MAN
SENT FROM GOD

I. His Boyhood Home

THE EARLY MORNING LIGHT FILTERED THROUGH THE LEAVES of the forest and shone on the new rifle. The boy carrying the gun moved silently, treading cautiously, like an Indian, on the damp leaves. The tall hickories, their leaves touched by the glowing hues of autumn, formed a bright canopy over his head. The boy halted, stood silent in the hardwood grove, and waited. All was still. Then a glossy black tail appeared among the leaves in a near-by hickory; the branches undulated and tossed; a hickory nut ripped through the leaves and struck the ground below with a sharp spat. The black squirrel barked excitedly. Other squirrels, gray and black, appeared in neighboring branches at work on the rich treasure of the trees.

The boy looked longingly at the squirrels, but he did not lift his rifle. He was after larger game. On the previous day he had seen a flock of wild turkeys feeding near the grove; he had made a turkey caller, fashioned from a turkey's wing; he seated himself in the protecting angle of an old rail fence; then, with great care, he sent out a succession of liquid notes, rising and falling, from the turkey caller held between his lips. Again and again he called; he was about to stand up and follow the squirrels, which were still at work in the hardwoods, when he saw the dark, ungainly form of a wild turkey come slowly from an adjoining field. The boy's heart beat fast as he repeated the call. Unsuspecting, the game bird moved nearer, and answered the seductive notes from the grove. The boy leveled the rifle, took steady aim, fired; and the prize was his!

21

Throwing the turkey over his shoulder, he strode happily home. His father, Congressman from the district, was in his office, talking to a visitor. When he had given the rifle to his son in his twelfth year, and the boy had promised him a wild turkey, the father had spoken with doubt concerning such an achievement. The boy knocked at the door, entered, and proudly displayed the prize of the new rifle. "Well done, Robert," said Congressman Speer to his son; and thus was initiated the long series of expeditions with gun and fishing rod along the streams and in the forests and the wooded valleys of the "mortal sweet hills of Pennsylvania."

Robert E. Speer's life is best understood when seen from the background of his boyhood. He was born in Huntingdon, Pennsylvania, a town named for Elizabeth, Countess of Huntingdon, and built on the site of Fort Standing Stone, one of the chain of forts spread across the Alleghenies to hold the French and Indians at bay. A replica of this original stone stands close to the house where Robert Speer grew up.

The feeling of the frontier was ingrained in the life of the town. The main line of the Pennsylvania Railroad connects Huntingdon with the cities to the east and the west and modern highways now bisect the state, but in Robert Speer's boyhood one had only to go a few miles north or south of the railroad to find oneself in almost primeval forests, with turkey, deer, and trout in abundance. Even now, when the highways cut through these forests, one still feels that primeval peace and strength.

This little town, with its frontier traditions, where every man had his gun and could hunt over a wide domain, was Robert E. Speer's home. Its people were individualistic, picturesque and strong, ranging widely from "Shackle-bony Chris," the vagabond, to the dignified judges, lawyers, and clergymen, who were his father's associates. The Presbyterian Church fostered high standards and unquestioning obedience to the Word and Law of God as understood by the Church.

His father's law office, next to his home, and the County Court House across the street, stood for intellectual discipline, honor and responsible citizenship. In this law office, the sons of Robert Milton Speer heard politics and history, the affairs of the community and of the nation, discussed by the men who were the strong nails holding together its economic and political structure. The law had always seemed to the Speer boys the natural course of ambition, and to be on the bench of the Supreme Court of the nation the highest of all attainments. In this law office local land titles were discussed, as were electoral districts for state and Federal representation, national policies and politics, murderers were prosecuted, and libel laws studied. Those who came to this office were a true cross-section of the life of the community.

When Robert E. Speer was nine, his mother Martha McMurtrie Speer, died, leaving five children: two daughters and three sons, of whom Robert was the second. His father did not marry again, and an aunt of his wife's came to keep house until Mary, the older daughter, could take over. One fancies that this great-aunt did not have an easy time with five vigorous, intelligent, strong-willed children to care for.

The first school for the Speer children was a "Dame School"; then came the public school, simple but thorough, exacting and democratic, laying strong foundations for the years at Andover and Princeton. But, above all, was their father's training in integrity, clear thinking, and public speaking, so that Robert grew up into a man who displayed the characteristics of courage and loyalty of a modern "Mr. Valiant for Truth."

The early death of his mother made the sensitive nine-year-old boy shy and deeply reserved. Inevitably he had to fight his own battles of wit and sinew with vigorous brothers and sisters, and this increased the natural reserve of his Scotch-Irish temperament; to talk of himself and his feelings was impossible for him. Ideas pent up at this time later found a clear channel in his lectures and preaching.

Hunting was a joy, and fishing was an even greater delight. Boys walked long distances in those days, with a lift now and then in a farm wagon. The trout streams, the thickets of rhododendron and laurel, the intimacies with nature in its secret recesses, all that he loved best, Robert found later expressed in Annie Trumbull Slosson's classic, *Fishin' Jimmy*. This out-of-door life, encouraged by his father, turned a delicate child into a man of extraordinary vigor and strength. An attack of erysipelas when he was ten was his only serious illness of childhood. His only other illnesses, until he underwent a major operation at the age of seventy-seven, were typhoid fever, suffered in Persia in 1897, and a bad turn of malaria after he had left China that same year.

Thus from his boyhood home in Penn's Woods Robert E. Speer drew stamina and endurance that served him well through his long and arduous career in his own country and overseas. "The strength of the hills was his also"; he grew into a "man as stiff as a Pennsylvania white pine and as clear as the spring beneath it."

II. His Ancestry and Background

ROBERT ELLIOTT SPEER WAS BORN IN Huntingdon, Pennsylvania, September 10, 1867. He came of old American stock, English and Scotch-Irish, and Swiss. All his ancestral roots were struck in the soil of Pennsylvania and in the religious tradition and temper of the Scotch-Irish Presbyterians; these two loyalties of State and religion ran vigorously in his blood.[1]

His great, great, great, great-grandfather was Henry Carpenter (Heinrich Zimmerman) who came to America from the Canton of Berne in Switzerland first in 1698; later, in 1706, he settled on a large farm in Lancaster County, combining farming and the practice of medicine. Robert Elliott, for whom Robert Elliott Speer was named, was one of his great, great, great-grandfathers who was born either in the north of Ireland or in Pennsylvania prior to 1730, for he is known to have been living in what is now Franklin County soon after 1730. His son Benjamin Elliott, who married Mary Carpenter, was a prosperous business man, one of the founders and the first chief burgess of the Town of Huntingdon just before the Revolutionary War. He was lieutenant and first sheriff of Huntingdon County in 1787, colonel of a Continental regiment, and an associate judge. He seems to have been the leading citizen of the county during and after the war and a man of courageous and independent convictions who, against the sentiments of his constituents, voted in the Pennsylvania Convention of 1787 for the ratification of the Federal Constitution, for which he was assailed at an assembly in Hart's Log Valley when he returned home.

On October 2, 1795, Benjamin Elliott's daughter Martha married David McMurtrie of Huntingdon, whose father David had come from Ayrshire in 1752, paying six pounds for his passage and two guineas for a cabin. Later he became a prosperous shipping merchant in Philadelphia.

The McMurtries were successful merchants, ironmasters, and landowners, operating in Maryland and Pennsylvania, and the second David's son William, after gaining a competence in the iron business in Frederick, Maryland, spent most of his life in Huntingdon, Pennsylvania. In his latter years he was a handsome white-haired old man, whom his grandson, Robert E. Speer, remembered for his dignity and geniality. Robert E. Speer recalled how his grandfather and his great uncle sat together on a bench before the old brick house, taking snuff and discussing politics and business, their loans and their farms. William McMurtrie was a man of intense convictions, unswerving loyalty, and stern integrity, plain-spoken and austere, but of a most tender heart toward his grandchildren.

The marriage of William McMurtrie's daughter, Martha Ellen, to Robert E. Speer's father, Robert Milton Speer, united two stalwart families. It is known definitely that Robert Elliott Speer's grandfather, Robert Speer, came to Huntingdon County from County Antrim in 1822 and in 1826 settled in Cassville, where he went into business and started one of the first iron furnaces in Central Pennsylvania. He was an enthusiastic, enterprising, sociable personality who found a needed and adequate balance in his wise, shrewd wife, Agnes Cowan, who mothered and molded the whole countryside.

Robert Milton Speer was the youngest of ten children. He attended the Cassville Seminary and then taught school and read law at the same time. He rose to the highest rank at the bar and was recognized as one of the ablest lawyers in that part of the country. For many years he was the leader of the Democratic Party in Pennsylvania, representing it in Congress and in national conventions. He was a man of handsome presence and extraordinary intellectual charm, and an unsurpassed platform speaker and advocate in court. A devout Christian man, he always had family prayers and grace at table, and for many years taught a large Bible class of men. Another task he set himself was to train his five children, whose mother had died when the oldest was only eleven years old, in memorizing the Shorter and Larger Catechisms and the great psalms. Robert E. Speer owed much to this brilliant Scotch-Irish father.

Robert E. Speer, writing for his own family and not for publication, described his boyhood:[2]

My earliest distinct memories of my father are in connection with the Congressional campaign and our time of residence in Washington. Our Congressional District then comprised Huntingdon, Blair, Cambria and Mifflin counties, and it was possible for a popular Democrat to carry it. Indeed, before the large Republican majorities in Philadelphia and Pittsburgh gave the Republicans control of the state there was a fair chance for Democratic governors, senators and congressmen. The rural counties were largely Democratic.

My father was elected twice, for the Congress of 1870 and the Congress of 1872. Often I went to the House with "Papa," as we always called him, and sat on the step in the aisle beside him.

Once he said something in Congress which earned the gratitude of James G. Blaine, then Speaker, and Mr. Blaine sent him a note reading, "You are a just man." Perhaps there were higher authorities on righteousness than Mr. Blaine, but at that time he was one of the most esteemed and popular men in America.

While we lived at one of the hotels, the Willard or the Ebbit, my brother Will and I had for a playmate the son of the proprietor. He had a room of his own for a playroom and a workshop. We three played all kinds of wild pranks there. The wonder is that we never burned the place down. I remember one glorious green powder explosion we produced in the open fireplace. Will and I possessed a dollar one day and decided to buy a muzzle-loading pistol. We went to the Capitol to get permission from Papa, fearing otherwise the dealer would not sell such a weapon to two small boys of six and eight. Arriving at the House of Representatives, Will sent me in as the younger to ask consent. My father was engrossed in some important matter and not taking in at all the nature of my proposal, he said, "Yes, yes, run away." So away I ran and bought the pistol and the powder and caps. I suppose no dealer would sell such goods to children today. We went under the big steps of the Capitol and had a grand time loading and shooting the pistol without bullets. That night at home our mother found the pistol in our clothes (*sic*) and confiscated it and we never recovered it.

My father was the most wonderful public speaker I have ever heard. He had a magnificent voice, clear, flexible, deep; and was capable of the most enormous driving energy. He was a very handsome man, with a high, white forehead, brown eyes, dark hair, with a curl over the side of the forehead; a half-curly brown beard. He was always well dressed in blue or plum-colored frock coat and striped trousers, or a gray or blue suit, with a silk hat.

In court he was complete master and he put all his power into every case, small or great. Once I was going past Mr. K. Allen Lovell's law office on Penn Street when I heard my father's voice. It was only some small matter but he was speaking before Mr. Lovell as justice of the peace with amazing eloquence and with the most complete and conclusive logic. He would do no work in a slovenly way. All cases were carefully prepared; all the litigants and witnesses on his side would be collected in the old law office and every point would be gone over and all the precedents marked and ready. How well I remember those motley, farm-smelling groups in the hot room. All these folk, ignorant and helpless in matters of the law, my father like a lion or an eagle in the midst of them, understanding everything, piercing through to the heart of things, gathering everything together in his masterful grasp, cutting away all that was irrelevant or cumbersome; authoritative and dominating, yet so winning and human.

There was one murder trial where I judge he saw no hope for the man he was defending except a straight appeal to human hearts. I remember him then, as so often the night before he was to make his final plea before the jury, walking up and down from room to room, going over his speech half aloud. On this occasion, he recited to the jury the old poem, "My Mother." One of us children had it in a large illustrated Christmas booklet. This he used.

> Who fed me from her gentle breast
> And hushed me in her arms to rest
> And upon my cheeks, sweet kisses pressed?
> > My mother.

The next to last verse read:

> When thou art feeble, old and gray,
> My healthy arms shall be thy stay
> And I shall soothe thy pains away,
> > My mother.

You may be sure that he had the old mother present in court, and when he got through the jury and courtroom were in tears. His client escaped the gallows. Indeed, I think that no one whom he defended ever was hanged.

He was always active in politics, and politics in Pennsylvania in those days were a lively concern. He was the undisputed Democratic leader of the county for thirty years, until his death. He was chairman of the State Committee in 1878. On the political platform and "the stump" he could not be superseded. He knew how to deal with human minds, thoughts, prejudices and wills, and his presence and speech were dominating.

In one campaign, he spoke with others at a great mass meeting in the Academy of Music in Philadelphia. He was one of the earliest speakers and had completely taken the audience in a short, clear, persuasive speech. I read it in the paper at the time but remember only this sentence "Let capital pause and be just." He made also a reference to his Irish ancestry. Some of the later speakers were ineffective, and in the midst of one address a not too sober Irishman in the gallery rose and cried out in a loud voice, "Enough of this, bring that Irishman back again!"

I remember his ever-tender care of my mother in her weakness. A bed was made for her in the living room downstairs. Then I remember she called Will and me in to kneel down beside her and promise we would never touch intoxicating drink. It has been no difficulty whatever to me to keep that promise.

My father bought her whatever he thought would please her. I remember especially the sealskin coat. When she slipped away from us, when I was nine, I remember my father taking all of us five children into the parlor and kneeling down with us around the coffin and praying that He who had promised to be a father to the fatherless would also be a mother to the motherless. That was in 1876. He died in 1890 but he did not marry again.

For some years, he taught a large men's Bible class, for which he prepared with care. He had a great law library and a fine general library, not too large but of the best books.

My father was a constant reader of the Bible. I can see him still with the familiar volume in his hands, sitting in the easy chair in the corner of the window looking up the street. We all went to church Sunday morning and to Sunday school, but were never required to go on Sunday evening.

Our father was absolutely lavish at Christmas time. He would go to Philadelphia on a shopping trip and combine it with law business, and on Christmas morning each of us would find a pile of treasures he had brought, and he would sit by enjoying it all. On Christmas Eve, he would have Mary or someone else read or recite " 'Twas the Night Before Christmas" and we all universally had a great outburst of joy over Santa's "little round belly."

I can remember my father coming back to our library after some especially important case, and sitting down almost discouraged, telling us how hard it had been to bring the truth, as he saw it, to the twelve men in the jury box. All day, he would say, truth had been blazing in him, but he could not burn it into the jury.

My memory of him is of a powerful, wholly confident, self-contained, righteous, broadly human personality, who feared no one but God, whom nothing could divert from truth and duty; a little lonesome with his wife gone and with no friend at hand who was his equal in intellectual thought. Generous and high-minded, using in a small place gifts equal to vastly greater occasions, but content to do work of the best and highest quality where he was, looking out meanwhile with the view of a philosopher and historian over the life of the nation and the human movement throughout the world and measuring it against eternity.

There were some odd characters in the town. "Aunt" Prudence Jackson sat in the pew adjoining ours. She was a spinster who lived across the street from us, who painted and powdered and dressed conspicuously and who in June, when Will came home from school or college, would come bustling up the aisle talking aloud to herself, and when she saw Will at the inside end of the pew, she would greet him aloud and kiss him before the entire congregation. After several such experiences, Will traded seats with me so that I would be a buffer. Aunty Prue saw me daily, so I got no kisses, but I would get her loud greeting of "Well, Robbie," and a firm but gentle refusal of my help when seeing Aunty Prue singing from her hymn book upside down at the wrong place I would offer to help her by offering her my book.

The first of our ministers whom I remember was Mr. Zahniger, who I think baptized all of us children. How well I remember his successor, A. Mason Hollifield. He was a Southerner who lisped. He was a good-looking young bachelor with a black mustache. "Aunty Prue" was greatly taken with him. "Ah, the dear man," she exclaimed in church, "what handsome legs!" He married one of the Cochran girls and the wedding was a great occasion.

The first Sunday school I remember was the infant class.

In the older Sunday school, under one teacher, we were an unruly group. I recall sitting down maliciously on Mr. Elderson's new black derby hat, and answering, smart-Alec fashion, to the question as to man's chief end, "his shirt tail." The only sermon texts of those far-off days which I recall were Mr. Hollifield's "Are not Abana and Pharpar, rivers of Damascus, better than the rivers of Israel?" and the thundering discourse of Professor Sargent of the Juniata College on "O Baal, hear us!" I know that if Baal didn't hear that roaring call, he was either deaf, a dead sleeper or dead altogether!

Our real religious education was at home. There were family prayers evening and morning and always a blessing at meals. After I decided to go into missionary work, I was bidden to lead family worship. In the early years, I would say my own prayers at family worship in the evening so that I would not need to say them upstairs. On Sunday we had to memorize and recite the catechisms. We tried to learn the portion before breakfast so as to have it over; we learned the Infant's Catechism, the Shorter Catechism and the Westminster Longer Catechism. Will and Mary and I did this. I have never met another human being who had memorized the longer catechism. Will thought he could escape the end of it by putting it off until he was due at The Hill School. But not a bit of it; he was not allowed to go until he had completed it. After Sunday dinner, we read or played in the yard, our father entering heartily as timekeeper in races. Then we had to recite psalms which we had learned, and read the Bible aloud, several chapters, verse and verse about, skipping nothing from Genesis to Revelation. When I went to Andover in 1883 we were engaged in memorizing the opening chapter in Genesis, and the discipline relaxed after this and Vic and Mig escaped the Larger Catechism.

It was a Puritan upbringing but it was never repulsive to us. Sunday had its own special treats of candy and books and a good walk in the evening. We often had church of our own at home, when one of us children would preach in imitation of old Mr. Prideaux or some other preacher of marked character, and our father would try to keep a straight face when he listened.

Life as a boy in Huntingdon in the early years and during vacations was a grand life—bass fishing with Carl Arthur on the Roystown Branch, deer hunting and trout fishing at Hiram Ross' in the Bear Meadows, boating, games, soldier companies, dances, camping parties at Juniata Crossing and elsewhere on the Branch, skating, coasting down the long Stone Creek Hill, sleighing parties, swimming and canoeing. I had my own good gun at twelve years of age and had an old borrowed carbine before that. The town was full of salty, eccentric characters. We collected stamps and made a great haul of Early American issues when the old court-house was torn down and we boys cleared the old records of their accumulated dust.

My first recollection of school is of being taken to Aunt Mime Whitaker's little school in the basement of the old Academy building. I remember the slate and the used reading book with a light purple back. On nice days Aunt Mime, my grandmother's sister, would take us out into the adjacent cemetery and the little school would sit down around her in a myrtle bed. Later the public schools improved and the old private schools disappeared. We had some good teachers, "professors," as we called them, White and Schimmel (afterwards State Superintendent) and Porter McHugh, who was a vigorous teacher. We were well drilled in mathematics. I had all the algebra and geometry necessary for college. We were well taught in English literature too, and I stored my memory with quotations from Swinburne's *English Literature* and Hart's *Rhetoric*.

On Friday afternoons we had declamations, essays and so forth. This was a great cross to me. I could not get through without breaking down. I tried Lincoln's Gettysburg Address and Whittier's "John Brown of Ossowatomie," and others, but it was a long time before I could get through a speech before breaking down completely. Mary could do hers with such dramatic fervor that I would hide my head with a sort of shame at her recital of "Curfew Shall Not Ring Tonight" with the most moving voice I can remember.

My older brother, Will, was a fighter and a fanatic of conscience from his earliest years. He and I rejoiced in continuous battle. In one of the encounters, as I pursued him with a birch billet, he fled to the back office door. I hurled the billet after him and in trying to catch the door which he had slammed, the edge of the door cut off the end of my right little finger. The end was clapped on at once and healed, but with a clear scar to this day.

Will was always ready to fight anyone. His nickname, partly from his fine, square, solid head, partly from his pugnacity, was "Beef-Head" or "Beefie" for short. Later a newspaper man and lawyer, he loved a fight—as at Albany over the graft in the state capitol, and as Corporation Counsel fighting the efforts to cheat the city in land values in connection with the "Catskill Reservoirs."

As I look back on it all, I think it was a glorious and wild life for boys. We lacked cultural influences of the time but we learned nature and life. I loved the country and the woods. Bob Mathews had an old carbine which we loaded with cork powder and marbles and gravel and used on it a percussion cap about as big as a 22-calibre short cartridge. With this we roamed over the hills. I remember the joy of the Christmas morning when I saw a gun standing with my presents. Before breakfast I went up to Chaney's hardware store and bought powder and shot and loaded some of the brass cartridges which I used at first and went down Stone Creek to try the gun. After that Friday evenings and Saturdays I would go out hunting.[2]

Robert E. Speer's love of his boyhood home and of his mother and his love for Christ are summed up in one of his early books:

In the central part of the State of Pennsylvania, on a little green hill that overlooks the valley of the Juniata, there is a grave.[3] I love that spot more than any other spot on earth.

There is only a white stone there, with the name on it, looking over toward the first rays of the rising sun. And underneath that stone are these words of John's: "And the blood of Jesus Christ, his Son, cleanseth us from all sins." There never was a human grave that less needed such words upon its stone, but the words are true words for every life.[4]

In a memorial of a boyhood friend who also lived in Pennsylvania, Robert Speer wrote of the beauty of his Pennsylvania home and of his love for his native state in words that applied truly to his own home and his affection for his early surroundings:

The green, fragrant fields of clover and timothy, the waving seas of wheat and rye and the rustling armies of corn; the sun-kissed, pine-fringed hilltops looking out over the rich valleys and the prosperous homes; meadows and orchards, woodland and forest were all dear to Hugh. Even now the sweet fields and swelling hills of Paradise can scarcely be dearer. . . . In such a community the social relationships and associations were all that could be desired for a boy, and there was all the freedom of country life with its wholesomeness and buoyant, purifying influence upon character.[5]

III. Andover and Princeton University

ROBERT SPEER ENTERED PHILLIPS ACADEMY AT ANDOVER, Massachussets, in September, 1883; his sixteenth birthday came on the tenth of that month.

He wrote his brother, Will, on September 9, 1883, a letter which will stir similar memories in the minds of other men as they recall their first days away at school:

Dear Will,

It's fearful tough work here. Our teacher in Latin, Comstock, uses a book of his own makeup, Comstock's *First Latin Book*. I know nothing about it. I studied Harkness. I can answer hardly any of his Latin grammar questions. He has divided the class into two divisions and I am in the second. He talks so fast, and sometimes I can't hear him, and he doesn't give time to answer anyhow. He says he may put some back into preparatory class. If he puts me back, as he probably will, I am going to write to Papa to let me stop Latin and take something of more use and let me go here but one year, and maybe only 'til Christmas, and then go home and study with Kidder a year, and then either study for a lawyer or do something else, whatever he wants me to. I haven't had enough time even to go to see the library and gymnasium. I studied all yesterday afternoon, too. I don't think college does you much good anyhow. Can you tell me anything better to do if I am dropped? Please answer right away.

What I said in regard to Latin should not apply to Algebra, Roman History and Greek, because so far, I have got along all right with Greek. You may think I am homesick because I write these things, but if I am dropped in Latin I must stay here at least three years before I can enter Princeton, and in Princeton four years, and then if I will study for a lawyer, it will be three years more, making me twenty-six years old and about two or three more years for a practice when I will be twenty-nine. Whereas, if I take my plan [meaning apparently to drop out and study at home] I will be only twenty-one or twenty-two when I would get through, or at the most I would be twenty-four.

Please write soon and please advise me what to do.

Your brother,

Rob.[6]

The Latin which he had found so hard was gradually conquered and in his second year at Andover, he had a 98 in the subject. He moved up to sixth place in his class in Latin, seventh in Greek, and first in French. In his last term at the school he stood fourth in his class in Latin and Greek and again led the class in History and French.

He took an active part in the extra-curricular life of the school, playing football in his second year, taking part in debates and prize-speaking, and in the schoolboy arguments and rivalries in the school societies. He was editor of the Phillipian and President of Philo.

One of the issues of the school paper, *The Phillipian*, carried a poem by Robert Speer, signed with his initials. Written after Andover had defeated Exeter on the football field, it was entitled "Exeter's Naseby—Adapted from Macaulay." [7] The epic began:

O! Wherefore come they forth, in triumph from their north
   With their caps and their tights and their raiment all red?
And wherefore did their rout send forth a joyous shout?
   And where are the grapes of the winepress which they
      tread?

The poem ends:

O! Evil was the root and bitter was the fruit,
And crimson was the juice of the vintage sour and cold,
For we trampled on the throng of the haughty and the strong
  Who came from northern Exeter to crush us of Phillips'
    fold.

R. E. S.[8]

Writing later in life for his children, Robert Speer described these Andover days:

Andover was a true world of its own. The school was a piece of real life. Dr. Bancroft and the faculty achieved the miracle of ruling without apparent rule a young, seething democracy. There were poor boys—many of them—and rich boys; self-respecting and respect-compelling poverty; and honorable and also snobbish wealth.

The Theological Seminary was a real influence. I attended school during the height of the doctrinal strife that raged within and without. President Park was still living, isolated from the liberal, almost controlling group. I used to see him with great awe, walking on Andover hills wrapped in a great shawl from which his high-browed, beak-nosed face looked out.

The Academy boys had to attend service twice on Sunday in the Seminary Chapel and listen to sermons which we did not understand. I remember Dr. Fairbarn's visit and the solidarity, but none of the substance, of his lectures and sermons. I attended a Sunday-school class taught by Miss Gulliver in the Chapel, and one vacation time on a cold day I pumped the organ for the Church service.

There were frequent lectures in the school. Daniel Pratt, the great American traveler, an eccentric of the past days, was invited to address us. Matthew Arnold lectured on Emerson in the back room at the top of the old Academy building. He wore a monocle and had his notes on a music stand at one side of the stage. He would consult his notes and then wander over the stage until he had to refer to his notes again. Once,

when at the opposite side of the stage, he said there was one
noble passage of Emerson's which he could never forget. He
forgot it, however, and in silence walked back to his notes to
see what it was he could never forget. We boys behaved de-
cently. There were not many of us there as the entrance fee
was fifty cents, as I remember.

There was a grand set of teachers for boys: Comstock,
Coz, Graves, McCurdy, Eaton, Gale, and Bancroft himself,
and Bierwirth, afterward of Harvard, and Clary. We used to
watch for Gale's reading in Chapel.

Robert Speer remembered that C. F. P. Bancroft, the
Principal, always took off his hat in passing Phillips Academy
boys, as though in recognition of a future President of the
United States. His reverence in conducting chapel impressed
the students, young as they were. The school combined work,
athletics, good fellowship, and religion.

Professor Comstock was relentless in his demand for exact
scholarship. As Robert Speer said later, 99.9 was not enough;
the student must score a 100, clear and clean. He was a cruel
master of sarcasm. In one of his classes, he caught a boy in a
reverie, his eyes charmed by a silver doorknob. Comstock
called on him: 'Bliss, you may recite!' Bliss did not even
know the place in the text. The professor let him flounder and
then remarked: 'That will do, Bliss'; and to the class: 'Where
ignorance is Bliss, 'tis folly to be wise.' " [9]

In after years Robert Speer expressed gratitude for the
early relentless insistence on accuracy.

After the morning chapel service of the school, a meeting
of the school body was generally held at which matters of
interest to the students were discussed and decided. Two
secret societies, K.O.A. and A.U.V., had been formed, without faculty recognition, and these two societies had elected
the captains of the football and baseball teams and many of the
important leaders in the life of the school.

Another student society, called P.A.E., was organized in

protest. This society was recognized by the faculty. Gradually, this society attracted boys of independent mind and speech who later became outstanding in the service of their country and abroad. Among its members were Henry L. Stimson, later Secretary of State and Secretary of War; George Carter, who became Governor of Hawaii; Edwin Morgan, later Ambassador to Brazil; James Hardy Roper, a distinguished theological scholar and professor; Arthur Goady, who became President of the Society of Psychical Research; Walden Myer, later Dean of the Washington Cathedral; Fred Bates Lund and Billy Groves, who became distinguished medical men in Boston.

Most of these fellow members of the society were older than Robert Speer, but he had begun to win attention as one of the stellar debaters and public speakers in Philo, the literary society of the school.

At a school meeting following chapel, the question of the secret societies was debated. Thomas Sawyer and Robert Speer had met frequently in debate in Philo, Sawyer speaking for the Republicans, Speer for the Democrats. On this occasion, Sawyer was champion and spokesman for the two secret societies (opposed, too, by the faculty); Speer spoke against them and in favor of P.A.E. A fellow student wrote of Speer's eloquence and force that won the day for the new society:

His handling of the two secret societies was spontaneous and decisive. He routed them, root and branch. We poured out of the chapel after the meeting, throwing our hats in the air and shouting at the top of our lungs. I have never witnessed a more complete oratorical triumph.[10]

Robert Speer wrote later that his best friends at Andover were: John Strong, John Crosby, J. H. Bonbright, Buxton, Walden Myer, George Hotaling, George R. Carter, Billy Graves, Cecil Bancroft, Charley Barry, O. Judd, Wilcox,

Carral Perry, Charlie Corliss, Talcott Banks, Darrogh de Lancy, Joe Lund.

If Robert Speer had remained at Andover for his Senior year, he would have had a leading place on the editorial board of the school paper, in the fraternities, on the football team, and in the debating societies. He was elected President of the Senior Class of '86, but he decided to arrange his work so that he could enter Princeton in the fall of 1885, and he did special studies that summer.

On July 29, 1885, Dr. C. F. P. Bancroft, the principal of the school, wrote to Robert giving him permission to leave Andover and enter the university. He wrote:

My dear Speer:

I send the required letter for Princeton and agree to let you off if you will find us two boys of the same sort to take your place! I hope you'll go on and win academic distinctions at Princeton. They are worth more than college boys think, if they can be attained without loss of health, friendships, and the incidental advantages of college life. It will, I hope, not be difficult for you to do this. It certainly would have been easy if you had taken the last year with us. It is not worth while to make them an absorbing end, but as giving direction and goal to your work, I think they will be exceedingly helpful.

I am sorry to have you go now, but it may be best in the end.

Ever truly yours,
C. F. P. Bancroft[11]

On the same day Dr. Bancroft wrote President McCosh:

To the Rev. James McCosh, D.D., LL.D., L.H.D.
President, College of New Jersey
Princeton, New Jersey

Dear Sir:

This is to certify that Mr. Robert Elliott Speer, of Huntingdon, Pennsylvania, has been for two years a member of the

Phillips Academy, Andover, and is now dismissed in good standing, and cordially commended to the officers of Princeton College as a young man of excellent ability, high scholarship, and unblemished moral character.

With great respect,
Your obt. servant,

C. F. P. Bancroft, Principal [12]

Robert Speer left Andover at the end of Middle year and by making up Homer's *Iliad* by himself in the summer, he entered Princeton in the fall of that year.

Later, he wrote: "I had four good growing years at Princeton," and the record of his life in college bore out that statement.

In Freshman year, he played on the Freshman football team as a linesman or "rusher"; he was on the Class tug-of-war team, and later was anchor of the Class team; he was elected Class President in Freshman and Junior years, and was offered that position permanently upon graduation, but refused because he expected to go abroad as a missionary. In Sophomore year he was a substitute linesman on the university football team, thus winning his letter, and he played as a regular member of the team in the line in Junior and Senior years, and, as was then permitted, for one year when a student in the Theological Seminary. He declined election as Captain in Senior year.

He was active in Clio Hall and was President of the Philadelphian Society (the student Y.M.C.A.) Managing Editor of the *Princetonian*, Chairman of the Bric-a-Brac Board, took active parts in the Dramatic Association, now the Triangle Club, won first prize in Junior Oration, was First Scholar Junior year, won the Baird Prize, was Chairman of Student Self-Government, part of the time managed the Tennis Association, and on Sunday was Superintendent of a local Sunday school for colored children. He was offered the Political Science Scholarship under Professor Sloane, who during the winter term sent him to New York to conduct a class in American Constitutional History for the men in Harvey Fiske's firm. He refused election to Ivy, one of the most popular eating clubs for upper classmen.

The characteristic and natural concern of a father in his son's career at college was expressed in letters from Robert Milton Speer, written during his son's Freshman year; and the boy's phenomenal collegiate record, curricular and extra-curricular, during his years in Princeton indicated that the admonition in these parental epistles brought forth rich fruit. Perhaps no student in Princeton was less in need of such stimulus and advice. One of the letters and extracts from three others follow:

January 16, 1886

You must put yourself down to earnest work. I fear that your thoughts run too much after light affairs and young folks' gossip. This is your period for stern study, and you should take off your coat, roll up your sleeves (metaphorically) and clear the rocks. The shotgun is not as deadly as the rifle. You must concentrate, remembering that there will be ample time hereafter for looking after other things than your books. You should stand at the head of your class, but whether you do or not, you should thoroughly understand what you are about, and lay deep and upon solid rock the basis for your future. Take a bull-dog grip of things, and go to the bottom of the problems that confront you and go forward and look upward.

Your father,
R. M. Speer

February 6, 1886

. . . At your age, deep impressions of God, His attributes, Sovereignty, and personal government, should be received and cherished as His merciful voice speaking unto you. Heed it, obey it—and it will lead you into paths of peace, duty, usefulness and safety. Remember thy Creator in the days of thy youth. Such remembrance will be a pure panoply against the temptations of the world, and the snares of the Evil One. We are pilgrims here, and there is a life beyond of perpetual blessedness to those who love and serve God. Open your heart to Him Who gave His life for you, and make it your supreme purpose of endeavor to love and serve Him. Go to Him in prayer for guidance, wisdom, and strength and He will hear and help you. . . .

Court will open on Monday.

February 13, 1886

. . . Do you take vigorous exercise daily? Don't suffer yourself to neglect to do so. Make it a rule of your daily life and observe it as regularly as you do the taking of your meals. . . .

You should be down to solid work now.

February 20, 1886

. . . How are you prospering? Is the circle of your thoughts growing larger? Is your mental horizon extending? Are you passing from milk to meat as an intellectual diet? *Toughness* is a good quality.

A story in *The Jamestown Collegian* for October 18, 1933, attributes the development of the line play of "boxing the tackle" to Robert Speer and to a Princeton team mate:

Boxing the tackle, a favorite maneuver of football players, was originated by an author and prominent churchman. Robert Elliott Speer, senior secretary of the Board of Foreign Missions of the Presbyterian Church, played a very important part in its creation.

According to the Football Annual of 1933, during a game between Princeton and Yale in 1888, Robert E. Speer, then a slashing Princeton end, teamed up with his tackle, Yup Cook, to form a two-man box around Billy Rhodes, Yale's right tackle. At the same time two more Princeton players took out Amos Alonzo (Lonnie) Stagg, right end for Yale, the same way.

The play was too revolutionary for the referee however. He ruled it illegal. Despite this decision, boxing the tackle and boxing other men on the line has become one of the fundamental plays of the game.

An interesting incident took place on the football field in the fall of 1886, Robert Speer's sophomore year and his first year on the varsity team. On Ocober 25, 1886, Princeton and Pennsylvania met on Franklin Field, Philadelphia. In those days football was a truly rough game, played with few pads, without the strict rules and regulations of the modern contest, and only the most rugged characters engaged in the sport. Robert Speer was playing against a Pennsylvania linesman. Describing the play, *The Princetonian* said:

At this point the Referee disqualified Speer for striking S——, the rusher opposite him. This was entirely unfair as S—— had been slugging Speer continuously through this half, and the Referee declined to disqualify both.

Robert Speer said later, "This is what happened. As you probably have heard, the scrimmages in the Penn-Princeton games of years ago were pretty rugged. The man playing opposite me had slugged me on a number of occasions. I finally went to the referee and called his attention to what was happening and warned him that if it did not stop I would have to retaliate. Several scrimmages later the Penn player again resorted to his unsportsmanlike conduct and when we rose up from the scrimmage I squared off and let him have it flush on the jaw in the sight of all the players and spectators. I was immediately ordered off the field but I went off clothed with a sense of righteous indignation." [13]

Robert Speer wrote later that his closest friends in college were Sailer, Mudge, Bovaird, Baer, Rollins. A life-long friendship began with George Merrill in Princeton, later Episcopal rector at Tuxedo, Buffalo, and Stockbridge.

A report was circulated for a number of years that Aaron Burr, of the Class of 1772, and Robert E. Speer of the Class of 1889, graduated with higher honors than had been won by any other Princeton students. Rev. Harry L. Bowlby, a member of the Class of 1901 at Princeton, and later Treasurer of the Class, wrote to the Secretary of the University, asking for the facts, and the Secretary, V. Lansing Collins, replied:

The rumor about Speer and Burr is a common and persistent one and, like most stories about Aaron Burr, is unfounded. . . . Aaron Burr, of the Class of 1772, received no honors at graduation. Robert E. Speer, of the Class of 1889, was graduated with the distinction of *Magna Cum Laude*, along with Lewis S. Mudge and Fred Neher of the same Class. All three were in First Group and received the same distinction. The actual final grades of the three '89 men were: Speer 1.02; Mudge 1.18; and Neher 1.27.[14]

We cannot anticipate or analyze the power of a pure and holy life; but there can be no doubt about its reality, and there seems no limit to its range. . . . In this strange and tangled business of human life, there is no energy that so steadily does its work as the mysterious, unconscious, silent, unobtrusive, imperturbable influence which comes from a man who has done with self-seeking.

FRANCIS PAGET: *The Hallowing of Work*

IV. The Choice of a Life Work

AT PRINCETON UNIVERSITY DURING THE EIGHTEEN NINETIES, class prayer meetings were held every Sunday night. At the first of these meetings, held in Robert Speer's Freshman year, in 1885, all those who were church members were asked to rise. Robert Speer was the only one who kept his seat. Later in Freshman year, however, he joined the church.

In his Sophomore year, John Forman, a Presbyterian missionary from India, and Robert P. Wilder, an active leader in the Student Volunteer Movement, came to Princeton and presented the appeal for volunteers for foreign mission service overseas. Following these meetings, Robert Speer made the fateful decision concerning his own career. He turned aside from the law which he had assumed he would enter, following the example of his father, and at once became an influential and outstanding leader in the foreign mission cause in his class and in the University.[15]

In his student days, Robert Speer was a forthright champion of integrity and purity of character. One day, after the decision for the foreign field, he came into a student's room, the walls of which were decorated by lewd pictures and photographs. The student who lived there was on the University baseball team. Robert Speer challenged him to a game of "burn" (throwing and catching a baseball with bare hands), the pictures to come down off the walls if the student lost the contest. The pictures came down.[16]

At one of the student conferences at Northfield, following

49

the decision as to life work, Robert Speer spoke on purity, quoting the lines from Tennyson's Sir Galahad:

> My good blade carves the casques of men;
> My tough lance thrusteth sure;
> My strength is as the strength of ten
> Because my heart is pure.

One of those who heard Robert Speer's speech wrote later: "We heard one of the most searching addresses on purity we students had ever heard; and we realized that Robert Speer had the same moving qualities as had Campbell Morgan, the great London preacher, who was also a speaker at the conference.[17]

An incident that occurred in the vacation following Robert Speer's graduation from Princeton University and before he entered the Seminary throws a revealing light on his humor and zest.

Robert Speer, T. H. P. Sailer, William Harris, later a missionary in Siam (now Thailand) and George Gillespie, a sub-Freshman protégé of Speer's, went to a student conference at Northfield. They lunched at New Haven where, to the delight of the group, a Yale Freshman asked Speer if he were taking the entrance examinations.

The group went to Springfield and stayed at the Massasoit House. For supper they had waffles and consumed tankards of coffee. They went to bed, but not to sleep. Their rooms adjoined, and during the night they wandered back and forth. Robert Speer and George Gillespie were good gymnasts.

The old-fashioned beds had high footboards; Speer and Gillespie took flying starts across the room, grasped the footboards and turned flipflops, landing on the bed with their feet hitting the headboards with a resounding crash. They finally stopped when the bed broke down.[18]

At the Northfield Conference later, Robert Speer led a Bible Class and Dr. Frederick J. Tooker, who later became a medical missionary in China and a generous benefactor of the work of foreign missions, wrote:

At that Northfield College Conference, Robert Speer led the course on the life of Christ, a very fine course. Emma Doll Bailey, a student from Bryn Mawr, was the only girl who attended, and it was somewhat difficult to keep one's eyes on the speaker.[19]

The life of a theological student combines sternness and levity, austerity and relaxation. In his Seminary days, Robert Speer was involved in one of the student plots and dormitory battles that had an unforeseen denouement. One evening he and a classmate planted well-filled pails of water on the stairway of one of the dormitories; they placed themselves in strategic positions at the head of the stairs armed with pillows; then an accomplice pulled the light switch, plunging the building into darkness. One of the Seminary professors who was a monitor in the building mounted the darkened stairway to investigate. Speer and his companions stood at the head of the stairs with pillows poised. The shadowy figure emerged, having climbed the stairs and having skillfully evaded the pails of water; Speer pulled back his pillow, ready to take a prodigious swing at the head of the unknown scout; unexpectedly the light came on; the two men, monitor and student, stood transfixed in a startled tableau.[20]

In his Foreword to this volume, John A. Mackay has written of the invitation that went to Robert Speer when he was still in Princeton Seminary to become a Secretary of the Presbyterian Board of Foreign Missions.

The invitation to join the Secretarial Staff of the Presbyterian Foreign Board was presented in a dramatic scene. Theological students in the 1890's were permitted to play on the Princeton University teams, and after three years as a tackle on the University eleven Robert Speer continued playing after he had entered the Seminary. One afternoon when Speer was a Middler, the representative of the Presbyterian Board of Foreign Missions, Dr. Purves, went to Princeton to see Robert Speer to offer him a position as Secretary of the Board. Not finding him in the dormitory or classrooms, Dr. Purves went to the football field where Robert Speer was scrimmaging with the Varsity eleven against the second team. Dr. Purves wore a dark frock coat and a silk hat. Robert Speer was excused from practice and came to the sidelines. A spectator described the scene:

Dr. Purves was stout and advanced in years, and in black; Speer was a giant and youthful and in football togs. The two made a striking contrast as they walked back and forth in earnest conversation along the sidelines.[21]

After consultation with several friends, Robert Speer accepted the invitation to become a Secretary of the Board of Foreign Missions, and left the Seminary in his Middle year.

A fellow student at the Seminary wrote to his mother about the election:

The position of Secretary has been offered to Speer and he has accepted. . . . He is a man of remarkable powers and is thoroughly consecrated. . . . He is not more than 24 years old and has had enough praise to turn the head of a score of strong men. He is not in the least affected, as far as I can see. I believe God has raised him up to be a mighty power in His Hands. . . . He is a hard worker with wonderful capabilities, both of mind and body, and a very tender, childlike spirit. I do not often grow enthusiastic over a man, but I am thoroughly so over Speer. His first name and initial are: "Robert E." [22]

In an address at the Third International Convention of the Student Volunteer Movement, at Cleveland, Ohio, in February, 1898, Robert Speer told of his own decision made in his sophomore year at Princeton to enter Foreign Mission Service:

I want to ask you to pause a moment in the midst of our meeting together to think of the meaning of this Movement which we compose. To the great world that lies just beyond us it has one meaning. There are many who regard us as possessed of a strange delusion, many who count us carried away by some fanatical madness, many who look upon us as following what, after all, though it be a noble dream, will turn out to be but a dream. I can remember as though it were yesterday the letters that came to me when I turned away from my intended profession of the law and wrote to my friends of my new interest in this work. I presume many of us can look back to that day in our lives, and thinking of it can appreciate something of the meaning of this Movement to which we belong, to those who have never come to view it as it is viewed by us.

This Missionary Movement has quite a different meaning to us. We look back to that hour when perhaps for the first time in our lives there was a hand laid upon our shoulder that once was nailed to the Cross, and there was lifted up before our eyes the vision of a new and larger life, and there came a new Heaven and a new earth for us. This Movement has a definite and vivid meaning to those of us who look to its first call to us as the spring of the richest and largest blessing of our lives. I can see still the little room in the North Middle Reunion at Princeton, where a little group of us met years ago in our Sophomore year and faced this question, and one by one sat down at a table and wrote our names under the words: "I am willing and desirous, God permitting, to become a foreign missionary." [23]

Amos Alonzo Stagg, who starred on the Yale football team in the later 1880's, and after graduation in 1888 rendered brilliant and able service in the field of physical education and as a football coach and physical director at the University of Chicago and at the College of the Pacific, has written of

Robert Speer's influence at the Student Conferences at North-field in earlier years:

The last of June and early July in 1888, 1889, 1890, and 1891, I was a member of the Yale group that went to North-field for the college student conference and I remember that most of these years Robert E. Speer, John R. Mott and Robert P. Wilder conducted the evening vesper services on Round Top, a little hill on the campus of the D. L. Moody Northfield School for Girls. My relations with Robert E. Speer were entirely as listener to his wonderful messages given mainly on Round Top.

The emphasis of those meetings was placed on winning the world for Christ in this generation and these remarkable young men pressed their message so strongly that some of us, I know, spent time and prayer on whether we were called to go to the foreign mission field. I remember that one starlit night I went off by myself into the loneliness of the surrounding fields and spent a long period in prayer on the question of preparing myself to go as a missionary into a foreign field. Years later, I remember Sherwood Eddy told of having had a similar experience at Northfield.

I recall that John R. Mott's messages were dynamic and those of Robert E. Speer were impressive spiritually.[24]

William Arnot Mather, later a missionary in China, wrote of Robert Speer's influence at Princeton:

Robert Speer was seven years before me at Princeton. My older sister told me not long ago of an address which he made nearly sixty years ago in her church in New York. He began his address by saying: "Friends, I want to introduce you to my dearest Friend, Jesus Christ." When I entered Princeton in 1892, the Philadelphian Society asked John R. Mott and Robert Speer to come to speak at the college. Sunrise prayer meetings were held every morning in the almost freezing temperature of the library of Murray Hall (the Y.M.C.A. center) and the evening meetings in the larger hall were always crowded. We all knew and loved our Princeton

athlete, scholar, and saint, "Bobby Speer." In all my four
years at college, these meetings had the most lasting effect of
any. One junior, who was anything but saintly, was so
soundly converted that he gave his after life to the Christian
ministry.[25]

H. Alexander Smith, U.S. Senator from New Jersey, has
written of Robert Speer during his student days:

Robert Speer was in the Class of 1889 at Princeton, and I
was a member of the Class of 1901. I recall vividly that when
I was an undergraduate, he and John R. Mott, who were
close friends, were active on their visits to Princeton, and
gave their attention to the spiritual welfare of the University,
and especially of the undergraduates. I remember that Robert
Speer was one of the speakers at the annual Northfield Conferences for students which I attended with a great deal of
interest during my years in college.

In later years I recall with a deep sense of appreciation
what his great character and his teachings did to my own
spiritual development and the building of my own faith. He
was one of the important friends that I had as a younger man
who helped me and others through the early stages of our
spiritual development. I feel that I owe him an eternal debt of
gratitude.[26]

V. Marriage and Family

by

MARGARET BAILEY SPEER

We know what home may be on earth—the place of love and peace, of confidence and rest, of perfect understanding, to which we look forward at the end of the day or the end of the Journey, and are sustained by the hope of it.

> "As when the weary traveler gains
> The top of some o'erlooking hill
> His heart revives if o'er the plains
> He sees his home, though distant still." [27]

A SHORT TIME BEFORE ROBERT SPEER BEGAN HIS WORK WITH the Board of Foreign Missions in New York his father died suddenly. The first year in New York must have been a lonely time for the hard-working young man of twenty-three, for although he had scores of close friends from school and college, he had no personal ties in New York and the city was an impersonal, dreary sort of place for one whose chief pleasure had been tramping with a friend and a gun in the woods of Pennsylvania. Although invitations to speak in colleges and churches kept him traveling whenever he could leave his office in the Board Rooms at Fifth Avenue and Twelfth Street there must have been many solitary evenings in the cheerless room where he lived on University Place.

In June of 1891 Robert Speer went to Northfield to lead a Bible Class at the YMCA Conference for college men. That year it had been suggested for the first time that students from women's colleges should join the conference, but, somehow, the plans fell through and the only young women to come were two freshmen from Bryn Mawr College—properly chaperoned, of course, and staying respectably in a near-by boardinghouse. One of these was Emma Doll Bailey from Harrisburg. In the following winter, at the suggestion of President Rhoads, she asked Robert Speer to come and speak to the students at Bryn Mawr and before the end of the year they were engaged. In the spring of 1893, when he was twenty-five and she not yet twenty-one, they were married.

For the next three years they lived in Elizabeth, New Jersey, and Robert Speer used the long commuter's trip to and from New York to read the volumes of history and biography and theology that he always carried in his heavy bag of papers. To the little house in Elizabeth began to come the stream of guests from many countries, who were welcomed for a meal or for a month's visit as later they were welcomed in the other houses in Englewood and Lakeville.

Emma Bailey was a gay and eager girl with a gift for attracting devoted and loyal friends. She was dark and tall and had so much of the same open, handsome look her husband had that they were often taken for brother and sister. She, too, came from a Pennsylvania family rooted in loyalty to the Church. Her father, Charles Lukens Bailey, came from a long line of Quakers, his great-grandfather having come, according to family tradition, from Bristol in 1682 to join William Penn's new community. When in 1856 Charles Bailey married Emma Harriet Doll, who was not a Quaker but a Presbyterian, this was considered by the elders in the Society of Friends not only so ill-advised but so wrong that he was "expelled from meeting." So young Emma and her four older brothers grew up as Presbyterians but were well acquainted with Quaker practice. Indeed, she remembers how one of her brothers showed the stuff he was made of by keeping perfectly still during a silent meeting even when he was stung by an un-Quakerly wasp.

Charles Bailey's mother was Martha Lukens, and his father, Joseph Bailey, was engaged with the Lukens family in the manufacture of iron and boiler plate at the Lukens Steel Company in Coatesville, Pennsylvania. Later he owned his own small plant, the Pine Iron Works, at Pine Forge near Pottstown. Charles Bailey became an ironmaster like his father. He was operating iron furnaces at Pottstown at the time of his only daughter's birth there in 1872 but shortly afterwards moved to Harrisburg, where he was president of the Central Iron Works and Chesapeake Nail Works and one of the leading citizens of the city.

Although the Bailey family had been peaceable Quakers, Emma Bailey's mother came from the same sort of Scotch-Irish pioneers as Robert Speer's forebears. Mrs. Charles Bailey's great-grandfather was John Elder, born in Edinburgh in 1706, a graduate of the University of Edinburgh, and famous in Pennsylvania history as "the fighting parson," pastor of the Paxtang and Derry churches east of Harrisburg. He preached at Paxtang and Derry on alternate Sundays, making the journey on horseback. The village of Derry is now the town of Hershey, the center of the chocolate industry. It was a family legend that he preached with a musket beside him in the pulpit, ready for Indians who might surround the church. A letter written some decades later describes one of his services to the Colonial cause:

At the time the British Army overran New Jersey, driving before them the fragments of our discouraged, half-naked and half-starved troops . . . the Rev. Mr. Elder went on Sunday as usual to Paxtang Church. The hour arrived for the church service when, instead of a service, he began a short and lusty prayer to the Throne of Grace; then called upon the patriotism of all effective men present, and exhorted them to aid in the support of Liberty's cause and the defense of the country.

In less than thirty minutes a company of volunteers was formed. Colonel Robert Elder, the parson's eldest son, was chosen captain. They marched next day, though in winter. . . .

The disaffected and Tories around (who were very saucy) raised a story on the old man's prayer of this Sunday . . . that he begged for and implored that Heavenly aid be given to the success of the American cause: "We beseech Thee, through our Lord and Saviour Christ, mercifully to give us triumph, yet not ours but Thy blessed will be done. And, oh, Lord God of the Universe, if Thou art unwilling by Thy Divine Grace to assist us, do Thou stand aside and let us fight it out." [28]

John Elder's thirteenth child was Samuel Elder, who was an officer in the military establishment of the new nation, in 1798 sheriff of Dauphin County, and an upright and respected citizen. His daughter Sarah married William Doll, son of Joseph Doll, a Dutch silversmith and expert clockmaker. Their fifth child was Emma Harriet Doll, who married Charles Bailey. Emma Speer's mother was as distinct and powerful a personality as Robert Speer's father, a beautiful and pious woman, with great executive and administrative ability, teacher for years of a large Bible class of men in the Market Square Presbyterian Church of Harrisburg and president of the Women's Synodical Society of Home Missions. She was a woman of many interests, loving and beloved, ready for adventure even at the end of her life when, at an age when her contemporaries sat quietly in rocking chairs, she went off to Alaska to visit the Sheldon Jackson mission there.

The Baileys and the Dolls were, like the Speers and the McMurtries, stalwart families. Some were fighting pacifists, some were peaceful militarists, and they fought against evil where they saw it with all the staunchness of the old Quaker of whom Charles Bailey loved to tell. He was attacked one night by a footpad demanding his purse. The old gentleman was heavy but alert, and tripping his assailant, he fell upon him and taking his walking stick, he rolled it up and down the rascal's face, saying quietly, "Friend, I may not smite thee but I'll rub thy nose."

Robert and Emma Speer had much in common but their interests were by no means identical. In politics the Speers were Democrats but the Baileys were Republicans. Young Emma Bailey had been conventionally brought up, the darling of her four older brothers. She was a far cry from a fighting feminist, but she had a mind of her own or she would not have been one of those to enter one of the earliest classes at Bryn Mawr College during the first years when M. Carey Thomas was its radical young dean and presidents of men's colleges were predicting the early nervous collapse of young women foolhardy enough to attempt the same curriculum that men followed at Harvard and Johns Hopkins. Fortunately she had learned to ride horseback on her father's farm near Downingtown in Chester County or she would never have been able a few years later to ride sidesaddle for days through Persian snowdrifts. But she never loved the rugged exercise that her husband enjoyed and she preferred the salt air of the sea to the high hills and trout streams of the North Country, where he liked to camp on holidays. Happily she liked to travel almost more than he did and boasted after several journeys to distant parts of the world that she had never missed a meal at sea, not even on a little Russian tramp steamer on the Black Sea.

Within the first year of their marriage Robert and Emma Speer took the first of many journeys together—a six-weeks' trip to Mexico with Dr. W. R. Richards. In the summer of 1894 they went to England, where Robert Speer spoke at the British Student Movement conference at Keswick. In later years their children were delighted and astonished by the tale of their return from this journey with exactly fifty cents in their pockets. The children knew their father as the thriftiest and most careful of planners, ready to take necessary risks but never foolish ones, and the picture of the young travelers who had spent everything but their last half dollar always seemed a summons to light-hearted adventure.

In 1896 Robert and Emma Speer started around the world on a visit to distant mission stations. This was long before the days of round-the-world pleasure cruises, and the journey would have called for physical courage and a tough quality of endurance even if it had not been complicated by Robert Speer's falling ill with typhoid fever in midwinter in Persia. ("Why did he not drink Poland Water?" an untraveled friend is said to have innocently asked.)

When they returned to America in the summer of 1897 they moved from Elizabeth to Englewood. Here in what was then a pleasant small community on the edge of the wooded Palisades their five children were born and here they lived for thirty years, until the youngest of the children was nearly ready for college.

Englewood was not then the mixture of apartment buildings and ranch houses that metropolitan suburbs have since become. It was a friendly little town where everyone knew everyone else. Most of the young men commuted to New York, but there were no highways and the rare cars that were seen on the streets were used for hazardous country excursions and not for the trip by steep hill and slow ferry to upper Manhattan. Commuters used the Erie Railroad and the downtown ferries. It was not hard to rush downhill in the mornings to catch the 8:13, but the same hill seemed longer and steeper to those returning on the 6:17 in the evening. Everyone walked to the station, although ladies going to town to shop might take one of Mr. Leary's open carriages.

Robert Speer's Princeton classmate, T. H. P. Sailer, and

his wife, came to live close to the Speers in Englewood, and many other young families whose names were then unknown found the little community a place where it was easy to make fast friends. The Dwight Morrows, the Thomas W. Lamonts, the Henry P. Davisons, the Frederick Duncans, the William Dulleses, the Edwin Bulkleys, the Sailers, and the Speers, all lived not far apart, went to the Presbyterian Church, and had exuberant fun together in the Shakespeare Club that met on alternate Friday evenings, at first reading and acting only Shakespeare but later reading interesting new plays.

For the children of these families Englewood provided streets on which it was safe to ride bicycles or to hitch behind the grocery wagon, hills that were perfect for coasting, woods that were full of anemones and dog-toothed violets in the spring, but where a sharp lookout had to be kept for copperheads and other snakes.

The Speers' first home was a white house on Chestnut Street, at the edge of the woods that stretched unbroken along the Palisades. Here their three older children were born—Elliott in 1898, Margaret in 1900, and Eleanor in 1903. In 1906 they moved to a larger house on Walnut Street, which, although it had been built in one of the worst of America's recurrent rashes of ugly houses, was comfortable and full of beautiful things and with ample room for a growing family and the endless stream of guests who came from all over the world.

Little three-year-old Eleanor died soon after the family moved into this house. Here the two younger children were born, Constance in 1907, and William in 1910.

As the two boys and two girls grew up they followed naturally many of their parents' interests. Elliott went to Andover, and although Billy went to Hotchkiss, both boys went to Princeton. Elliott, after Princeton and some study at New College, Edinburgh, was ordained as a Presbyterian minister and was for two years Chaplain of Lafayette College, before being asked at the age of twenty-seven to become president of the Northfield Schools. The story of his tragic death there only a few years later is told in another chapter.

Both daughters went to Bryn Mawr College. Margaret went in 1925 to teach English at Yenching University in Peking, China, where she served under the Presbyterian Board of Foreign Missions until the outbreak of war with Japan put a temporary end to university work. After being interned in a Japanese internment camp, appropriately enough in what was left of a Presbyterian Mission compound in Shantung, she came home in 1943 on the repatriation ship *Gripsholm* and soon after went to the Shipley School in Bryn Mawr to become headmistress.

Constance interrupted her college course to go with her parents to the International Missionary Council meeting in Jerusalem and the meeting of the World's YWCA in Budapest in 1928. Immediately after college she married Dr. Robert Freeland Barbour of Edinburgh. The families had become friends at the time of the International Missionary Conference in Edinburgh in 1910. Constance and her husband have spent most of their married life in Bristol, England, although during part of the wartime blitz, while Dr. Barbour was serving with the Royal Army Medical Corps, she brought the three children to stay with her parents, who were then living in Lakeville, Connecticut. The three little Britishers, like many other children before them, fell under their grandfather's spell. During recent years some of Constance's boundless energy has gone into work with the British YWCA.

William, except for an interlude with the Navy during World War II, has been a teacher and school administrator, first at the Asheville School for Boys, then at the Shady Hill School, Rutgers University, and Loomis Institute. He is now associate dean of students at Massachusetts Institute of Technology.

Elliott's marriage in 1921 to Charlotte Rose Welles of Wilkes-Barre and New York, and William's marriage in 1940 to Elizabeth Lester, daughter of Dr. and Mrs. John A. Lester of The Hill School, brought into the family two gifted and interesting young women, who are most congenial daughters-in-law.

Although Mr. and Mrs. Speer became increasingly busy as their children grew up and as they were both called on to take more and more responsible positions in church and community affairs, they managed in an extraordinary way to combine their work for organizations around the world with a warm-hearted, close-knit family life. The big house in Englewood was always full of people—retired missionaries enjoying a rest, visiting speakers from England or the Continent appreciating their first glimpse of American life, or classmates of the children just having a good time.

Mrs. Speer early found in the growing work of the National Board of the YWCA not only an outlet for her lively interest in people and in their welfare but also a source of constant growth and enlargement. In 1913 she became the second president of the National Board and has been one of the pillars of that forward-looking organization. For many years she was almost as much a commuter between Englewood and New York as her husband.

In 1926, when the children had scattered, the big house began to seem too big, and the trip by tube and train from New York began to seem like an unnecessarily tiring end to the day's work. The Speers reluctantly left Englewood to take an apartment in New York for a few months. They thought they were leaving only temporarily but they never went back. One day, after ten years' residence in New York, Mrs. Speer went to Lakeville, Connecticut, to see Billy, the youngest of the family, who was down with measles in the Hotchkiss School infirmary. On the way from the train to the school the jitney, which she was sharing with a stranger, stopped at an old white house commanding a wide view of the Connecticut hills. The house was for sale, and with characteristic decision Mrs. Speer signed an option for it within a few days, and in two weeks the house was theirs. "Rockledge" became at once their summer home, while they spent the winters in a New York apartment at 24 Gramercy Park, a short walk from Mr. Speer's office. When he retired from service with the Board of Foreign Missions in 1937 they made "Rockledge" their permanent home.

Robert Speer combined physical strength, imagination, and simplicity in a way that made him an irresistible companion to children, his own five, and, later, his nine grandchildren. Several small English refugees during the war came often to play with his Barbour grandchildren at "Rockledge." They all called him "Robbie," and one day at lunch the littlest laid her small hand on his large one and said, "Wobbie, you are the nicest man in all the world."

Father was famous as a storyteller. On the rare Sundays when he was at home there would always be a walk, either to Eleanor's grave in the quiet Brookside cemetery, or through the woods to Clinton Point high over the Hudson. On the way he told endless tales—stories of early American folklore like the tale of how Jane McGuire escaped the Indians by hanging onto the tail of a madly dashing cow, or an original and highly imaginative serial about Farmer White's adventures in the Friendly Woods, or robustly humorous stories such as the one about the bear named Horace who would eat up respectable citizens until his figure bulged and "the bulge was Benjy."

On winter nights or summer Sunday afternoons he read aloud to us, beginning with Uncle Remus and later reading Kipling and O. Henry and Irving Cobb. At the funniest bits tears of enjoyment would stream down his cheeks as he read and we rolled on the floor. The Irish brogue with which he read the dialogue of *Soldiers Three* may not have been authentic but it was convincing.

One of the exciting annual events was "The New Missionaries' Party." Each June there would be a conference for all new missionaries about to go abroad, and, after an afternoon of games, Father would invite to our house for supper all the new missionaries for whom he was the responsible secretary. There would always be some furloughed missionaries, too, and there would often be seventy or eighty people, some very shy and needing to be put at ease. Many of them had long admired Father from a distance, and looked on him with a mixture of awe for the prophet and respect for the boss. Now they saw him for the first time as a simple, friendly, fun-loving person. We children quickly learned how to make ourselves useful on these occasions and to have a good time in the bargain. We learned how to avoid the effusive head-patters—"How much you look like your father, dear!"—and to attach ourselves to the people who brought curious foreign objects out of their pockets and who had stories to tell of Kurdish chieftains or Japanese volcanos. We put up the folding chairs, brought out the equipment for potato races and obstacle races, passed the fruit punch, and when we felt in need of a rest retired to the kitchen to make inroads on the chicken salad and the ice cream.

Father could always beat us at tennis but he never took up such suburban occupations as golf. When he had a free Saturday afternoon, which was seldom more than once a month, he would rake leaves or trim shrubbery, wearing such shabby old working clothes that more than once ladies coming to call, in days when formal callers wore heavy white kid gloves, mistook him for the gardener. He did not take up gardening as a true hobby until he began to work on the ten acres at "Rockledge," but during the First World War, when manpower was scarce and it was less common than it is today for "gentlemen" to mow their own lawns, he took over the care of the Englewood property. When Dominico, the Italian gardener, came back from the war and discovered who had done the work in his absence, he thought it highly improper. "My God, Mrs. Speer, you put Mr. Speer in the garden!"

In those days all the families we knew had a blessing at meals but there were not many families who had family prayers regularly, as we did. Breakfast was at 7.30 and prayers began promptly at 7.20. Any guests who might come chattering down the stairs a minute late froze at the bottom as they came upon the family and the household helpers kneeling by their chairs in the living-room. In the summers at Diamond Pond there would be family prayers in the evening as well. We knew one family where children were called on without warning to say a prayer or a verse but this we considered barbarous. We "said our psalms" on Sundays, taking pride in rattling through them without mistakes, and sometimes we would, with fair warning, be asked to read Bible passages at prayers, but we thought praying was Father's business and it was our business to listen. This was not hard, for he prayed with the utmost sincerity and simplicity. God's blessing was asked on all our affairs, large and small, but never in such a way that a child could feel that his small privacy was being violated.

An invention of Father's which became an institution with the small fry of the neighborhood was the game of "Bear." In our large old house the floor of the front hall was covered by a huge rug which Mother and Father had bought during their winter in Persia. On those rare Saturday afternoons when he was at home Father would establish himself as The Bear, with this rug as his base. The children of the family and half a dozen of our friends would rush from room to room across the hall—from front door to living room to dining room to library and back again, shrieking defiance at The Bear. The rule was that he could not leave the rug. While he would chase one child, another would daringly come behind to tag him and The Bear would turn with terrible growlings, while the adventurous one fled to the safe areas beyond his reach, but his arms were long enough to catch many a child dancing impudently at a supposedly safe distance.

We could not imagine why Father should ever be thought solemn or grave. To us he was the most hilarious of companions. He told outrageous stories with a poker face and we loved to watch guests grow more and more puzzled until they realized at last that he was ribbing everyone. He went to great lengths with elaborate practical jokes designed to surprise and fool us all, never unkind or hurtful to anyone's feelings, but effectively pricking any tendency to pompousness or self-importance. He was a master of the delicious art of teasing, not the sort of teasing that ridicules the defenseless but a skilful and affectionate use of humor so that childish sulks would disappear in a burst of laughter.

The best part of each year was the month at Diamond Pond in northern New Hampshire. Here he took the boys on hard, long fishing trips where they learned to use an ax, to carry a heavy pack, to treat "the woods" with respect, and much more besides. His daughters were taken on easier trips; that is, easier for them, but hardly easier for him, since he had to carry the extra loads, cut the balsam for beds and all the logs for the fire.

Not all the expeditions were into the deep woods. We walked up and down the valleys where the farms were lonely and far apart and where anyone who had once met Father was glad to see him come back. One family of Irish farmers, the Carrs, liked to have him come to dinner. They fed him homemade ice cream from a huge soup bowl. One day he weighed before and after dinner and seemed to have gained twenty-five pounds, but no one knew then that he had slipped some old horseshoes into his pockets!

I remember one day stopping with him for a drink of water at a distant farm where we had never been before. The rather querulous old woman who came to the door said, "I don't see many people now, I'm so near gone." "Oh, no," Father said, somehow conveying his own idea of death, "don't say, 'Near gone'; it's 'Near come.' "

On August Sundays he often preached at the simple morning or evening service attended by both summer visitors and near-by farming people. His talks were full of illustrations from the things that young and old had been doing together during the week, and they provided many sayings that became family bywords. There was, for example, the advice for a camping trip in the deep woods which could be applied with equal effect to any other adventure: "Prepare for the worst; expect the best, and take what comes." It was a precept he lived by all his life long.[29]

VI. His Service with the Board of Foreign Missions

The missionary movement has been given its direction and has achieved its effects scarcely more through its agents on the field than through the men who have been its representatives and administrators at home.[30]

ROBERT E. SPEER SERVED AS A SECRETARY OF THE BOARD OF Foreign Missions of the Presbyterian Church in the U.S.A. from 1891 to 1937, a total of forty-six years.

When Robert Speer came to the Board in 1891, the Secretaries were Frank Field Ellinwood, John Gillespie, Arthur Mitchell, and John C. Lowrie, who had retired but still came to the office. John C. Lowrie was the son of J. Walter Lowrie, United States Senator from Pennsylvania, the first Secretary of the Board. William Rankin, who had been Treasurer from 1850 to 1888, still came to the office.

In 1891 there were 598 foreign missionaries; 28,000 native Christians were related to the Presbyterian work overseas; the total income of the Board was less than a million dollars. At the General Assembly of 1893 it was reported the Board's income had exceeded a million dollars and much enthusiasm greeted that report. In 1891, the reserve funds of the Board were $110,000, compared with $16,000,000 in 1943; the receipts on the field were $38,000, compared with $2,000,000 in 1943. John D. Wells was President of the Board. Of the members and officers of the Board, serving in 1891, the only ones living in 1943 were Robert Speer and Miss Susie Pinder in the library. The only two missionaries in active service in 1943 who were serving in 1891 were Mrs. William Harris, of Siam, and Mrs. J. A. Funk, of Iran.

In 1891 the Board offices were in a three-story brownstone mansion at 53 Fifth Avenue, New York, on the northeast corner of Fifth Avenue and Twelfth Street. The home had belonged to James Lenox and his two sisters and had been acquired by the Foreign Board in 1887. Fifth Avenue was cobbled and the carriages made a constant rattle and noise, making talking in the summertime, with open windows, difficult on the Fifth Avenue side of the office. The noonday prayer meeting of the office staff was begun in 1892, in the room of the Secretary for Special Objects, Mrs. Fry, whom Robert Speer described as "a dear little white-haired lady." Robert Speer wrote later: "Those were days of small things compared with today, but of the same great spirit and joy."

In 1895 the Boards of Foreign and Home Missions of the Presbyterian Church completed the erection of a thirteen-story building at 156 Fifth Avenue; and "156" became known throughout the world as the headquarters of these two organizations and of their missionary and secretarial personnel.

The Presbyterian Church takes its name from the Greek word *Presbyteros* (πρεσβύτερος), translated in English, "elder." The organization from the beginning of the Church in America in 1789, when the first General Assembly met, has been that of representative government. The Mission Stations are composed of missionaries located in a town or city or area; these Station groups make up a larger unit of a Mission. In certain fields the Missions send their representatives to a Council. This arrangement was put into effect in China and India and has been adopted in some other smaller Mission areas. The decisions of the Stations on policy, reinforcements, and property go to the Missions, which usually meet once a year. After full consideration and open discussion, the Mission decisions go to the Board in New York for consideration by the Executive or Secretarial Council, which, again after full consideration and discussion, presents its recommendations for action by the Foreign Board. The missions have Executive Committees and Chairman or Secretaries who are responsible representatives elected for specific terms. The organization from Station to Mission to Field Council to the Board and finally to the Assembly is built on actions and functions of the *presbyteros*, the elected representative, rather than on those of an *episcopos* or bishop. In recent years there has been a tendency to sharpen this organization by election of Field Representatives who will be more directly representative of the Board.

During the term of service of Robert Speer the Board met once a month. For a number of years the Foreign and Home Base Councils, composed of Secretaries of the Foreign Department and the Home Base Department, met on Thursday and brought their decisions to the full Executive Council on Friday; after further discussions, the decisions of the Executive Council and its recommendations were brought to the Board for action on the following Monday. Special problems and those of controversial character were brought before the Home Base and Foreign Committees and the Policy and Methods Committee of the Board before being presented to the Board for action. The Minutes of the Board recording discussions and decisions were presented to the General Assembly once a year and were subject to review and approval by the Assembly. The whole process was that of representative and democratic government, similar to that of the government of the United States.

The staff members of the Foreign Board during Robert Speer's later years included A. Woodruff Halsey, for twenty-two years, from 1899 to 1921 Secretary in the Home Department. Dr. Halsey was a graduate of the Class of 1879 at Princeton and was elected its permanent president. Woodrow Wilson was his classmate and a warm friend. After Dr. Halsey's death, in 1921, Wilson wrote:

As his classmate at the University and his friend and frequent companion in subsequent years, I had ample opportunity to know the fine qualities that endeared Woodruff Halsey to so many friends and that won for him the well-deserved confidence of the Church.

I am deeply grieved that he should be taken away. He will be missed in every relationship of life and not least by those who have known him the longest.

He will be remembered always as a man worthy of trust and affection.

That description of Dr. Halsey and his work could be applied also to the character and service of his colleagues. These included Arthur Judson Brown, a Senior Secretary of the Board who served with Robert Speer from 1895 to 1929, and is now Secretary Emeritus, a distinguished author, an eloquent spokesman for the Foreign Missions cause, the recipient of a number of honorary degrees, from Yale and other universities; Dwight H. Day, a graduate of Yale in the Class of 1899, and later an elder in the Fifth Avenue Presbyterian Church of New York, who began in business selling bonds, and became phenomenally successful, Treasurer of the Foreign Board for eighteen years, from 1906 to 1924, a man of warmth of heart and kindness, always thinking of deeds of helpfulness and generosity in behalf of the missionaries and his friends; William P. Schell, a graduate of Williams in the Class of 1901, who was on the Secretarial Staff of the Board from 1913 to 1948, and became Senior Secretary and then Secretary Emeritus, who succeeded Woodruff Halsey as Executive Secretary of the Home Department, an exceptionally gifted extemporaneous speaker, a man of courage and quick decisions, who almost invariably diagnosed the issue when a question was up for discussion, and was able to state his views clearly and concisely and with conviction that often carried his audience with him; George T. Scott, who was on the Board Staff from 1913 to 1920 as an assistant to Robert E. Speer and to Arthur J. Brown, and as Secretary for Higher Education of the Board, and then Secretary in the Foreign Department from 1920 to 1940, a Princeton graduate with some years of teaching experience in Beirut and at Hampton Institute, a member of the family and firm of Carson, Pirie Scott of Chicago, a huge man six feet four inches tall, with exceptional capacity for administrative detail, and with conservative judgment which helped to balance the views of some of the more liberal members of the Council; Russell Carter, a graduate of Princeton in the Class of 1888, who entered business after college and came to the Board as Assistant Treasurer in 1914, who later became Associate Treasurer and then Treasurer and served on the Executive Council for twenty-seven years, a man who faithfully fulfilled the functions of a Treasurer as guardian of the financial goal line of the Board, a loyal friend and admirer of Robert Speer who always supported him in the discussions and actions of the Council; Gertrude Schultz, an Executive Secretary of the Home Department from 1923 to 1945, of whom a church member once remarked, "That woman has power," a leader beloved throughout the Church; Ann T. Reid, Candidate Secretary and Area Secretary in the Central Area, from 1921 to 1948, who radiated common sense, sincerity and humor; Edward M. Dodd, M.D., a graduate of Princeton in the Class of 1909, a former medical missionary in Persia, who as Medical Secretary since 1924 brought judgment and sympathy to the performance of his professional duties in the Council; Orville Reed, a Yale graduate, a former leader of the Yale Glee Club, a man of conservative theological viewpoint but of sweetness of spirit as of voice, who served fourteen years as Assistant Secretary in the Candidate Department; Stanley White, a graduate of Princeton, Corresponding Secretary for the Chile, Hainan, Hunan and Syria Missions and Secretary of the Candidate Department for seventeen years; George H. Trull, who served for thirty years as Sunday School Secretary, and Secretary for Specific Work, a patient and indefatigable secretary, with a burning zeal in behalf of the service of Christ; Cleland B. McAfee, who, after years of conspicuous service on the faculty of McCormick Seminary, and in the Church of which he was Moderator, came to the Board as a Senior Secretary, and served from 1930 to 1936 with ability and distinction; Webster E. Browning, who came to the Board as Secretary for Latin-America and West Africa, from 1936 to 1940, after having served as a missionary in Latin-America, as Principal of the Instituto Inglas, in Santiago, Chile, and as Educational Secretary for the Committee on Co-operation in Latin-America, who was given an honorary degree of Doctor of Literature by the University of San Marcos in Lima, Peru; Clarence A. Steele, a former missionary treasurer in Siam and later assistant Treasurer and Treasurer of the Board, a devoted and dogged defender of the Board's financial resources, who invariably sided with Russell Carter and Dr. Speer when his support was needed; Ruth Elliott, a Wellesley graduate, a member of the Executive Council from 1927 to 1954, who was Secretary for Specific Work and later for Special Gifts and Annuities, who combined judgment and grace; Mrs. Mabel Roys, who had served as a missionary in Shantung with her husband Charles K. Roys, M.D., and after her husband's death returned to this country and for a number of years was a Secretary in the Foreign Department and then a Board Member, who was much in demand as a speaker, who later became Dean of Wells College; and William N. Wysham, a former missionary in Persia, who has rendered versatile and effective service as Acting Candidate Secretary, Western and Eastern Area Secretary, and Secretary for Literature and Publications.

The Secretarial Staff included also Lindsay S. B. Hadley, the Candidate Secretary for six years, a former missionary in North China; Miss Helen Kittredge, Assistant Treasurer of the Board, a sister of Thomas J. Watson, who, with Miss Mary Moore, later Mrs. Robert N. McLean, made a remarkable deputation trip to the Missions overseas, carrying a message of buoyancy, good cheer and courage around the world; Marcia Kerr, a Wellesley graduate, later Mrs. Graham Hunter, whose versatility was revealed in her capable filling of several positions on the Secretarial Staff; Frank W. Bible, who went to China as a missionary in 1904, became the outstanding leader in the Central China Mission, and on his return to America was appointed Secretary in the Home Base Department in the Central District, a forceful speaker and successful solicitor of gifts; Francis Shunk Downs, who came from a family of influence in business and politics in Pennsylvania, who served for seven years as an Associate Secretary in the Home Department; Herrick B. Young, a missionary in Persia engaged in educational work, who was brought into the Board service in America to direct the Centennial celebration and to lead the campaign for funds during that celebration in 1937, who served as Personnel Secretary, and was later President of Western College in Oxford, Ohio; Miss Irene Sheppard, who came to the Board in 1925 after service with the YWCA in South America, and was an associate secretary in the department of Latin America and West Africa; Ernest F. Hall, who served as secretary in the Western and Eastern Areas, and in the Department of Annuities and Special Gifts; and Weston T. Johnson, a former missionary in Japan, later Western District Secretary of the Board, who rendered able service as a translator and advisor for the Army during World War II.

Individual members of the clerical staff include those who have given long years of service in carrying forward the detailed work that must be done in an organization whose scope is world-wide and that reaches throughout the bounds of the home church, in this land and overseas.

The staff in Robert Speer's office included Miss Johanna Connell, who for many years was Dr. Speer's secretary, who deciphered his indecipherable calligraphy and served with rare fidelity; Miss Edith Dickie, who later served with devotion and grace in China; Mrs. Charles Bidwell; and Miss Alice M. White, who has written of her memories of Dr. Speer on pages 85 and 86.

Board members included: George Alexander, pastor of the First Presbyterian Church, New York City, a member of the Board for forty-six years, and President for twenty-one years (Dr. Speer's tribute to him appears on page 98); Charles R. Erdman, of the Princeton Theological Seminary Faculty, President of the Board from 1926 to 1940, a man of sound scholarship and delightful humor; W. E. Stiger, a Yale graduate in the class of 1866, a lawyer whose blindness did not prevent his serving as legal counsel of the Board with rare fidelity and ability; Alfred E. Marling, President of a large real estate firm in New York City, a layman much in demand as a public speaker, who brought original and unusual gifts of mind and spirit to his service on the Board; Peter K. Emmons, pastor of the Westminster Presbyterian Church in Scranton, Pa., and President of the Board of Trustees of Princeton Theological Seminary, and of the Foreign Board from 1951 to the present.

Other Board members were: Margaret E. Hodge, a Vice-President, a member of the well-known Hodge family, whose brother Cortland Van Renssaeler Hodge, M.D., was killed by the Boxers in Paotingfu in 1900, a leader in the Church of outstanding influence; Mrs. John Finley, wife of the Editor of the New York Times; Mrs. D. Johnson Fleming, who had served in India, and was an able speaker for the foreign mission cause; Edwin M. Bulkley, senior partner in the firm of Spencer, Trask & Co., in New York, Chairman of the Finance Committee of the Board, Robert Speer's close friend and a near neighbor, an elder in the First Presbyterian Church in Englewood, New Jersey, a man tall in stature and Victorian in dignity, whose generous gifts to the work of the Board and individuals in need were a continual inspiration and help to a wide circle of friends; James M. Speers, President of James McCutcheon & Co., an elder in the Central Presbyterian Church of Montclair, N.J., the father of six sons, two of whom entered foreign mission service, two became ministers, and two entered business in their father's firm; John T. Underwood, President of the Underwood Typewriter Company, an elder in the Lafayette Avenue Presbyterian Church of Brooklyn, an influential member of the Finance Committee of the Board; John A. Mackay, who came to the Board from service as an Educational Missionary in YMCA work in South America, who, because of his ability in the Spanish language and his scholarship, was given an honorary degree by the University of San Marcos in Lima, Peru; who from 1932 to 1936 was Secretary for Latin America and West Africa of the Board, and was called to the Presidency of Princeton Theological Seminary, who became a Board member and President, and later Chairman of the International Missionary Council, an author of several influential books, both in English and Spanish, dealing with foreign missions and Latin America, who was elected Moderator of the Presbyterian Church for the year 1953-54; John L. Severance, a patron of the arts, a financier and philanthropist of Cleveland, Ohio; and Cheesman A. Herrick, President of Girard College, whose realistic judgments and decision and force of character and wide experience in the educational world were valuable assets in the administration and formation and execution of Board policy.

These were Robert Speer's associates, men and women in whose selection for service with the Board he had had an influential part—associates and friends who were loyal to him and to the Church and to the Master whom they together served.

Perhaps never in the history of the Foreign Board did its membership include abler and more influential men and women, particularly laymen, devoted to the Foreign Mission Cause than during the service of Robert E. Speer, the magnet and admired leader and friend who had drawn them to the work with him.

For over twenty years after his election as Secretary, Robert Speer handled all the details of his administrative work in the Foreign Board. The feeling grew among the Board members that he should be relieved of much of this detail so that his time and thought could be devoted to the larger issues of the Board and of the Church. A Board member came into the office one day and found Dr. Speer occupied with pursuing the details of a missionary's home allowance and with action concerning his furlough. The Board member exploded in a Committee meeting, asserting, "We are wasting Dr. Speer's time! He ought not to have to be occupied with such relatively trivial detail."

But Dr. Speer resisted these efforts to separate him from the detail of administration and contact with the missionaries, and until the last year of his service with the Foreign Board retained the duties of a Foreign Secretary of the Board for the India and Persia Missions, although he did relinquish the Secretaryship of the Central China and Kiangan Missions. He felt he could be in closer touch with the work and more truly identified with it if he had intimate and direct personal contact with individual missionaries and individual Missions.

Robert Speer and Arthur J. Brown, the Senior Secretaries, took turns in presiding at the Council meetings. The sessions of the Councils were carried through with a minimum of waste of time and with intense concentration on the business in hand. Members of the Council soon learned the need of careful and full investigation and preparation before bringing up matters for action; the penalty for carelessness or superficial preparation and presentation was defeat of the action proposed or delay in decision, and request for further study and investigation before action. Usually the views of Dr. Speer and of Dr. Brown were approved, but at times they were voted down, and Dr. Speer took such decisions in the best of spirit and with no rancor.

I remember vividly the first Council meetings I attended and the first action I presented for approval. That was in the spring of 1921. I had been brought into the Council after the sudden death of Dr. A. W. Halsey, beloved Secretary for Latin America and Africa and head of the Home Base Department. One of the first matters to be presented on my docket was a request for increase in salary that came to me from a missionary in Colombia. When I presented the request, the two watchmen of the Treasury, Russell Carter, Assistant Treasurer, and Robert Speer, Senior Secretary, bowled me over, stating the Council and the Board could not act on a request from an individual missionary. I reported this to the missionary who told me there had been Mission action on the request and a Secretary of the Board had stated the matter would be considered when appropriations were made up the following spring. After strenuous research in the files, in which I found that both the Colombia and Venezuela Missions had asked for increases, that all the other Missions outside of Latin America had been given increases, I asked permission at the meeting of the full Council the following day for reconsideration of the vote approved the previous day. I did this with considerable misgiving and trepidation, as it seemed hardly fitting for me, a young missionary and newcomer in the Council, to challenge the opinion of veterans like Dr. Speer and Mr. Carter; but I could not believe the decision which had been reached had been right, so I asked the opportunity for reconsideration. I stated the matter as clearly as I could, and then made the motion for approval of the increased salary for both Colombia and Venezuela, and I was greatly heartened when the vote was taken to hear the deep voice of Robert Speer recording a resounding "Aye."

Never did Robert Speer harbor resentment for being outvoted. Once in a Board meeting it was reported that a matter had been approved by the Councils despite Robert Speer's negative vote. One of the Board members asked in surprise, "Why, Robert, are you ever in the minority?" Dr. Speer replied in good spirit and with a twinkle in his eye, "I live there."

Once, after a long and tedious discussion in one of the Councils, I said to him, "I think you're very patient with the Council," and he replied, "Well, this is a democracy." Never did he try to use his prestige and standing to force through a vote against the judgment of his colleagues, but patiently and carefully he would explain why he favored or was opposed to the action being discussed. Often he reminded me of Lincoln in his dealings with his own argumentative and obstructive Cabinet.

Robert Speer's patience and open-mindedness were described by his assistant, George T. Scott, who came into his office in 1913.

George Scott wrote that his first assigned task was correcting galley proofs of the report of a conference in Latin America which Robert Speer had organized and led. George Scott had been a member of the faculties of the Syrian Protestant College in Beirut and Hampton Institute in Virginia, and had had experience in correcting papers and essays of his students. Orville Reed, a secretary in the Candidate Department, came in to see how the new assistant was progressing in his work. Dr. Reed saw the galley proofs were well marked up and inquired, "Do you know who wrote that report?" George Scott replied he did not, and Orville Reed said, "That's a speech of Robert E. Speer exactly as he delivered it." Dr. Scott replied, "The grammar needs correction." Dr. Reed left the room in consternation. Later, when Dr. Scott informed Dr. Speer about the corrections, Robert Speer laughed and told him he had been quite right and thanked him for correcting the address.

Official correspondence was a large part of Robert Speer's duties, but he also wrote many letters to individuals, in which his tact and courtesy were beautifully and clearly shown. In pure and tender consolation and sympathy his letters to bereaved individuals remind one of the letters of Abraham Lincoln.

When a missionary was blocking progress, "former football tackle Speer would take him out of the play with the best Princeton technique." Once a missionary was not doing his work well and Robert Speer was the Secretary who was designated to tell him that for the good of the service he should resign. George Scott related how this was accomplished:

Mr. Speer brought me a three-page typed letter and asked, "How will this do?" His letter was a magical composition which I do not yet understand; in its beginning the man was a friendly missionary apparently in good standing but at its end, without any noticeable intervening change, he seemed not to have the slightest relation to the Mission or Board. I searched that letter for evidence of the transition and could find none. I had a much-needed lesson in letter writing. In due time and in fairly amiable spirit, the missionary's resignation arrived.[31]

As George Scott pointed out the perennial issue in all enterprises, "staff officers" (in the Board this would include secretaries in New York) versus "line officers" (executives in the Missions), at one time caused the Board much concern. Robert Speer was at the center of the conflict because he was senior staff officer and because he believed in centralized and responsible administration. Two strong Missions, led by a few determined drivers in each, demanded field autonomy, and agitated through the General Assembly at home the setting up of a special commission on this and related issues. Heat was engendered and friendly ties were strained. In the hearings of the Commission Dr. Speer carried the main burden of the defense of the Board. One missionary, the leader of the majority party in the Mission, closed his rhetorical address with the question, "Under the great Presbyterian Board is there not room for a missionary like *me?*" Rising for a defense of the Board, Dr. Speer quietly replied: "Of course there is a place for you, Dr. ———. That question is not before the Commission. The question to be considered is: Under the Presbyterian Board is there room for a missionary *not* like you?" After nearly two years of hearings, definitions were agreed upon in the administrative relations of Board and Missions, with fuller autonomy being given the latter under locally elected executives.[32]

Robert Speer did not like to give advice, particularly on personal problems. He seemed to feel that some individuals in coming to him for help in making such decisions were avoiding the hard-thinking and courageous choices necessary in their own character and careers. When consulted in regard to such decisions, Robert Speer would listen thoughtfully and ask a few revealing questions, which usually would clarify the situation and lead the inquirer to reach his own conclusion.

Personal financial appeals Robert Speer would meet from an amount kept by the Board Treasurer marked "R.E.S.

Trust Fund." This removed the personal element from the transaction and saved friendships so often impaired by direct beneficence. "Robert Speer was short on promises but extremely long on performance." [33]

In his public addresses and in his personal bearing Robert Speer gave the impression of earnestness and gravity. This was due to his intense preoccupation in the work at hand. But his sense of humor was known to personal friends and associates and often helped to liven and brighten the routine of everyday tasks. Just as Lincoln relieved the tension of a Cabinet meeting during the Civil War by reading a story from Artemus Ward, so Robert Speer knew how to introduce humor to relieve tension.

One day during a meeting of the Executive Council, when discussion had continued for a long period and patience was wearing thin and tempers were rising, Robert Speer, who was presiding, noticed that the Treasurer of the Board had brought with him to the Council meeting a bag of round, hard candies, shaped like marbles. Dr. Speer placed one of the candies in the center of the long table, asked the Treasurer for another candy, and holding it, he knelt down, closed one eye and took careful aim. With his index finger he shot the candy down the table, hit the other piece and knocked it off the table. Then he stood up, resumed his seat, and said, "Let us now proceed with our discussion." [34]

Shortly after Woodrow Wilson defeated Charles E. Hughes for the Presidency in 1916 the staff of the Foreign Board held its annual dinner at a hotel on lower Broadway. The toastmaster announced that a distinguished citizen had just arrived at the hotel and had accepted an invitation to address the dinner guests. The door opened and in walked Charles Evans Hughes, with silk hat, whiskers, cutaway coat, striped trousers, gloves and cane. It was Robert E. Speer! His address, "Why I Lost the Election," captivated and convulsed the audience. This performance was so popular that he was persuaded to repeat it at subsequent dinners.

At another staff dinner, Dr. Speer came in as a musician with a jazz band, banging on a tin pan with a large spoon. At a staff dinner just before his retirement in 1937, he gave an address on "Why I Am Glad to Retire," the principal reason being because he would no longer have to go to the General Assembly.[35]

A member of the office staff of the Presbyterian Foreign Board wrote of a revealing incident that occurred one day in March when the bell was rung for the brief noon worship service held every day in the Assembly Room of the Foreign Board offices at 156 Fifth Avenue. When the secretarial staff and stenographers gathered for the meeting, they saw Dr. Speer standing by the door. He was scheduled to lead the service and he announced: "This is St. Patrick's Day, and only those who have remembered to wear a bit of green are privileged to occupy the front seats, which have been specifically reserved for the faithful." Then the staff noticed that he himself was wearing a tie of Ireland's favorite color.[36]

One of Dr. Speer's personal secretaries has written of her work with him:

As one of Dr. Speer's staunchest admirers for his efficiency, saintliness, brilliance, oratory and humility, I appreciated most of all his warm friendliness and sense of humor in the everyday work of the office. His desk was bare to the general public, but he could produce voluminous correspondence which he read when he was away from the office. Those letters he carried in a large attaché case. He dictated speeches after, and not before, delivery. Poetry he recited from memory. When people would criticize him, he would remark, "This is *good* for one." One of his stock paragraphs in correspondence would be under the heading "reading," which changed from week to week, an amazing list.

After an appeal for funds Dr. Speer would often receive large checks with a notation that "this is a tribute to you as a man." This would disappoint him, as he wanted everyone to be interested in the work. He was asked many times to write prefaces for books. He did this at times but felt a book should stand on its merits.

As Dr. Speer's time was valuable, he would be apt to dismiss a well-known person rather quickly, but would allow ample time to less known people. Many callers were mature ministers who said their one meeting with him when they were young had changed their lives.

I liked to tease Dr. Speer and told him he seemed just about perfect to me except for his politics. He was a Democrat with what seemed to me a Republican make-up.[37]

One of Robert Speer's associates in the Secretarial Staff of the Foreign Board wrote of another incident which occurred during discussion in the meeting of the Executive Council. She was then Acting Candidate Secretary and brought to the monthly meeting an item for clearance. As the debate began to develop, taking the time of the whole group, Dr. Speer spoke rather sharply, stating the subject should have been cleared with those concerned prior to the meeting, and as Chairman he shut off the debate. Later, he pushed a note across the table to his associate in which he had written, "Forgive my peevishness." The Secretary stated that Dr. Speer had been absolutely right and he had no need to apologize, but what he did revealed his humble spirit.[38]

On another occasion a number of callers had come into Dr. Speer's office, the last one being Mrs. Speer. Mrs. Bidwell, Dr. Speer's secretary, opened the door to the inner office and announced Mrs. Speer's arrival; she saw Robert Speer rise from his chair and heard him say, "You are not the first lady who has come into my office this morning, but you are the loveliest." [39]

Clarence A. Steele, a former Treasurer of the Siam Mission and later Assistant Treasurer and Treasurer of the Foreign Board, has written of his joy in the work in the office in New York with Robert Speer. He spoke of Dr.

Speer's ability to keep figures in his mind and memory. On one occasion the work sheet had been prepared for Dr. Speer's study and use. This work sheet records the amounts the various Missions and Mission Stations ask in their estimates from the field. The sheet indicates the estimates for the eight classes of work and is a compilation of figures so extended that the paper covers the whole top of a desk. This document was always presented to Robert Speer before the appropriations were brought to the Board for action. Mr. Steele spoke of his amazement at Robert Speer's grasp of the figures, and his accurate memory of the requests from previous years. Once Mr. Steele related that Robert Speer inquired if requests in one of the Mission's estimates had been verified. Clarence Steele replied in the affirmative. Later, on investigation, he had to report to Dr. Speer that those who had made up the appropriation in the Treasurer's office had overlooked certain details which Dr. Speer had recalled "with his uncanny memory for figures." [40]

When Robert Speer was on a deputation trip to Siam in 1914, he and Clarence Steele called on Prince Damrong, who held the position corresponding to United States Secretary of State. Robert Speer guided the conversation into a discussion of Buddhism, and the Prince explained his position, which was, of course, along the line of the Buddhist religion, though he was very sympathetic with the Christian service in Siam. Dr. Speer was able, in a conference the next day, to outline fully the Siamese Prince's discussion and trend of thought on our Mission problems. [41]

At the annual meetings of the General Assembly, except for the times when he was scheduled to speak, Robert Speer was seldom seen on the platform with the Moderator or other leaders of the Church. At a meeting in Cincinnati, the representative of the Foreign Board who addressed the Assembly on Foreign Missions referred to Dr. Speer's coming retirement and paid a tribute to him for his influence and leadership during the years. The audience rose to its feet, applauded and called for Robert Speer. He was sitting on a camp chair behind the piano, hidden from the audience, and, as a spectator wrote, "He had to be dragged to the front of the stage, where he received a tremendous ovation."

At another Assembly, the Moderator asked William P. Schell to find Robert Speer and bring him to the platform to confer on a matter of importance with the Moderator. Dr. Schell looked all through the auditorium without success, and finally went to Dr. Speer's hotel. There he found him in bed in his pajamas, with a board resting on his knees, writing an article for *The Missionary Review of the World*. Dr. Schell told Dr. Speer of the message from the Moderator, and Dr. Speer asked that the Moderator be told he had gone to bed and that he would see the Moderator in the morning.

Robert Speer believed that history moved in cycles, and that a knowledge of history could prevent repeating the errors and mistakes of the past. When someone would enthusiastically propose action on a certain matter in the Executive Council, Dr. Speer would say, "Yes, that was tried out some years ago. It didn't work then but it might work now. Try it and see." Or, again, referring to past history, he would argue against a repetition of a previous error.[42]

The schedule of addresses and almost continuous travel both in the homeland and overseas placed an obvious strain on Robert Speer's strength, but he wrote his wife of his true satisfaction in that service: "It is tiring work, speaking three times a day and talking incessantly, riding in slow trains; days like these are not bodily restful, but this is a fruitful expenditure of life."[43]

Mrs. Speer records:

His letters speak of the constant travel, the small local country hotels, the connections that did not connect, the meals that were missed with no dining car and no chance for lunch or supper. "One of our cars jumped the tracks and we arrived five and half hours late at 1:30 A.M. Nothing to eat since noon yesterday; to cap it all, we were at first told there were no rooms for us, though reservations had been made some time before. However, at last we got good quarters and I could sleep from 2 until 7:45.

Later, when airplanes made the journeys shorter, there was always the risk of bad weather and of missing the engagements altogether. So he gave up air travel and stuck to railroads. Once, when a difficult journey had been made to keep an engagement of long standing, he wrote: "Last night's Missionary meeting was a fizzle. There were less than fifty people there. It had evidently been no one's business to work it up. However, with a handful of earnest souls, one could always have a good time." Another difficulty was being engaged to speak three times and being expected to speak six.

Once, after a day with several speaking engagements, followed by a restless night on a train, Dr. Speer tried to secure some sleep in a hotel bedroom before an evening speaking appointment. He fell asleep and was aroused by a pounding on his door and by the message that he was overdue at the evening meeting. He hurriedly threw on his clothes, finished dressing in a cab, and made the address almost as if in his sleep. This was one of the two times he forgot an appointment, the other occasion being when he completely failed to remember a speaking engagement; but that was on the day his first child was born.[44]

His constancy in prayer and his reliance on prayer were realities concerning which he seldom spoke. On one occasion, as he was starting off on a long deputation trip overseas, he wrote to a friend who had sent him a copy of a book by John Masefield to read en route: "The book has been a real source of pleasure and help. I had to read and pray to keep happy and steady, and prayer has never seemed so sweet." [45]

VII. His Service with the Board of Foreign Missions (*Con't.*)

A POST-WAR CONFERENCE OF REPRESENTATIVES OF THE Missions and of the Foreign Board was held in Princeton, New Jersey, from June 19 to 27, inclusive, 1920. Its purpose was stated in the letter sent to the Presbyterian Missions on January 25, 1919: "The main business of the Conference should be to face frankly the solemn questions of world evangelization in the light of the conditions which the war has created, and to consider earnestly and prayerfully how we can more effectively meet them."

One hundred and fifty-two delegates and representatives met on the beautiful campus of the University, the Theological Seminary and the Graduate School. George Alexander, President of the Foreign Board, presided at all the sessions or appointed a substitute.

On "stunt night" Robert Speer took his part with able mimicry and humor, making a "missionary address" by retelling some of the tall tales of Owen Crimmins, contained in the book by that title, which he had written about this former woods partner and guide, and poking fun at his senior colleague, Arthur J. Brown, for his justifiable pride in two of his best-selling books on Missions, *The Why and How of Foreign Missions*, of which over 200,000 copies were sold, and *The Mastery of the Far East*, published by Scribner's. Robert Speer described these two books as "The Whereabouts and Whatabouts of Foreign Missions," and

"My Mastery of the Mystery of the Far East," and at a later meeting made the concluding address of the Conference, "Our Future Policy as a Whole."

He spoke of the "broad question of the further expansion of the work." Where shall this expansion come and in what order? Perhaps the criteria of judgment would be: (a) sole occupancy or the measure of our separate territorial responsibility; (b) the responsiveness of the field; (c) the strategic importance; (d) human need.

This presentation was listened to with concentration of mind and heart by the missionaries whose fields were being discussed, and Robert Speer's sympathetic understanding and his sense of humor were revealed in a statement he made as he was completing this address:

I marvel at my hardihood in casting out so recklessly such a bushel basket of apples of discord; but either you must make a better and juster list or we must go on with the old opportunist method, balancing the conditions annually as fairly as possible, and seeking to adjust each year's contemporary needs and supplies. Which is the wiser course? Or perhaps the best and indeed the only thing we can do is to look at our field in five great divisions, the Far East, the Mohammedan World, the old and still kindred religious mass of Hinduism and Southern Buddhism, Latin America, and Africa, and to move steadily along the five lines of activity essential to deal with these five areas of need, not attempting to judge any one of them to possess any claim of exclusiveness or continuous precedence.

Dr. Speer went on to consider the question of new fields and also the respective functions of Foreign Missions, of the Christian Church, and of Christianity, and the fact of the divine government of the world. He concluded: "There are two words of Our Lord which sometimes appear contradictory but which are really supplementary and that provide us with the true principle of comprehension for our

missionary program: 'He that is not with us is against us,'
but also 'he that is not against us is for us.' " [46]

Robert E. Speer was not only the chief spokesman for
the Foreign Board and its chief administrator but he was
also the most powerful and successful promoter of its work.
A memorable example of that service was during the year
1923-1924, when the Board faced a deficit of approximately
half a million dollars in its current budget. This debt was
due to the increase in appropriations following recommendations of the Post-war Conference held at Princeton, N.J.,
in 1920. I remember vividly the meeting held in the daily
prayer service of members of the staff of the Executive
Council when Robert Speer spoke of the situation the Board
was facing. He said: "We are facing now a true test of
God's power and of the fulfillment of His promises; Christ
has said that such work as we are trying to do is His work
and that God will care for it and will bless it; the situation
we are now facing will prove if these promises are true."

Robert E. Speer led the staff in the drive for increased
gifts for the work to meet the new deficit and the current
budget. He wrote a moving appeal for aid from the Church
and from individuals, "Our Foreign Missions in Peril,"
pointing out that the cause of the deficit was not the character of the missionaries and of their work, asserting that
the missionaries were the truest Christians in the Church
and deserved support, and ending the statement, "Never did
we appeal so earnestly for your support. We beg your aid
to avert disaster."

At that time I was Executive Secretary for the Latin
American and West African Missions and had returned from
a six-months' deputation trip to Mexico, Colombia, and
Venezuela. The deputations always find a need for securing funds for the property and budgets of the Missions
visited, and I returned with the burden of a special need
in the Colombia Mission, where the outstanding girls' school

in Barranquilla was facing the loss of its property and the
need of funds for new buildings. A total of $40,000 was
being asked for these needs. This sum, if met, would be
an additional financial burden on the Board.

Hearing on my return from the field in April, 1923, of
the great deficit which the Board was facing in its current
obligations, I offered in the Council meeting to give up the
campaign that was being planned to secure the $40,000
needed for the property additions in the Colombia Mission,
so there would be no diversion of gifts from the regular
budget of the Board to these property needs. Robert Speer
spoke with appreciation of this offer, but told me to go
forward with the plan for a campaign in Western Pennsylvania to secure gifts for the Colombia Mission property needs.
The campaign was carried out in the fall of 1923 with the
generous co-operation of the Presbyteries of Blairsville,
Clarion, Erie, and Kittanning; three members of the Colombia Mission participated in the campaign with the Executive Secretary;[47] the Church members of the four Presbyteries responded generously, and with the aid of a grant of
$10,000 from the Sage Legacy Fund the full total of $40,000
needed was secured.

In one of his pithy statements, Robert Speer summarized
the two essential factors in such efforts. "Work without
prayer is ashes; prayer without work is a dream." And,
again, he once said, speaking of the prevalent and extreme
reliance upon money alone in Mission work, "We have re-
versed a saying of Christ's, and we assert that with God
an action may be impossible, but not with money, for all
things are possible with money." After approving of the
property campaign for the Colombia Mission, he threw his
own strength and great power into the campaign to meet
the current deficit; the members of the Executive Staff and
of the Board and of the Missions who were in this country
joined in the effort, which extended throughout the Church;

and in a most dramatic way the Church responded; gifts totaling over a million dollars came in; and the Board went into the new fiscal year beginning in April, 1924, with the burden of debt rolled away and with deep gratitude to the Lord of the work, to the generous and sacrificial donors throughout the Church, and to Robert Speer for his courageous and inspiring leadership.

Edward M. Dodd, M.D., a medical missionary in Persia and later Medical Secretary of the Board, wrote of Robert Speer:

I first knew Dr. Speer when I was a student at Princeton and during those years he and Woodrow Wilson, at that time President of the University, were the greatest inspirations in my life.

One of Dr. Speer's books, *The Marks of a Man*, made a deep impression on me. I little thought that his chapter on the lie never being justifiable would be like a beacon to me when as a young medical missionary, alone with heavy responsibility, in a beleaguered Iranian city during World War I, I had to face a potential choice between hazards. The Mission station at Urumia (now Rezayeh) changed hands several times with chaos and devastation and massacre between, the main protagonists being the Russians of the old regime and the Turks, with marauding Kurdish tribesmen intermingled. During these tense and trying years we were completely cut off from outside mail and almost completely from outside news. We did not know until weeks later that the war was over and that the Allies had won.

During these years we had an immense sense of backing in Mr. Speer as our Secretary at Board headquarters in New York. We knew he was there, doing all that could humanly be done, praying, upholding our hands. It was like having the Rock of Gibraltar back of you.[48]

George H. Trull, who served on the secretarial staff of the Foreign Board, for thirty years, wrote of Robert Speer:

He believed in strict adherence to the rules and regulations of the Board's Manual for the conduct of its work. He deprecated missionaries asking for property items and for activities that did not have the sanction of their Mission, for this tended to divert funds from the Board's regular budget. . . . Dr. Speer hated debts and believed in strict economy, especially in overhead expenses. He regarded all the funds received by the Board as a sacred trust, to be expended without waste of any sort. . . . He loved beauty everywhere, chiefly the beauty of holiness in Christ his Lord and wished his own life and the lives of his colleagues to be "unspotted" and "consecrated" in service.[49]

Robert E. Speer was thrifty and economical in his personal expenditures. He was a member of the Princeton Club in New York City, but rarely ate there, usually having his luncheon at a Child's restaurant near his office or at a stand-up lunch counter. He avoided using taxicabs whenever he could walk. I remember that when he came to Auburn Theological Seminary to speak while I was a student there he walked the half-mile up hill from the railroad station to the Seminary, carrying his bag, heavy with books and papers. After his retirement, he wrote nearly all his letters in longhand, avoiding the expense of having them typewritten.

Robert Speer's sympathy for those who had lost loved ones was deepened by his own experience in making his way through life after he was nine years of age without his mother to cherish and guide him. A letter written to John E. Williams, Vice-President of the University of Nanking, after the death of Dr. Williams' mother, is revealing:

I have just learned from Mr. Scott of the great sorrow that has come to you in the death of your mother, and I send you my deep and loving sympathy. I rejoice with you that you have had your mother with you for so many years. My mother died when I was a very little boy, so that my sympathy with those who have just lost, as you have lost, has always been touched with a little envy that they had possessed for so many years the richest of all wealth. I am glad that you could be at home for the last days with her, and I know the new strength of your ties with the unseen and the eternal which is the one compensation for sorrow so deep and measureless.[50]

William N. Wysham, who served in Persia from 1920 to 1938, with two years in the office in New York, and is now Secretary of the Division of Literature and Publications, wrote:

In Persia, Dr. Speer was our beloved corresponding secretary and we felt that he never lost sight of the interests of the Persia Mission and of each one of us as individual missionaries. . . . From the time that I began my new work in Christian literature in Iran in 1926 Dr. Speer was my enthusiastic supporter and without fail commented on my annual reports. I quote from one of his letters:

"I have read with deepest interest and satisfaction and joy the report of your Literature Committee for the year ending this summertime. It is an immense encouragement to see what you have been able to accomplish in just a few years. What you have done shows what could be done, I presume, in almost any mission field in the world by a little group who would give themselves intelligently and devotedly to this important matter of the development of Christian literature. I trust that you may be able to go on with this work until Persia becomes, as it has well-nigh become already, a model for all the missions in the world as to what can be done in this field."

In his personal correspondence, Dr. Speer never confined himself to mission matters alone. He was always trying to help us to become more useful, and made frequent references to books and other broadening influences. For example, he wrote on August 5, 1929: "I read through on the trains a few weeks ago one of the most interesting and refreshing books that I have read for a long time, Karl Barth's *The Word of God and the Word of Man*. Barth was one of the new theological school in Germany which has swung clear to the opposite extreme from the old emphasis on human experience as the source of religion and of theological doctrine. This new German emphasis is now wholly on the overpowering sovereignty of God. No doubt the reaction is due in part to the war, with its demonstration of the futility of man's plans and with its mighty stroke of Divine Judgment. We felt very strongly this new German tendency in the German and Scandinavian delegation at the Missionary Council meeting in Jerusalem. . . ."

It is interesting that at the very beginning Dr. Speer picked up the significance of Karl Barth, who is now a household word across the world, and is the father of Neo-Orthodoxy.

My last contact with Dr. Speer was at the Synod of Pennsylvania, meeting at Wilson College in the summer of 1947, just a few months before he died. He was still at the height of his power and led a never-to-be-forgotten series of devotional services. He was, in my opinion, the greatest Christian of his age.[51]

At the memorial services for George Alexander, who had been a member of the Presbyterian Board of Foreign Missions for forty-six years (the same span of years that Robert Speer served the Board as Secretary), and was President of the Board for twenty-one years, Robert Speer made three contributions to the services and to the memory of this much loved leader and friend. He gave his personal tribute to him, he drafted the Memorial Minute, approved by the Board at its meeting, December 15, 1930, and he made the prayer at the funeral service at the First Presbyterian Church in New York on that same afternoon.

One of Robert Speer's characteristics was his refusal to follow the easiest way in preparation of his addresses on a topic designed for different audiences, and his avoidance of the repetition which others with less high standards would have employed. Instead, he always presented an original and individual statement or contribution, and on no occasion was this more evident than in the three products of his pen, of his heart, mind and voice, that he supplied at the death of George Alexander, whom he deeply trusted and warmly loved. His triple tribute to his friend after his service of nearly half a century could be applied justly to Robert Speer himself:

No part of the foreign mission field and no missionary problem or human need was alien to him.

No member of the Board was more active and intelligent and devoted. He was invariably present at all meetings of the Board and of the committees to which he belonged, and his counsel and prayers were the most precious human resource in the work of the Board. His annual Communion Service for the new missionaries at the New Missionaries Conference each June was the richest spiritual experience of the year. He had a place which no one else has held during the past half-century in the affection and trust of the Board and its members and its missionaries, to all of whom he was endeared by the noble qualities of his pure and genial and gracious spirit. By reason of his long service he has had to do with the commissioning of more missionaries than any other Presbyterian in Christian history, and his death will awaken more personal and affectionate memories around the world than that of any other man. . . .

George Alexander was the good, great man of whom Coleridge wrote:

"Hath he not always treasures, always friends,
The good, great man? Three treasures, love and light
And calm thoughts, equable as infant's breath:
And three fast friends, more sure than day or night—
Himself, His Maker and the Angel Death." [52]

I remember with special gratitude the farewell service led at 156 Fifth Avenue by Dr. Speer when Mrs. Wheeler and I and our three sons went back to China in 1932. I had been a member of the council of the Board for eleven years as Secretary for Latin America and Africa. We had always hoped to return to China, and when John A. Mackay had become available for the Latin American and African Missions, I renewed my request that we be allowed to return to China. This request was approved, and in August, 1932, with hearts full of joy, we sailed again for the Far East. Our three sons came to the farewell service in the Board Rooms at 156 Fifth Avenue, and Dr. Speer led the meeting. He took for the reading the third Epistle of St. John: "The elder unto Gaius the beloved, whom I love in truth. Beloved, I pray that in all things thou mayest prosper and be in health, even as thy soul prospereth. For I rejoiced greatly, when brethren came and bore witness unto thy truth, even as thou walkest in truth. Greater joy have I none than this, to hear of my children walking in the truth."

We left the Board rooms with the benediction of these beautiful words of the Beloved Disciple and of Dr. Speer's prayer and blessing, spoken with depth of feeling all the more moving and memorable because of his restraint.

Peter K. Emmons, pastor of the Westminster Church in Scranton, Pa., since 1930 a member of the Foreign Board and later its President, wrote of Robert Speer:

My very first contact with Robert Speer gave me a personal sense of appreciation of his spiritual leadership. He brought help to me at a critical and decisive moment in my own intellectual and spiritual experience, during my undergraduate days at Princeton University. Like many students in those days, my Christian faith was sorely tried by my introduction to science and philosophy by teachers who seemed to delight in shaking our beliefs. Just when I was ready to turn my back upon all teaching of the Church and home, this renowned World Christian came to the campus of the University. He gave us this simple, yet profound challenge: "If your faith is being shaken and God seems to be losing His reality for you, start praying this prayer, 'Lord, help me to *love* Thee more.' " I went to my room and began to pray that prayer and I found a new intimacy with God which changed my whole outlook on life.

Years afterward, I had the privilege of being closely associated with him in the work of the Presbyterian Board of Foreign Missions and the Board of Trustees of Princeton Theological Seminary. This was during days of tension. This man of God stood like a soldier, unmoved by the swirling currents of theological controversy and ecclesiastical strife. With a deep sense of mission to a lost world and an abiding confidence in God's power to fulfill His purposes, he marched straight on, unembittered and unafraid. Thus, Robert E. Speer proved himself in the truest and highest sense a prophet of the Most High.[53]

Arthur J. Brown, Secretary Emeritus of the Presbyterian Board of Foreign Missions, for thirty-four years a colleague of Robert Speer, has written of their work together:

It is not easy for me to speak of Robert E. Speer in terms of moderation. My association with him was long and intimate, official and personal. For thirty-four years we were coordinate administrative secretaries of the Presbyterian Board of Foreign Missions, New York. We occupied adjoining offices. We were in frequent conference on the numerous problems of the Board's large evangelistic, educational, medical and humanitarian work in Asia, Africa, and Latin America. We served together on a number of interdenominational and international committees and organizations. We were intimate friends as well as official colleagues, and we usually lunched together when our engagements permitted.

I mention these associations to justify my testimony that Robert Speer was one of the best men that I have ever known. Many men that the world deems great have defects of character or conduct that are not suspected by people who see them only in public. Dr. Speer was as great in private, as in public; he was a strong, masterful man, a born leader, but he kept his temper under perfect control. He never attempted to dominate others or to push himself forward. He was always the Christian gentleman, a genial companion, temperamentally reserved, but among his friends a brilliant conversationalist.

In this greatest of all causes, the world-wide work of the Christian Church, he was everywhere recognized as a great statesman, an able administrator, a wise counselor, an eloquent advocate. For nearly sixty years he was a popular and impressive speaker in colleges and conferences of various kinds, so that there are clergymen and laymen in hundreds of cities who were influenced by him. Few religious workers of the last half century were so widely known. He traveled extensively in other lands, published many books and countless articles, and received every honor that churches and universities could bestow upon him.

His interests extended far beyond denominational lines. He gave whole-hearted support to union and co-operative movements with adherents of other churches as well as his own. He was a member of a large number of committees for the promotion of human welfare. He was one of the charter trustees of the Church Peace Union, founded and endowed by Andrew Carnegie in 1914, for the promotion of international friendship, and he actively served on that Board for thirty-three years.

I have grateful memories of my long fellowship with this notable man, a true nobleman in the Kingdom of God. Reginald Wheeler is rendering an inestimable service in making available to this generation and to generations to come a record of that life of radiant faith, utter consecration and apostolic power.[54]

Charles T. Leber, who was called from his pastorate in Scranton, Pa., in 1936, to join the Executive Council of the Foreign Board and later became its first General Secretary, has written of Robert Speer's final year of service with the Foreign Board:

The first time I ever saw Dr. Speer was when, as a boy, I sat in our family pew in the Brown Memorial Presbyterian

Church in Baltimore. There in the pulpit stood a man I almost deified. He was the personification of all the mystery, romance and call of foreign missions and of magnificent faith in Jesus Christ. . . .

The last year of Dr. Speer's service on the Board, the one year I worked under him directly, was a severe and emotionally difficult one for him. He drew very much into himself as he prepared to lay down the leadership of the many and heavy years. . . . The concerns of the years seemed to be gathered into his mind and heart. He had set the course and had led the movement far on its way. Now it was up to those who should carry on. . . .

Although we did not talk much with Dr. Speer during the last year, his presence among us was always evident. When he spoke at our meetings, we listened as one listens to authority, and with reverence and with sacred affection. Administrative matters were interpreted by him in the depth and length and breadth of the Spirit. I recall the closing sentence of one of his office memoranda. I believe it was the last one he sent around. It read: "Build ye more stately mansions, O my soul."

At the dinner held by the Board upon the occasion of Dr. Speer's retirement in 1937 he spoke at length. And at the close, in his final words as an Executive of the Board, looking at us, Board members, members of the Staff, missionaries, as from the heights of terrific testimony and humble glory, he literally and wonderfully thundered: "Don't quit! Don't quit! Go ye . . . ! Carry on!" [55]

VIII. Foreign Journeys in the Old World and the New

We are grateful for the privilege of this visitation. From first to last, we have been with the men and women who most richly embody the Christian spirit and who are most nearly reproducing the work of the Apostolic Church. All the affection which we already felt for them has been deepened, and our one desire is better to serve them and better with them to serve our common Lord.[56]

—Robert E. Speer: "Report on India and Persia, 1922."

IN THE HOMELAND ROBERT SPEER'S WORK WITH THE FOREIGN Board included Board administration at 156 Fifth Avenue and field work throughout the Church; on the foreign field his service included visitation of the Missions and the Mission Councils overseas. As representative of the Board, his foreign journeys carried him on trips to the Missions in Persia, South America, Mexico, China, Japan, India, and the Near and Far East.

On his first journey, to Mexico in 1894, he went with his wife and Dr. W. R. Richards; his second journey, in 1896, was with Mrs. Speer, when they went together around the world. Mrs. Speer has written:

Going overland to Odessa in Russia we joined Dr. Joseph Cochran, one of the most beloved and distinguished of the Persia missionaries. He had been sought after by the Shah but preferred to stay in Urumia with the Mountain Nestorians, whom he dearly loved. To enter a city with him was an experience. A company of Persian officials, gorgeously mounted and in full uniform, would come out to meet him to show their respect, often riding like mad. And when he left the city there were led horses and many colorful ways of showing honor for him. His sister had married a Russian diplomat and Dr. Cochran's account of his visit with them made the Russia, through which we had passed a reality. From Urumia we went on to Tabriz and then down to Hamadan, where illness delayed us until the winter and early spring of 1897. With a few weeks in India, cut short because of typhoid in Persia, we went on to China and Japan, returning in September of 1897.

In 1909 Robert Speer went to South America with Joseph Cook as secretary; in 1915 to Siam, the Philippines, China, Korea (Chosen), and Japan, with Guthrie Speers as his secretary; in 1916 to a conference in Panama; in 1921 and 1922 to India, Persia, and China, with Russell Carter, with Henry Welles III as secretary; in 1925 he and Mrs. Speer went to the Congress on Christian Work at Montevideo and visited Missions in Brazil, Uruguay, Argentina, and Chile. In 1926, again with Mrs. Speer, he went to China for Evaluation Conferences and for visits to Japan and Korea. In 1928 they went to the World Conference at Jerusalem, followed with a month in the Near East. In addition, he made four other trips overseas: in 1894 to England to attend the Student Conference at Keswick; in 1900 to London for a British Student Volunteer Conference. Early in 1910 he and Mrs. Speer went to the World Missionary Conference in Edinburgh. His last trip was the only overseas journey made for purely personal reasons— a holiday with Mrs. Speer, visiting their daughter and her family in England in 1939.

Robert Speer's physical stamina was tested in his deputation trips to the field. Anyone who has gone on one of these trips knows they are full of blessings and rich fellowship but that they also combine the experiences of a campaign tour and an endurance contest.

George T. Scott wrote of Mr. Speer's service in these journeys:

Official visitation to Mission Fields abroad is a significant phase of a foreign secretary's service; here reference is made only to the New York end of such trips by Mr. Speer, who administered the Brazil, Persia, and Japan Missions and the Missions in China and India. This wide geographical spread, coupled with slow travel and the constant demand for his presence in America, made it impossible for him to visit his fields as often as he would have liked. Before leaving, he made careful preparation and discussed with other secretaries the issues in all Missions that he would visit. His magnificent service of many kinds on these long, difficult, and exhausting tours is related by others. His reports to the Board (like his regular semimonthly presentations) were detailed, comprehensive, masterly and convincing; one or another personal friend, to save Board money, would gladly meet the cost of publishing these reports in book form. After his visit to the Far East in 1915, Dwight H. Day, Treasurer of the Board, told me: "I heard Robert speak 180 times on the trip and never repeat himself except for an illustrative anecdote which he told twice."

But from his reports the reader would have no idea of the tremendous contribution made by his addresses. To economize Board funds, Mr. Speer was accustomed to secure special gifts for his own modest expenses and for those of his traveling companions who did not provide their own. Regarding these visits the Board received gratifying reports from Missions and missionaries, frequently of other denominations. Mr. Speer knew his Missions (probably better than anyone else in his time) and the Missions knew he did.[57]

Letters written by Mrs. Speer give a vivid description of the journey to Persia in 1896-97, of Robert Speer's illness in Hamadan, and of the experiences on their first journey to the field.

Sunjud, Persia
Tuesday, October 27, 1896

Dearest Mother and Father:

It won't do any good to take out an atlas and look up this place, for it is only a little red-mud village of about a hundred families, on the road from Tabriz to Hamadan. I have wished many times a day that you, Father, could see this country, this scenery, these people, and their oriental ways, unchanged, I fancy, since the time when Abraham left Ur of the Chaldees. I don't think that Mother would enjoy it much, the stopping places at night do not afford good enough beds, and the whole method of traveling is too rough. For instance, to-night we are all four of us—Mr. Coan from Urumia, who is taking us to Hamadan, Miss Lincoln, also from Urumia, who is taking advantage of our going to go to Hamadan, and Rob and myself in one room, and here we spend the night. O, if you could only see it! The floor is roughest mud, with a few dirty pieces of felt laid over it. The walls are of red mud, with a few little shallow holes dug in it for closets. The door is a frame work of branches, with twigs woven through them, and mud plastered on the inside. The roof is something of the same sort, with a few holes in it for windows and chimney, and the sole furniture is a few rough implements for cooking and some huge clay receptacles for flour and wheat. In the middle of the floor is the bake-oven or "tandour"—a yawning hole into which we are in great danger of falling, but the people are the soul of kindness.

Hamadan, Persia
November 5, 1896

We have accomplished the long horseback journey from Tabriz to Hamadan, and are now enjoying the delights of civilization for a while. Rob has started for Teheran and I am here alone for ten days, staying with delightful people, Mr. and Mrs. Hawkes, who almost make me forget that I am away from home. Mrs. Hawkes and I have a great deal in common, and know some of the same people at home. Her sister, Miss Margaret Sherwood, is a member of the Wellesley

Faculty and has lately written a delightfully clever little book, published by Macmillan.

Every one was amazed at the quick time in which we made the journey from Tabriz to this place. Most caravans take seventeen days but we did it in eleven and a half, doubling every stage but one, and riding one day for eleven hours, another for ten, and almost every other day for seven or eight. The route was over the mountains most of the way, but the road was pretty good—for Persia, be it understood—so we could go fast. We would get up at three or four and start out in the moonlight about five. It was cold in the mountains at that hour in the morning. It is a great mistake to think that Persia is a warm country. The climate is just about like ours, and you know what it is like at five o'clock on a November morning at home. Fortunately we have plenty of warm clothing and have not caught bad colds.

My horse is a jewel. He is a light gray, strong and well-formed, and has absolutely perfect gaits, a fast walk, smooth pace and the easiest canter imaginable. We call him "The Country Gentleman," because that so exactly expresses his character. Rob's horse, a darker gray and not so pretty nor so easy, is "The Plodding Farmer." I wish I had even half a hope that you were getting our letters. . . .

Your Emma

November 27, 1896

Dearest Mother:

I had meant to write you a long happy letter by this mail about my visit here while Rob was in Teheran, but instead there is very woeful news to send home. We came here from Tabriz as I wrote you on our arrival here, with Mr. Coan of Urumia, a man thoroughly experienced in Persian traveling, knowing always the best and easiest ways of managing on these long, hard horseback journeys. The day after we arrived, Rob and Mr. Coan started "chappar" or post (i.e. on post horses without their servants or any outfit) to Teheran. They reached there early the following Sunday, having had a very hard, rough ride. They were caught in a blizzard on the mountains and were thoroughly chilled and soaked and had the worst sort of places to sleep in at nights. They stayed in Teheran until a week from the next Monday, and reached here late Thursday night. Rob had worked very, very hard in Teheran and was utterly tired out and the hard journey back was more than he could stand. At one place he had to get off his horse and lie down on the hard earth, he was so worn out. As soon as he reached here, we gave him a hot bath and put him to bed, and the next day he was up and better. He rested a little from his journey, but last Sunday he began to have fever, and though he seemed bright in the mornings, by 2 o'clock he would be utterly listless and very drowsy and weary. I realized from the time he arrived that he was ill, for the journey alone would not have used him up so, hard as it was, and I thought it was a bad attack of malaria, but on Wednesday night Dr. Holmes said it was typhoid. You can imagine what that meant to me. Here we are twenty-four days from the nearest railroad, sixteen days from the Persian Gulf and English steamers, and in a place where we cannot send cablegrams nor receive them, and from which it takes a letter six weeks to reach New York, with high mountains (14,000 ft.) all around us and the winter storms just beginning, with just eleven English-speaking people in a Persian City of 80,000 inhabitants, and Rob—Rob who had never been ill since I have known him, who hardly ever was tired even, has typhoid fever! To say that I felt as if the foundations of the earth were passing away would not half express it. Fortunately for me there was work to do and plenty of it, taking care of Rob. I could not stop to let myself think for half a minute, never mind what happened, and when Rob was asleep, I had to face it and think the whole thing out. However, several things soon stood out very clearly. First, that if I had any good stuff in me, now was the time to show it. Second, that God would take care of us here just as well as in New York, and that His way was always loving, no matter how hard it might seem. Third, that I had unspeakable reasons for thankfulness that we were not in some little hole on the way to Baghdad, as we should have been had we carried out our original plan. Fourth, that Dr. Holmes is a man we have every confidence in; he has lived in Persia for twenty years and is probably one of the most honored and respected men in the country. The new Shah tried very hard to induce him to come to Teheran and be his personal physician, but he would not leave his missionary work. He has pulled the missionaries through typhoid and smallpox, and every one of them regard him as a good angel. In addition to him, there is Dr. Wilson, a woman, and Mrs. Holmes, who was a practicing physician before her marriage, both of whom have a full knowledge of nursing. Mr. and Mrs. Hawkes could not be more kind if they were our own flesh and blood. They have no children, and have given up their whole house practically to us. Rob's temperature has not yet been above 104. The doctor said it is a light case with no bad symptoms, and this morning he said that Rob was decidedly better than he had expected to find him, so it is not as bad as it looked at first. However, I want you all to know about it, and by this mail a letter goes to Dr. Potter in Teheran, enclosing a cablegram which he can send from there in English over the European line to the Board in New York. It ought to reach you by Wednesday of next week. It is as follows: "Will remain in Hamadan until further notice. Robert has fever. Full confidence in physician. Will cable weekly. Notify Speers, Bailey etc." Please send this letter to Mary Speer, Mother dear, as I will not have time to write another. Oh, what would I not give for a sight of you all! It is mail time now and the mails go only once a week, so good-bye. Love to everyone.

Hamadan, Persia
Friday, December 11, 1896

Dear Father and Mother:

By this week's mail to Teheran, I have asked Mr. Potter to cable, "Convalescing," but Rob is not getting well quite as fast as I had hoped. He has a very sore leg, which the doctor fears will develop into an abcess, and that or something else has given him a fever again. Dr. Holmes says it is nothing to be alarmed at, but it means a longer stay here. Oh, if we were only coming home after we leave Persia! There is not time to write much. I spend the days in reading to Rob, after his room and mine are in order, and I try to read to him a great deal, for he cannot read or write himself yet, and for him of all people, it is very hard to do nothing. I wish I could one-half tell you how kind Dr. Holmes and Mr. and Mrs. Hawkes have been. The Holmeses send Rob all the milk from their cow so that he can be sure of pure milk and if you knew Persia and the great difficulty of getting good milk, you would understand how great a boon this is. Mr. and Mrs. Hawkes think no trouble too great. It is not only the things they do, but the way they do it, that makes it so lovely. They do not ever seem to think anything a trouble, and one might imagine from what they say that we are doing them a great favor by camping down on them in this way.

> With much love to all,
> Your affectionate daughter,
> Emma

Dec. 11, 1896

. . . I wish you could hear the noon call to prayer that is being sounded now from all the house-tops around us. The "Ahzan" they call it. I don't know all they say, but it begins with "Allah Akbar," repeated many times and the A's drawled out as long as they can hold their breath. Here in Mr. Hawkes' house, which is so cozy and comfortable, I forget sometimes where we are, but such things as this "Ahzan" remind me of the differences between this far-away land and the dear home country.

To return to the subject of Rob—we have read two books on Mohammedanism, an autobiography of Finney, the Evangelist; Freeman's *The Turk in Europe*; Mrs. Ewing's *Jan of the Windmill*, part of *Alice Through the Looking Glass*, and various short articles from the *Century* and other magazines, and a charming old Scotch story by James Hogg, "The Ettrick Shepherd, called the Brownie of Dodsbeck."

I wish you could know Mrs. Hawkes—she is one of the nicest people I have ever met. Of course I would think so after the thousand and one things she and Mr. Hawkes have done for us.

Rob has a poem about Mrs. Hawkes' two beautiful Persian cats that have fur two inches long. One is all black and one is all white and I am deeply attached to them. They are so funny and so attractive but Rob doesn't like them. Here is his verse:

> "They live with us, the cat, and cat:
> And both these cats are very fat.
> One cat is black and one is white,
> And both these cats I dislike quite,
>   I dislike quite.

> "But strange to say, Emma does not:
> These nasty cats her love have copt.
> For though she hates the general brood,
> Toward these she has a different mood,
>   A different mood.

> "Upon her love these cats impose.
> A cat is selfish, each one knows,
> (Except the old Englishman on the *Pavonia*);
> Yet Emma pets them just the same;
> But I these cats no more will name,
>   No more will name."

New Year's Day 1897

The Busrah mail has come in and brought nothing for us and this is a bitter disappointment, although I had tried not to set my heart on having letters today.

Rob is better again and sitting up in the invalid chair once more. The relapse was worse than the first attack and kept him in bed almost three weeks. . . . He feels quite like himself again, except that he is very weak. The relapse came apparently because the poison of the fever had not run its course and was still in his system. This time I hope there will be no second relapse. His appetite is tremendous and Rob

begs all the time for "more" like Oliver Twist. The difficulty now will be to keep him here until he is really strong
enough to travel and to stand the long and tiresome journey
of eighteen days to Bagdad, which will now have to be taken
in the dead of winter instead of in good fall weather as we
had first planned.

New Year's Day 1897

Rob, as you know, thinks everything must give way to
enable him to accomplish all he has planned and he talks of
leaving here in two weeks, when he can scarcely walk from
his bed to his chair yet! We have daily battles, but I shall not
leave Hamadan one day before Dr. Holmes assures me that it
will be perfectly safe for Rob to travel. Traveling, you
know, means eight hours a day in the saddle, over the roughest
mountain roads, and at night cold, damp, dirty, ill-ventilated
rooms, and always very poor food. It may be the first of
February or the first of March before Rob can endure that
sort of thing.

Our Christmas here was a very nice one; we thought of
you all, all day, and wished much that we could know just
what you were all doing. The people here knew how much
we would miss you, and everyone tried to do all he could to
make us feel less lonely and far away. The servants showered
all manner of Persian blessings on us; the day was bright and
clear with the mountains dazzling white with snow, and it
was the first day that Rob's temperature had come down to
normal, and in proportion as his temperature fell our spirits
rose.

Rob sends a great deal of love to all and wishes you a Most
Happy New Year.

Very, very lovingly,
Emma

On January 21, 1897, after being delayed in Hamadan for
two months, Robert Speer and his wife started on their
journey again. Mrs. Speer wrote her mother that day:

We start on the road for Baghdad in an hour, a three weeks' winter journey, but summer is waiting at the end of it, and for the winter part we have bedding and blankets enough to supply six people, and clothing and warm wraps enough for a dozen. Everyone here has contributed something to keep us warm. They have stocked our larder too with all manner of good things and in fact have done every kind and thoughtful thing anyone could think of, so we will make the journey as comfortable as possible. Of course it won't be any fun, this winter traveling, but it is the right thing for us to do and so it will be all right.

They rode horses belonging to Mr. and Mrs. Hawkes. Mrs. Speer's horse had an Arab strain. Mr. Speer and Mr. Hawkes rode horses of a Percheron strain. Mrs. Speer using a side-saddle especially ordered for her in New York, a gift from their friend, Henry Grant. Mrs. Hawkes lent them her experienced Persian cook, Kazim.

On February 16, 1897, after twenty-six days on the road over high mountains and deep snow, sometimes with moments of real hardship and glimpses of surprising beauty, Robert and Emma Speer reached Bagdad. The kindness of the Persian women in their "manzils" was unforgettable, and the appeal of their poverty and their helplessness in illness is vivid after sixty years. Mrs. Speer wrote from the steamer on the Tigris of the last stages of the journey on land:

Friday, February 19, 1897. This is a fine chance, while we sail down the Tigris, to catch up on all one's arrears in writing. Nothing distracts one's attention. We have nothing to read; Rob and I are the only cabin passengers, and one hour of watching the banks of the river is enough, for the same Arab villages of black hair tents and rushes, the same irrigating appliances, the same pitifully ragged children and lines of donkeys, are repeated over and over again. But the joyous thought that the hours of weary horseback riding are in the past, relieves all monotony!

Last Saturday, February 13th, we left Khannikeen, arising
at the fearful hour of 2:30, breakfasting, packing and starting
at 5:30 in order to make two stages in one day. We said good-
bye to Mr. Hawkes in the dark and to the taciturn Japher,
and rode away by the light of one small paper lantern, feeling
a good deal like the Babes in the Woods, although Khan-
nigheen streets did boast of some lights, and the houses
seemed picturesque and substantial compared with those of
Persian towns. The mud and stones were almost as bad as in
the streets of Kirrind, and it was very poor fun to go along
in the dark with one's horse slipping and stumbling at every
step, and having to cross a rushing river that sounded like a
flooded torrent. Some little streams had to be crossed on unguarded bridges, and just at the edge of the town we had to
plough through a real morass. But that was the last of the bad
roads, and the first light of the morning, a pale, clear, yellow
shining behind the black palm trees in the gardens, was so
beautiful that it well repaid one for the mud and stones. After
the town and its gardens were passed, the road was hard and
gravelly. It was a delight to ride over it past the lines of caravans, watching the sun rise in the cool morning air.

The first break in the level road was in crossing the low
range of hills that we had seen from the frontier. The road
led through the narrow defile and it was startling to have an
Arab horseman, whom we overtook at the foot of the hills,
spur on his horse and run shouting past us to the top of the
pass, as if he meant to summon a robber host. But he disappeared in the gullies at the top and we saw nothing more of
him nor of his "forty thieves."

As we came to the valley, we met a long line of laden
camels, and my horse, who strongly dislikes them, tried to
walk straight up the side of the ravine rather than encounter
the ugly brown beasts. There is something most amusing in
his avoidance of camels. He does not fret or fuss at the sight
of them; he merely goes quietly and resolutely as far away as
possible.

This morning when we woke we found ourselves on the
way down the Tigris. We like the *Bloss Lynch;* coffee at

seven-thirty; breakfast at nine; tiffin at one, tea at four, dinner at seven. Nothing will ever again seem so blissfully civilized and comfortable as this little steamer, where it is no longer necessary to pack our bags and bedding every morning and jog for weary hours over the endless plains. A long chair on deck under an awning; plenty of rugs around us; pelicans taking clumsy flights along the shore; illustrated Christmas magazines, property of the captain, it all seemed too good to be true. The captain, first officer, and purser were all very kind, and, as we were the only cabin passengers, it was like being on a yacht, except that we could have the interest of watching the deck passengers, women huddled in little tents; Turkish soldiers, pilgrims returning from Kerbala, Persians and Indians. The windings of the river had a very odd effect. A devout Moslem would try to say his prayers toward Mecca but before he finished he would be faced North, South, East and West, usually without knowing it.

About nine o'clock, we passed the ruins of Ctesephon on the left bank, the famous arch standing out clearly, but disappointing utterly any expectations of architectural beauty, wonderful as its construction may be. It's hard to associate the mud brick ruins with the stories of the wealth found in this city at the time of the Arab conquest. A little farther down the river on the other bank, was a mound which is said to be the ruin of the end of the wall of Babylon, which in its glory reached to the Tigris. These two landmarks are all that is left of the great civilization.

At tiffin time we passed the junction of the Euphrates and the Tigris, the Euphrates a clear blue stream with a rocky bed, very different from the muddy river that flows from Nineveh. The tomb of the Prophet Ezra, with shining dome of greenish blue tiles, was a short distance from the junction, and near it is the Arab site of the Garden of Eden, containing the original apple tree! But having seen Eden once before under Ararat's great shadow, our faith was not as deep as it might have been. From the junction down to Bozrah the great Shat-el-Arab (River of the Arabs) is lined with palms and gardens and is much less dreary than the Tigris. At five we reached Bozrah, or that section of it that is on the river, and it was exciting to see European houses and Englishmen.

Rob went ashore with Dr. Worrall of the Dutch Reformed Missions stationed in Bozrah and when he came back, we said good-bye to the *Bloss Lynch* and its officers, and in Dr. Worrall's boat went out to the British India steamer, *Pemba*, which seemed to our unaccustomed eyes most gorgeous and spacious.

In Baghdad they met the Dutch Reformed Missionaries, who showed them every kindness, and Mrs. Speer's diary says:

It was very nice both on the *Bloss Lynch* and on the *Pemba* to see how high in everyone's opinion the Dutch Reformed missionaries were held. They seemed to be universally respected, and of Samuel Zwemer especially they could not say enough of his courage, his zeal, his tact, his charm and his untiring work.

After shifting from the *Bloss Lynch* to the *Pemba*, again with an unbelievable sense of luxury, we landed in Karachi, and the order and control that one felt arriving in British India in 1897, after the feudalism of Persia, and the dead hand of Turkey in Mesopotamia, made us friends at once with the British Raj. There were weaknesses no doubt in their rule, but the contrast between the medieval Asia we had left behind and this land of firm and just controls gave us great relief.

There was a brief stay in India, where we had revealing visits with great missionaries who could see the magnitude of India's problems and needs, the dark side of Hinduism, and the courage of the Indian Christian leaders. From Calcutta we went on to China, over Kipling's "Seven Seas," with passengers that brought Kipling near, young tea planters from Assam on their way to "Raffles" for a holiday.

In China we met the missionaries who had laid firm foundations in Canton and the south. A dreamlike trip up the Lien Chou river in a flower-decked houseboat in May, "li-lamed" by coolies, who lived on the stern platform of the boat and pulled us up stream, chanting as they pulled, with Dr. and

Mrs. Kerr as guardians, was again a royal progress, for at each village stop there came crowds to greet the doctor who had relieved the suffering of thousands in his hospitals in Canton.

The visit to the remote station in Lien Chow was enriched for me by a friendship with Eleanor Chestnut, young, lovely to look at and to know, who had worked her way through Park College and the medical school, "to go where she was most needed" and to die soon after in a mob attack on the Mission because she stopped on her way to the river and safety to bind up the wounds of a boy hit by stones meant for her.

Then came Shanghai, Japan, Chefoo, and a glimpse of Korea. While I stayed in Chefoo, Mr. Speer was in Korea, and I learned from Mrs. Nevius, whose guest I was, something of the courage and faith that took the early missionaries to China in sailing ships. I met the brave Chinese woman who through Mrs. Nevius had been the first Chinese woman to study medicine and who started the first anti-foot-binding society. In Japan there was a memorable Mission meeting in Karuizawa, whose message to the world, had it been heeded, would have meant a different world for us today. "Japan is ready for Christian leadership. Ready to receive the best the Christian Church can send." Our churches were busy at home and German militarism had its chance and took the leadership we missed.

Unforgettable faces and scenes come back, like old films newly developed; and the last is of moving away from the dock at Shanghai into the muddy waters of the Whangpo and on into the Yangtze, and Mr. Speer, looking back and saying "The junks of China are bound for the open sea." It was not long before the storm of the Boxer Rebellion burst in its fury, and the quiet of the old Empire was ended forever.[58]

After his first visit to Asia, Robert Speer foresaw and foretold many of the policies related to the needs of the underprivileged people throughout the world that have now taken shape as our national responsibility.

Guthrie Speers, Robert Speer's Secretary on a Deputation

trip in 1915, wrote of an incident on their visit to the Philippines:

In 1915 we literally blew into the little harbor of Ilo Ilo in the Philippines on the wings of a typhoon. That evening there was a large mass meeting of students at which Mr. Speer was to speak. All during the service the wind was howling around the building and threatening to lift the roof off. Mr. Speer had just begun his address when the lights went out. The auditorium was in complete darkness. Mr. Speer never hesitated but went right on with his address. Indeed, the very strangeness of the situation made his address more impressive. He was speaking to those students from the text, "Remember now thy creator in the days of thy youth." [59]

Margaret C. McCord, a member of the Siam Mission who went to the field in 1905, has written:

I have a vivid recollection of Dr. Speer's visit to Thailand with Dr. Bovaird and Guthrie Speers in 1915.

When we prepared to attend one of his meetings at the Bangkok Christian College I was told by one of the Siamese teachers that the cook must be allowed to go with us.

"But this meeting is only for those who understand English," I remonstrated. "There will be no interpreter."

"Please let her go too," the teacher begged. "She has already received a great blessing just by watching Dr. Speer's face."

The daughter of that cook is now a student in New York. She is a Christian because of what her unlettered mother taught her of Christ.

We missionaries with our vexing problems certainly did wear Dr. Speer out. He was much more weary when he left than when he came. After leaving us, he sent a letter from the ship with this jingle,

> "The sunset is a glorious red
> Is that my chief delight?
> Oh, no, it is I go to bed
> At eight o'clock to-night."

I cannot fully describe the impression of Christian fellowship and peace he left with us. Our next Mission meeting was
in a greater spirit of harmony and consideration for others
than any meeting I had attended before.[60]

The Rev. Edward Adams, Field Representative of the
Korea Mission, who has spent thirty-two years in Korea, has
written of Robert Speer's kindness in sending Christmas
presents from the Speer children to the Adams children, and
also of an incident that took place when Mr. Speer was on
the field as a member of the deputation of the Board in 1921:

The first is a childhood memory. At that time the Goop
books were very popular. I can remember my brothers and
sisters and myself being brought up in proper manner by the
reading of these books. The front leaf had written on it
"Merry Christmas from the Speer children to the Adams children!" In the early beginning days of the Student Volunteer
Movement my father and Dr. Speer were quite intimate, so I
judge that this gift was a result of the friendship made at that
time.

The second recollection has to do with a trip he made to
Taegu shortly after my arrival as a missionary there. My
parents had already left the field. I think that I was the
youngest member of the Station. We were in conference,
various opinions were being expressed, and Dr. Speer was asking questions. Suddenly, without warning, he turned to me
who, because of my youth, had been keeping pretty quiet
and asked me, "Ned, are you going to advise your son to look
forward to Korea as a mission field?" The question somewhat
took my breath away but I remember collecting my thoughts
sufficiently to reply, "If the Mission program can keep a frontier in two directions—first, on reaching out to the non-
Christian population and, second, on helping the Korean
Church to expand on new projects—there will be a place for
my boy to work in Korea." The fact that impressed me most
at the time, however, was that he was thinking so far ahead
and eager to get the advice of a green missionary.[61]

Mrs. John E. Williams, wife of the Vice-President of the University of Nanking, wrote later of Robert Speer's visit to Nanking in 1921:

I saw him for the first time in June, 1899, when we went to New York for the Conference of Out-going Missionaries. He was then in the full tide and power of his splendid young manhood. I remember with what awe I looked up to him as he spoke and as he led us in the Consecration Service. I was timid and unsure of what was ahead of us and I needed the power and strength of his wonderful prayer of Consecration which gave courage to my heart. I never dreamed that one day I would come to know him as a life-time friend. He was the one who helped my husband decide to become a missionary.

Years later, in 1921 he was our guest in China. Our son, Richard, was about four years old. As the guest of honor, Dr. Speer was given the "prophet's chamber." Richard, in our rather crowded house, had a little bed just outside on the veranda. Our anxious Amah strictly forbade him to trouble the "great foreign guest." But Dick, waking early, not only went into the room, but climbed into bed with him, where, I understand, they had a happy visit, to the horror of the Amah. Dr. Speer, who was far from his own children, then tucked Dick into the carriage as he rode about the city, and always called him "My little pal!" [62]

In 1921 Robert Speer wrote from Shanghai of the Board's Deputation to China:

The last night before we reached Shanghai, I went out alone on the forward deck to look off across the quiet waters toward China, and to contrast our approach with Robert Morrison's more than a hundred and ten years ago. He came alone in the face of opposition of the greatest commercial organization in the world, the East India Company. No one was waiting for him. He would find no home prepared to welcome him, no facilities for language study, no readiness of the people to receive him. They wanted nothing that he had to offer. They had awaked as yet to no realization of their need and no thought that the outer barbarian world had any thing to give to them. No doubt on his last night as he drew near the China coast, Morrison had gone out under the stars alone to reflect on his mission. Before him, as before us, the Scorpion stood out clear and sharp in the southwestern sky with the Archer over against it, and Vega must have shone as brightly above him as it did over us, standing out as brilliant and almost as near as a green light at the masthead. The same God looked down from the same heavens over his ship and ours.

But how immeasurably different our missionary situation from his! Thousands of missionaries were settled now over the whole of China. Missionary agencies were at work there as powerful almost as all the Christian forces in Great Britain in Morrison's day. Our company would be welcomed in Shanghai by hundreds of missionary friends and would find a living Chinese Church established over all the provinces. The same Scorpion would be in the sky, but it would be a very different dragon upon the earth that we would find, a China humbled now, full of friendliness and good will, dissatisfied with the past, and eager for all the help that it could receive.

But most of all I was interested in contrasting our ship's company with Morrison's. It is true that he came out on one of David Oliphant's boats, and Mr. Oliphant was one of the early American merchants to whom the extension of the Gospel was as deep a concern as his own business. But it was interesting to reflect how much more our ship represented. There were perhaps a hundred and fifty missionaries, old and new, half a dozen of our American boards being represented by from twenty to forty missionaries each. The most powerful commercial agency in the world was represented, not directly, of course, but by a deputation of thirty or forty men and women, led by Mr. John D. Rockefeller, Jr., that was coming out to China to express its unselfish interest in the people and to dedicate in Peking a great institution which was being given to China for the relief of suffering and the promotion of Christian sympathy and progress. The universities of America and Great Britain had provided a deputation of some of their ablest men and women under the chairmanship of Professor E. D. Burton, which the Foreign Mission Boards of the United States and Canada were sending to study missionary education in China, with a view to making it the most effective agency possible in building up the Christian Church and in helping the Chinese people. A group of Chinese students, men and women, who had been educated in the United States and Europe, were going back with Christian principles and Christian purpose to serve their nation. American experts in finance and education and medicine like Mr. Frederick Stevens, the American representative on the Consortium in Peking, Professor Monroe of Columbia University, and Dean Holgate of Northwestern University, and Dr. William H. Welch of Johns Hopkins University, and many others were also going out with the true missionary spirit. So I might go on. In truth the *Empress of Asia* on this trip was just one huge expression of the missionary ideal. And standing under the stars that night and looking back to Japan and on to China across the tranquil waters of the Eastern Sea, I thanked God for the progress of the century past and was glad that from his place in the great cloud of witnesses Robert Morrison could look down and see to what his enterprise for China has grown.[63]

IX. His Work with Students

To R. E. S.

Perhaps the words you speak seem vain, all vain;
Perhaps the boyish heart seems always turned
Aside to worldly things, that should have burned
Beneath your pleadings; mayhap, all in pain,
You seem like one who fiercely strikes amain
Upon some door that's barred, your knocking spurned
By revelers within, who well have learned
To ope to none who will disturb their strain.

You have disturbed their strain; your ringing word
Breaks through the barrier and assails the heart;
And even he who fain would not have heard
Has heard, despite; nor can there e'er depart
From that young heart the cleanness that you preach,
Nor from his soul the honesty you teach.

—HOWARD BEMENT[64]

WITH HIS RECORD AS AN OUTSTANDING FOOTBALL PLAYER, A tackle for four years on a Princeton University team who was offered the captaincy in his Senior year; with his high scholastic stand as Valedictorian of his Class; with his exceptional gifts as a speaker, and with his idealistic dedication to an absolute cause in mission service overseas, Robert Speer appealed to students as a natural leader in the student world of his generation and in the generation to follow.

Robert Speer deprecated the application of this term to

himself and to his work, and again and again said the ideal should be, not to be a leader of men, but rather a follower of Christ. This spurning of human popularity, and his other-worldly emphasis only served to increase his influence and power.

After he made his decision for foreign mission service in his Sophomore year at college, Robert Speer was increasingly in demand as a speaker at schools and universities and as a leader at Northfield and other conferences.

Professor and Mrs. John Meigs, Michael F. Sweeney, and Morgan H. Bowman, on The Hill faculty, were warm admirers and supporters of Robert Speer. He spoke in The Hill School pulpit and to Hill students in informal gatherings every year from 1891 to 1939, and several times after that year, his last sermon being preached at a Hill Commencement in 1947, the year of his death. *The Hill School News* recorded the titles and texts of these sermons and addresses of Robert Speer. They show his versatility of thought and the wide range of his interest. The complete list is given in the Appendix.

Hermann Hagedorn, poet and biographer, a graduate of The Hill and of Harvard, has written of his student impressions of Robert Speer:

Robert E. Speer was an exceptional man. He came to The Hill three or four times a year. . . . He did not actually preach hell fire, but he pictured the black awfulness of sin in a way that was vivid enough to make me still feel the atmosphere of the old schoolroom where he preached . . . and hear again his voice pronouncing his text: "Be strong in the Lord and in the power of his might. . . . Put on the whole armor of God, that you may be able to stand against the wiles of the devil. . . ." There was greatness in him, the greatness of complete giving to the Master he served with single-minded devotion.[65]

A Hill student, a former football captain there, wrote:

"He was a stalwart, manly young preacher, with a pleasing, deep voice and a shining face. Even to us students, he had the mighty power of one who dreamed great dreams." [66]

In one of his talks at The Hill, Robert Speer described an incident in the athletic life at the school. One of the best players on the football team played all fall under the handicap of anxiety about the illness of his father. His father had been blind for some years. The father became worse as the football season progressed and died before the championship game. The coaches were uncertain how the father's death would affect the boy and did not know if they could count on him to play in the final contest. But after the son had been to his home and to his father's funeral, he returned to The Hill and played in the championship game and he helped to win it. Later he was asked how he had been able to meet that test so bravely and well, and he answered: "That was the first game my father had ever seen me play." [67]

At the Hotchkiss School in Lakeville, Connecticut, Robert Speer spoke every year from 1904 to 1924 and frequently thereafter. The Headmaster during those years, Hubert Gray Buehler, and his successor, George Van Santvoord, were also admirers of Robert Speer. William Speer, the younger son of the Speers, was a student at Hotchkiss from 1925 to 1929. The move to "Rockledge" in Lakeville in 1926 brought the Speer family into close contact with the school. Robert and Mrs. Speer often had guests from overseas at their home, and those who were interested in American schools would be taken to Hotchkiss, and there shown details of significance and value in the school life and property. George Van Santvoord recalls how Robert Speer brought to the services his tiny, well-worn New Testament, and how he would read the Scripture lesson from that cherished book before he spoke.

Dr. Van Santvoord testified that Robert Speer's clarity and forcefulness in speaking showed no decline as he grew older, but rather that he gained in strength and vigor, and that his increased certainty of position carried increased conviction to his hearers.[68] After the death of Elliott Speer, Mrs. Speer wrote to Dr. Van Santvoord: "You see he feels he is speaking now for Elliott too." [69]

In his talks to college audiences and to preparatory students, Robert Speer always appealed to the heroic in a man. Duty was central; a man should be honest and courageous. His duty was to do what he believed to be right, to be loyal to Christ. These two notes, duty and loyalty, were the keynotes of his messages to students. Duty and loyalty were a recurring refrain in his compelling address, later widely distributed in printed form, "What Constitutes a Missionary Call." "Duty is clear; Christ commands; we obey." [70] Another address was on the verse: "A great door is open *and* there are many adversaries." He pointed out that Paul did not say " '*but* there are many adversaries.' That is a phrase we use when we look for excuses! When a door opened for Paul the adversaries were not excuses but opportunities." [71]

Loyalty to truth, loyalty to Christ, courage in facing adversaries, these were the keynotes of Robert Speer's talks to students. Finally, he drove home the appeal of needy people. The whole world was his parish.[72]

In his talks to students he also developed and emphasized the fivefold theme of an early book: *The Marks of a Man.* This book contained the record of five addresses made at Ohio Wesleyan University on truth, purity, service, freedom, progress and patience.

When Robert Speer told his father of his decision to enter foreign missionary service, his father sent him a diary for the year, as was his custom, and inscribed on the first page: "Do your duty."

During the months that Robert Speer served as a traveling secretary of the Student Volunteer Movement in 1889-1890, he secured over a thousand student volunteers. In the mid-1920's he became Chairman of the Executive Committee of the Student Volunteer Movement, and was a wise counselor until his death. Thomas Sharp, the Secretary of the Movement, wrote of his service:

No one, save possibly Dr. John R. Mott, participated in more Student Volunteer Conventions, and no one ever made such a deep and lasting impression on those in attendance at the Conventions. He differed from other men in that he was guided by basic principles from which he never deviated. He never quibbled or compromised and expediency was not in his vocabulary. Those who idealized him when they were students, idealized him still when they had occasion to be associated with him in later years, because he grew in stature, intellectually, morally and spiritually. He was the incarnation of the spirit of the Student Volunteer Movement and he influenced the Movement and those who attended its meetings by his character, his words, written and spoken, and his life more widely and deeply than any other living man.[73]

Another note Robert Speer struck constantly was his emphasis on Bible study.

The students accepted Dr. Speer as tops in Bible exposition and application. When a new book by Robert Speer was announced, I have known students who went without a third meal to save enough money to buy the book. We wore his books out.[74]

In an address made at the Student Volunteer Movement Convention held in Cleveland, Ohio, in February, 1898, Robert Speer spoke of the Student Volunteer Movement: "Let us bear in mind that the person who puts his money into the Student Volunteer Movement touches all springs of the all-embracing Church of Jesus Christ, touches all nations, touches all races. There is no form of investment which reaches more springs of influence."

A former secretary of the Y.M.C.A. who served in this country and overseas in a national position stated that in his student generation Mott and Speer were "almost one word of two syllables." He first heard Robert Speer at a student conference in the Blue Ridge Mountains, and shortly after heard him again at the Student Volunteer Convention in Nashville, in 1906.

Mott's address [he wrote] was to the mind and will; Speer's to the mind and soul. . . . There was a vibrant quality in what Robert Speer said and in the organ-like voice with which he spoke, which literally made my soul tingle in response.

At the dinner we arranged for Dr. Mott in 1946, on his return from Oslo where he had gone to receive the Nobel Peace Prize for that year, Dr. Speer was among those who spoke on that occasion. Many of us had not seen these two men, Mott and Speer, together in twenty-five years. As one saw them together and heard them speak that night, one's thoughts ran literally to the ends of the earth—where so many men and women have gone as Christian missionaries because of the influence these men had upon their lives back in college a generation and a half ago.[75]

Of these student conferences Robert Speer wrote:

These summer conferences of students are as free and simple almost as was the school of Jesus on the hills and by the brooks and blue waters of Galilee. . . . The mornings began with some conference as to the methods and need of Christian work in college. This was followed by Bible classes, one designed to teach the devotional use of the Bible for spiritual growth and the other its practical use in dealing with men and endeavoring to lead them into Christ's discipleship. After these came one or two earnest, direct addresses, designed to produce result in resolution and character. The afternoon was free for recreation or quiet study and fellowship. In the twilight as the sun slipped down, and the hills flung their lengthening shadows across the lake, men gathered on the grass under the trees for a meeting to consider the great field of life opportunity and service and the day closed with a general meeting, like the last meeting of the morning and in quiet little gatherings of the students from each college, apart, to gather up and seal the influences of the day.

These summer gatherings of students have become a valuable part of the Christian forces working for young men. They began in the summer of 1886, and about 200 students accepted Mr. Moody's invitation to spend some weeks at Mt. Hermon, Mass., for a study of the Bible and for a general conference on Christian and missionary work. The next year this gathering was held at Northfield, Mass., about five miles from Mt. Hermon, and the place of Mr. Moody's home and the seminary for young women which he had established. At Mt. Hermon was his school for boys. Each year since, such a conference of students from colleges, universities, and preparatory schools has been held. . . . The students who attend the Conferences live under the trees and largely in the open air. It is a good place to meet the Master. Such spots have ever been dear to Him.[76]

These student conferences combined earnestness and devotion with light-hearted enjoyment and relaxation. A full schedule of Bible study classes, missionary seminars and addresses was maintained in morning and evening, relieved by athletics and other diversions in the afternoon. On one evening, usually the Fourth of July, the students and speakers let off steam by a tremendous out-of-door parade, a towering bonfire, and a final gathering in the auditorium, in which the various student delegations gave their college cheers and songs and indulged in other extra-curricular activities.

The Cornell students would seize John R. Mott, the presiding officer, and would rush him up and down the platform, ruffling his dignity. Princeton would do the same with Robert E. Speer. Sometimes the Princeton students trundled a stuffed tiger on to the platform. Then someone would yank a large halyard on a great Princeton banner hanging over the platform and would let loose a shower of orange and black tissue-paper hats. Robert Speer, with a big grin, would catch one of these hats and put it on his head.[77]

At one of these boisterous gatherings in the auditorium at Northfield, when invited to the platform to address the audience, Robert Speer read three letters which he told the audience he had received from individuals who had problems to present:

Geneva, New York
July 2, 1908

Dear Sir:

I am a stranger to you but I know your interest in young men, and as the mother of two of the students who will be at the Conference, in Northfield, I venture to write to you.

In the first place, won't you please warn the students against excessive frugality? Nowadays students do not spend nearly enough money. My husband is greatly troubled because my sons spend only 7/4 of his income. Please beg the students to avoid any strictness of economy in their expenditure of their father's money.

In the second place, I beg of you, entreat them not to study too hard. I have known students so eager for knowledge that they go back and repeat a whole year they have already taken. All my sons have done this. . . .

Lastly, I think that students should be taught to make themselves heard. You never know a body of students any more when you see them. They are so quiet and still. Can they not be taught to use their voices—in singing and cheering? Please urge this point, especially on the evening of the Fourth of July, when I understand some attention will be paid to this matter.

With loving interest in you and your work, I am, as ever yours,

Respectfully,
/S/ Sarah K.

President's Office
Yale University,
New Haven, Conn.
July 3, 1908

Dear Mr. Speer:

I am a good deal troubled over athletics down here. We are in a bad way. We especially need some men who know how to play baseball. Could you find me three first class men at Northfield? I am willing to pay $50 a month and board, with a bonus of $10, if we beat Hotchkiss.

Yours sincerely,

/S/ Arthur T. Hadley
President

P.S. Don't get Harvard men. The Librarian has just had all our books nicely arranged and we don't want any of them taken from the shelves.

Vassar College
Poughkeepsie, N.Y.
June 30, 1908

Dear Mr. Speer:

I saw a picture of Mr. Mott and you in the paper telling about Northfield. I like Mr. Mott's picture very much, especially his bright, mischievous smile, and the playful twinkle in his eyes. He must be great fun, but I am going to write to you. I understand the young ladies often confide in you. I would have gone to the Conference myself, but I was told that Mr. Mott did not like pretty girls to come. That shuts me out. I enclose my picture. Don't you think so? Why can't we come? They let us into Heaven if we are good, even if we are pretty. Why can't we come to the Conference on the same terms? I am awfully sorry that we are not allowed.

But, anyhow, I am going to write to you and ask you a favor. Will you please pick out a nice student and give him this letter and ask him to write to me? At first I thought I would like him to be a West Point man, but my mother says that "all is not gold that glitters" and that "you can't judge from the wrapping paper." My father says that "a captain of

industry is the only kind of a soldier who can afford me." I
will leave it all with you.

Yours devotedly,

/S/ Alice J.[78]

John Sutherland Bonnell, pastor of the Fifth Avenue Presbyterian Church of New York City, has written of Robert
Speer and his work with students:

On the morning of December 31st, 1913, I was ushered
into Convention Hall, Kansas City, Kansas, and seated directly beneath the speakers' platform. My friend and I were
students of Prince of Wales College, Charlottetown, Prince
Edward Island, Canada. If someone with prophetic foresight
had said to me, a high-school graduate in Canada, "Twenty-
one years from now this man, Dr. Robert E. Speer, seated
before you on the platform, will address you as the newly-
installed minister of the Fifth Avenue Presbyterian Church,
New York," I should undoubtedly have thought that the
prophet was mad.

Promptly at the appointed hour, John R. Mott rose and
tapping the gavel, called the meeting to order. Beside him on
the platform sat Robert E. Speer. This was the first time I
had ever looked upon his strong and kindly face. Throughout
the meetings of the Convention I was gripped by the compelling, statesman-like addresses given by Dr. Speer. His deep
earnestness was unmistakable and his love for Christ shone
forth in his face and was reflected in his heart-warming
words.

In one of the opening addresses of the Convention, Dr.
Speer spoke on, "What Is God's Will?" He concluded his
address in words that brought me and many another in that
audience of 7000 persons face to face with the necessity of
surrender to the will of God. Said Dr. Speer:

"Not a man or woman that has come here today need
wait another moment before he or she shall receive that
which God has brought us here to give us, if only now
we will just forget ourselves . . . and will remember

God, and in that great and absorbing remembrance of Him rest upon St. John's word that is carved, in part, on Mr. Moody's gravestone: 'And the world passeth away and the lust thereof, but he that doeth the will of God abideth forever.' That will is not in tonight's session, nor tomorrow's, nor some other day's; it is now. That will is nearer to us now than our neighbor is, as near as our own soul, and it is waiting this moment to be given the mastery."

During the years that followed, while I continued my studies in university and seminary, I read book after book that had come from the pen of Dr. Speer and in those formative years felt on my life the impact of his virile and radiant faith.[79]

Luther Weigle, for twenty-one years Dean of the Divinity School, Yale University, former President of the Federal Council of Churches, and later President of the Board of Trustees, Yale-in-China Association, has written of Robert Speer:

The college students of the late nineties found their most inspiring Christian leadership in Dwight L. Moody, who was approaching the close of his great career of Christian service, and in John R. Mott and Robert E. Speer, who were in the early years of theirs. Speer was just thirteen years and one day older than I was, and I looked up to him, when I graduated from college and entered the theological seminary, with all the respect that twenty has for a vigorous and effective thirty-three.

For some years he helped me most through his books. One of these particularly—*The Principles of Jesus*, published in 1902—is so clear and resourceful a guide to the study of the principles of Jesus' life and teaching that I have used it many times with Bible classes, and it remains today, after fifty-one years, one of the "live" books on my shelves, to which I turn from time to time with some problem or need.

"Following in Jesus' steps is not wearing the sort of clothes

which He wore," says the author in the Introduction to this
volume. "Neither is it merely the possession of a sweet feeling
towards all men irrespective of the moral life. It is the application to conduct today under its changed conditions of the
principles which found expression in the life and teaching of
Jesus nineteen hundred years ago, but which, because they
are principles, are not local, transient and personal, but universal and abiding." [80]

The Rev. John G. Magee, of the Class of 1906 at Yale,
who prepared for college at Hotchkiss School, and later had
a distinguished career as a missionary of the Episcopal Church
in China, has written of Robert Speer's influence on his life
decision and on that of other students:

Dr. Speer came for his first Sunday at Hotchkiss during
my second year there, the school year from September 1899
to June 1900. For a number of years after that, as I remember
it, he came twice a year to the school. He must have spent a
great many of his Sundays at schools and colleges during that
period of his life, for I kept hearing about the influence he
was having among students everywhere.

I shall never forget his first address at Hotchkiss, a sermon
on "Hate Lies." I had never been moved so deeply by a sermon before and could hardly walk out of the chapel afterwards. I do not remember to this day any sermon which has
touched me as this first sermon of Dr. Speer's at Hotchkiss.
During the subsequent years his sermons and addresses always
spoke to me as the sermons of very few people ever did,
whether at Hotchkiss, Yale, the Northfield Student Conferences, or at any of the great quadrennial conventions of the
Student Volunteer Movement. Many years later, on one of
his visits to China, he brought to me the same uplift and inspiration. One address to the missionary body at Nanking, I
remember, was on the importance of missionaries loving one
another. One of the very real problems on the Mission Field
is the mutual irritation of several strong-minded persons
cooped up in a small community where they have so little

outside social diversion. He had no doubt encountered this in his visits to various Mission Fields, and in that address, which I imagine he repeated elsewhere, he was trying to help a group of missionaries triumph over this problem.

As I think over the years, it was not just what he said that helped me, stimulating as his words always were, but the strength of the man that spoke through his whole personality. It was the integrity of a man of unusual intellectual gifts who had dedicated his whole life to Jesus Christ as Lord. That was apparent in all he did and said.

On the return journey from the Nashville Convention of the Student Volunteer Movement in 1906, I happened to be in the same Pullman car with him and a number of delegates. I think it was one of the Erdmans who gave an amusing account of Columbus' discovery of America at which Dr. Speer roared with laughter. This human side of him I had not seen before.

As I look back to my school days it is clear that he was the most important influence in my youth. I remember saying to myself at Hotchkiss after one of his visits, "if I could only be with him all the time, I could be good!" It was probably after one of his visits to the school that I asked him for the names of some books to read. He gave me quite a list, among them being a life of Bishop Coleridge Patteson and another with some such title as *Heroes of the Mission Field*. There were also a number of books by Henry Clay Trumbull, such as *A Lie Never Justifiable, The Blood Covenant;* and I remember another book of Trumbull's on prayer. Coleridge Patteson became my first missionary hero, and there is no doubt but that these books stimulated my faith and my mind, and helped to strengthen my missionary purpose. Dr. Speer was interested in studying what boys were thinking and reading, and once gave a questionnaire to some boys at Hotchkiss asking us what books we read and liked, and what it was that appealed to us in the books we liked. I don't doubt but that this helped him understand what was going on in the minds of the boys, and thus enabled him the better to speak to their needs.

The first thought of being a missionary came to me while reading my Bible in the winter of my second year. This became my greatest ambition after hearing a missionary from India speak at Northfield the following summer. It was undoubtedly Dr. Speer, however, more than anyone else, who nourished this initial enthusiasm to a mature purpose. I doubt very much whether I would ever have gone to the Mission Field if his influence had never touched my youth.

During my first summer in China I was invited to take my vacation at the home of one of our Episcopal Church missionaries at Kuling in the mountains of Central China. One evening my hosts invited to dinner Dr. Samuel Cochran of the Presbyterian Mission in Hwai Yuan, a Princeton graduate, and Bishop Huntington of Anking, a Yale graduate. I happened to say that I did not think I would have been in China had it not been for Robert Speer. Both Dr. Cochran and Bishop Huntington surprised me by saying the same thing. A few nights later I was at a dinner party at the home of the Murdock sisters of Hwai Yuan and happened to speak of the coincidence of three of us at dinner a few nights before discovering that we were all in China owing to the influence of Robert Speer. Two or three people immediately said the same thing, among them one of the outstanding missionaries in China, Bishop Logan Roots, a Harvard graduate. I am sure that if a questionnaire had been sent to all American missionaries in China many more men and women would have given a like testimony. I am sure also that the same result would have been found in any of the great Mission Fields of the world where American missionaries were at that time. God alone can measure the influence of this great, good, and humble servant of Christ, both to the cause of Christian Missions and to the upsurge of Christian faith among students in our schools and colleges at that time.[81]

Sherwood Eddy, a contemporary of Robert Speer, a member of the Class of 1891—of the Sheffield Scientific School at Yale, who went to India in 1896 under the YMCA, who became Secretary for India and Asia, and by his books and

addresses, had a powerful influence among students and supporters of foreign missions throughout the world, has written:

Robert Speer became the dominant influence at Northfield
in the deepening of my spiritual life far more than any other
man. Northfield was my Waterloo. I had all my plans made
to go out and make money—because I believed that money
was power—when I was bowled over by Moody at my first
student conference in 1889. I decided to give my life to
Christ and turned from the ambition of making money to the
making of men.

When I was taking my last year in Princeton Theological
Seminary before going out to India, Speer was the most
powerful and most deeply spiritual speaker at our large band
of student volunteers. He had the same deep influence and
authentic message as he met the missionaries of his Board all
over the world, and often all the missionaries in a local station. He was always in truth a world missionary. And he was
always traveling. I can still see him carrying his suit case, and
walking to the train after a conference. I can still see him
playing on the Princeton football team as tackle, opposite
R——— on the Yale team. R——— was not his equal as a
man or as an athlete and resorted to tricks which Bob Speer
would never do. Throughout his life he played a clean game.
All his life he was a spiritual athlete, always in training. His
whole life was Christ-centered. He was one of the most loyal
followers of Jesus I ever knew.

After college we both came to work in New York City the
same year, 1891, I in the YMCA, Speer as Secretary of the
Presbyterian Board. When I went to his room in the evening
his influence was again powerful. He was more mature than
I at that time, both intellectually and spiritually. I was amazed
at his wide reading revealed in every address that he made and
in every interview.

When I went to India in 1896 and we held conventions for
the deepening of the spiritual life both for students and missionaries, again Speer was the most powerful speaker we
could call in.

Ruth Rouse told me of the world-wide and eternal influence of a single address that Speer made to an early British Student Conference at Keswick, before the student movement had any conference site of its own, like Northfield. His subject was the watchword, "The Evangelization of the World in This Generation." After the meeting British students went silently out into the fields and hills to pray. The biographies of these leaders, written decades later—men like Oldham, Gairdner and Thornton of Cairo, Donald Fraser of South Africa—show that lives were changed that night forever. Donald Fraser spent the whole night in prayer. When he came back to his student group the next morning no questions were asked, or needed. He was transparently a changed man. Fraser was the acknowledged leader of the student movement in Britain and of missions in Scotland for that generation, as the great Alexander Duff had been in his. Some of those Scotch leaders told me that Speer's flaming missionary messages in Scotland were the greatest heard since those of Duff himself, and reminded them of Duff.

Two men towered head and shoulders above the rest of us throughout our entire student generation—Mott and Speer: Mott the statesman and Speer the prophet, Mott the organizer and Speer with his messages for the deepening of the spiritual life of his time—for students, missionaries, ministers, and laymen of the churches. I think I can see him in the great world beyond. No harps, no golden streets for him! A happy warrior on some far-flung battle line, to win some new planet in the evangelization of the universe.[82]

Rev. Samuel M. Shoemaker, who served as a missionary in China, and had a fruitful ministry as rector of Calvary Church in New York City before going to Calvary Church in Pittsburgh, has written of Robert Speer's influence on life's decisions:

John Magee told me that years ago in Kuling, Bishop Roots, Dr. Sam Cochran, and Bishop Huntington were together in one room and one of them said, "I would not be here if it had not been for Robert Speer." Thereupon every one of them echoed exactly the same thought. I believe he was a determining influence in the decisions of the majority of the missionaries who went out in those rich years when his leadership first began. I will never forget the first time I heard him at Northfield. I can hear John Mott now, saying, "Bob Speer is coming up here this year under greater conviction than ever." It was at one of those evening meetings that Dr. Speer spoke on "The Light of the Knowledge of the Glory of God in the Face of Jesus Christ." It seemed to me that I had never seen our Lord so lifted up before. It was impossible to estimate the extraordinary influence he had on large numbers of people.[83]

Anson Phelps Stokes, former Secretary of Yale University and later Canon of the Washington Cathedral, wrote of Robert Speer:

When I was an undergraduate at Yale, Robert Speer was one of the most effective preachers in the College pulpit and one of the men whose addresses in Dwight Hall were most inspiring to the student audience.

Later, as Secretary of Yale University, I was also Secretary for over twenty years of the Committee on the supply of the University pulpit, and nearly all University preachers, including Mr. Speer, spent the Sundays of their New Haven visits at our home. Thus we came to know him well and gained increasingly deep respect for his character and faith.

I think it is fair to say that in the last years of the Nineteenth Century and during the first three decades of the Twentieth Century, Mr. Speer was one of the three or four most popular and influential Yale preachers. His friend, John R. Mott, and Lyman Abbot were certainly two of the others. They were very different but were all effective.

An incident in connection with Mr. Speer's visits to New Haven was related to the founding of Yale-in-China. This incident is recorded in full in Henry Wright's life of Thurston. It was the meeting in front of the fireplace in my house during a week-end when Mr. Speer met Thurston, Williams, and others who were interested in the founding of a Yale Mission and asked and secured his advice and support. This event is commemorated, including the use of Mr. Speer's name, in the memorial plaque which was erected a year ago last spring over the fireplace in our old house in New Haven.

I remember well a remarkable sermon that Mr. Speer preached with some such title as "The Goal of Life." In that sermon he ended with an illustration of a Yale-Princeton football game in which the Princeton man was carrying the ball toward the goal but could feel the breath of the nearest Yale runner on the back of his neck. He, however, saw behind the goal sitting on the bleachers the girl whom he loved, and this stimulated him to superhuman effort, and he made the winning touchdown. He then turned the metaphor and said that the goal was the goal of life and that the girl in the bleachers could stand for our Master beckoning us forward! His illustration was an almost impossible and daring one, but was carried through with such extraordinary skill and power that there was no adverse reaction in his audience. At the close of the service President Hadley, referring to Mr. Speer's sermon and especially to his concluding illustration, said: "I never realized why the Greeks called their orators gods until after hearing Mr. Speer's sermon this morning." [84]

The Right Rev. Henry Knox Sherrill, Presiding Bishop of the Protestant Episcopal Church, who was a member of the Class of 1911 at Yale, has written of Dr. Speer's influence and his part in the Bishop's decision to enter the ministry:

My first recollection of him was hearing him when I was ten years old and had just entered the Polytechnic Preparatory School in Brooklyn. He came and told the story of some man, as well as I can remember it, who, after over fifty years, had gone into the desert and had devoted his life to transforming the desert sands into a garden plot, and he used that as an illustration of what our lives ought to be in redeeming service. I remember the tremendous response of the boys on that occasion, and how deeply he impressed me at the time. Later on I went to Hotchkiss, where he came and preached, and then I heard him many times in the Yale Chapel, as well as at the Student Volunteer Convention in Kansas City, in 1914.

The depth of his own Christian conviction, the seriousness with which he presented the challenge of the Christian life to young men and boys, made a great impression upon me, and he had part in my deciding to enter the Christian ministry. I can hear now the depth of his tone, and the earnestness with which he always spoke.[85]

George Stewart, clergymen, author, soldier, has written of the service of Robert Speer and of his associates at these student gatherings:

In those days, men who had started the student work of the YMCA and those who had founded the Student Volunteer Movement were still living. They stirred us with memories of those beginnings. Joined with them were their younger associates: Charles Hurrey, David Porter, Sherwood and Brewer Eddy, Henry Wright, Henry Hallam Tweedy, and always missionaries from far places, the Humes of China and India, Cyril Haas of Turkey, Dr. Paul Harrison and others. We were hero worshipers but we had men of heroic stature to worship!

At Northfield Dr. Speer would stand before us on the high platform in the auditorium, straight as a spruce tree against the sky, usually grave but frequently smiling too, never talking down, never given to colloquialisms, an intellectual making simple the deep things of the spirit, his fine voice matching the eloquent flow of his ordered thought. Echoes come back across the years: "The Gospel is either true for all, or it is not true at all!" He never dealt in small matters; always he spoke to us upon full enlistment in the cause of Christ, about the unoccupied fields, about the chance to invest life among the pagan tribes, or in old but static or decadent civilizations, in great centers of the East, in the less known regions of Africa, along the desert wastes of the earth, from Casablanca to Karachi, up in the mountains of Persia or Kurdistan, among people by the rivers of China, in Japan, Malaya, Borneo, Latin America, and in the far corners of the earth. For us he associated geography with mankind and adventure with faith. He deepened our insight and widened our horizons.

As we knew Dr. Speer, he never considered ideas as something to play with but rather as fertile seed to sow into the furrows of his generation. He was in the highest sense an acknowledged and unashamed propagandist for the Faith.

We felt the spiritual pressure of his will; he *was* trying to persuade and to convince. His invitation to service and to loyalty to Christ was insistent, but the invitation was made in full respect for other minds. He never considered other religions were as good as Christianity, and men of other faiths valued him for the fair way he presented his own convictions.

He had a way of suggesting books and authors which made us want to read. I do not believe I ever heard him make a major address that I did not immediately visit the book stores. I have heard others speak of this quality of his addresses. He was a Johnny Appleseed of the spirit.

Never was Robert Speer at greater advantage than when standing before those student audiences of many colors and races and creeds, giving the full thrust of his study and experience in setting forth reasons for the supremacy of the Christian gospel; a knightly figure, a modern intellectual Bayard, the kind of man the modern student would instinctively trust and follow. He laid the deep imprint of his mind and heart upon the plastic stuff of our lives for our healing, for our guidance and our dedication.[86]

John R. Mott, Chairman of the National and International Committees of the Y.M.C.A., has written of his friend and colleague:

I have been asking myself why this one man's influence widened and deepened, and was ever more helpful from college days through the long years. First and foremost, Jesus Christ constituted the cornerstone of his faith, of his life, and, therefore, of his influence. This cardinal fact stands out with a more vivid and attractive clearness and convincing power in his books, pamphlets and addresses than any other theme or personal experience.

His long life abounded in well-directed activity. I never saw him when he was not busy. One of the last occasions was in a railroad station in Cleveland, Ohio, when, with little more than twenty minutes to wait, he had his books and papers spread out before him and was hard at work. He employed the means which experience and the study of biography reveal to have the greatest influence. He always brought men to the point where they faced the living Christ. . . .

This inevitably involves the employment of another means which Dr. Speer used faithfully from his student days through all the years, namely, that of fostering the reverent and thorough study of the life and work and words of Christ. He believed with Chrysostom that the cause of all our evils lies in our not knowing the Scriptures. . . . An entire and extensive treatise might be written of his work as a Bible teacher and normal class leader. . . . Literally thousands of young men and young women trace to him their interest and passion for fostering this vital ministry with its inevitable results. Co-ordinate in importance was his emphasis on the Christlike practice of prayer.

Still another means he employed was his effort to multiply the number of unselfish Christlike workers. . . . A real life story could be written of Dr. Speer's interviews with literally thousands of students on the question of their life and vocation. Around the world one constantly meets missionaries and laymen who trace their life investment in Christian work to his faithful dealing with them. Some of his most effective work along this vital line were letters he dictated under the pressure of office detail. . . .

Robert Speer was never stopped by baffling, or what looked like impossible, difficulties, but rather used them as a means to greater heights of achievement. . . .

He never tried to make the Gospel easy. As I review in

memory his writings and addresses, but more particularly his travels and statesmanlike and courageous programs and summons to the Churches to advance, I am impressed anew with his courage and faithfulness.

Dr. Speer's lifelong practice did not permit him to confine his work of administration to his office chair. Instead, he mingled efficient work, in administration and attendance upon countless committees, with many prolonged and exacting tours to the most difficult fields of the Near and Far East, India, and, very especially, to those in Moslem and Roman Catholic lands. This involved the paying of great prices shared cheerfully by members of his family. One of his priceless possessions was a very happy home life, which broadened his sympathies and was a great factor in his work with other individuals.

As I look back over his years crowded with glorious life, I cannot overlook his recognition of the strategy of boyhood and the time and attention he generously devoted to young people of all ages. I believe that one of the most fruitful parts of his life work was a long series of unhurried, intensive visits he paid to The Hill School at Pottstown, Pennsylvania. Possibly I am prejudiced by his influence on one of my own boys, but I think not as I remind myself of hundreds of college students and graduates who, across the years, have shared with me the most formative and vital influences of their lives.

If I were to sum up the marvelous influence of this man— which will gather momentum as the years pass—I would trace it to the attitude and practice of the Society of Friends in their exemplification of two passages of the Christian Scriptures—

"My soul, be thou silent unto God," and
"Speak, Lord, for Thy servant harkeneth."

As a lifelong friend and companion from the late eighteen eighties down to his permanent entrance upon the blessed ministries of the Heavenly Host, I have no question that these two verses set forth the practice and experience which explain his vital and enduring influence.[87]

X. His Attitude Toward War

ROBERT SPEER'S ATTITUDE TOWARD WAR AND HIS CONVICTIONS in regard to the duty of individuals to their country in time of war were clear, courageous, and forthright.

In the first chapter of his volume, *The Stuff of Manhood: Some Needed Notes in American Character*, The Merrick Lectures for 1916-1917, Robert Speer described the qualities, discipline, and austerity generally regarded as characteristic of the soldier, and spoke of the need of those qualities in American life today:

Whether there should be compulsory military training in America is a question to which some people will answer yes or no according to their general theories and others according to their observation of the actual effects of such training on moral character. But whatever our views may be on this familiar question, whether we regard military service as ethically helpful in its influence or as morally injurious, we cannot differ as to the need in our national character of those qualities of self-control, of quick and unquestioning obedience to duty, of joyful contempt of hardship, and of zest in difficult and arduous undertakings which, rightly or wrongly, we consider soldierly, which we attribute in such rich measure to our forefathers, and which the moral exigencies of our national task today so peremptorily demand. To put these primary and elemental needs as sharply as possible, let us call them discipline and austerity. Our American character needs more of both.[88]

We know how Jesus' exultation in difficulties, this love of hardship, this scorn of ease, became the characteristic note of early Christianity. And when Paul comes to write his conception of the happy warrior, we find him setting this quality in the foreground: "Endure hardship, as a good soldier of Jesus Christ." [89]

As Chairman of the General Wartime Commission of the Churches, which was organized September 20, 1917, Robert Speer took a leading part in the drafting of official statements by the Wartime Commission and in presenting its views to the country and to the churches during World War I. The Commission was organized with Robert Speer as Chairman, Right Reverend William Lawrence, Bishop of Massachusetts, Vice-Chairman, and William Adams Brown, as Secretary. At later meetings Rev. Gaylord S. White was chosen Associate Secretary, and Rev. Harold E. Tryon, Rev. Samuel M. Cavert, Rev. Eric M. North, and Rev. Stuart Cramer were made Assistant Secretaries. The smooth working of the various war commissions was assisted by the appointment of a small committee of informal character; the Chairman of this Committee was Father John Burke; other members were Captain Harry Cutler, of the Jewish Welfare Council, John R. Mott representing the Y.M.C.A., and Robert Speer.

At the beginning of the War, Robert Speer made a statement which was widely misinterpreted.

He pointed out that we were not without error ourselves and, although he believed we had to fight the war, we could not think of Germany as wholly evil and ourselves without sin. To his surprise and indignation, he was violently attacked in *The New York Times*, although he had many letters from students, both graduate and undergraduate, who saw clearly the point he had been trying to make and felt it was something greatly needed. But war hysteria had risen fast and the *Times* attacks spread like wild-fire. The Board of Foreign Missions was attacked because he was on their staff and there were letters from hot-headed patriots who said they would never contribute to foreign missions again as long as Robert Speer was a missionary secretary. His only answer was to state just what he had said and why; that he was not a pacifist and not pro-German. In time the fury died down.[90]

During World War I, Robert Speer often spoke and wrote of the challenge to the Christian of the courage and fidelity of the soldier. "Every soldier dying on the battlefield is a challenge and a summons to those of us who have accepted the Christ of the Cross, but not the Cross of Christ. If they can give so freely to their lords of death and destruction, why should we not give even more freely to the Lord of Life and Peace?"

During the last year of World War I Robert Speer put his thoughts concerning war and the duty of a Christian in relation to it in a book entitlted, *The Christian Man, the Church and the War*, which was published by Macmillan and received wide attention. In a letter to his son Elliott, Robert Speer outlined the contents of the book and his purpose in writing it:

I have just finished reading the galley proofs of the little book on *The Christian Man, the Church and the War*, and am hoping to get the page proofs shortly. I do not know whether it will convince anyone who does not already agree with the positions which it takes, but I hope that it may be helpful to some. I expect it to be criticized both by ultra-militarists and by ultra-pacifists, but I think its positions are right, or as nearly right as I can see in these very mixed-up and confused days. In the first chapter, I have tried to state clearly that I believe as a Christian man the present war is just and necessary. In the second chapter, I have dealt with the problem of the Church and the war and what the spirit and functions of the Church ought to be in times like these. The third chapter is an attempt to analyze some of the elements of the world problem and to show that the only possible solution is to be found in Christ.[91]

In this little book of only 105 pages, written during the suffering and strain of war, Robert Speer expressed ideas which later were expanded in his larger volumes: *The Church and Missions, Race and Race Relations, The Stuff of Manhood,* and *The Finality of Jesus Christ.*

Can anyone deny that there have been wars which on one side at least were right? If there is any truth at all in the Old Testament records, it is clear from them that again and again men were convinced that they were fighting with the very help and warrants of God. In our own national history, who is prepared to say that both the Revolutionary and the Civil Wars represented no right principle for which the nation was justified in contending, even to the death? The New Testament itself recognized the legitimacy of military service for Christian men as it certainly could not have done without sacrifice of its moral authority if it be true that war cannot be morally allowed in human life. And in all later days many of the noblest and purest Christian spirits have been soldiers. . . .

Jesus clearly bade us to yield our own rights, but He did not bid us to yield our duties. If one smites us on our own cheek we are to turn to him the other, but if he smites a little child on one cheek he will not smite it on the other if we have the strength and love of Christ in us. Set in the duty of service we are to stand immovable, faithful unto death, shielding the helpless, protecting the weak, overthrowing the evil. . . .

Let it be said again that the time will come when all this sort of argumentation will seem to men the talk of a forgotten day. But the day is not now forgotten nor the time bygone. . . . We shall never bring that other and better day in if we do not do our duty now. Our duty now is to refute the false ideals of military hypocrisy and willful power. To check and throw back national ambition that ignores the rights of the weak and aims at usurpation and dominion, to destroy at any cost to ourselves the principle of war, to deliver mankind from the unbearable burden of armaments and dread of attack. It is not tolerable to live in such a world. And if there is

no other escape from it than by the death of men in war let
us die so, in order that other men may live in a different
world.

The problem of war to the Church is even greater than its
problems for the Christian man. . . . I believe that Jesus and
the New Testament keep the relativity of the right of life and
the absoluteness of the claims of truth, and that these are the
fundamental issues of the present hour. If the principle of life
is absolute and of truth relative, why should men die for a
cause, how can a cause ask men for their lives? But I believe
it is truth and righteousness which is the absolute and sovereign value for which alone we have a right to war, and to
count life in comparison a secondary thing to be poured out
without reserve. To these principles the Church needs to bear
an unmistakable witness and to build them as a great rock
under our national thought and purpose. The certainty of
victory is with those who see the principle of truth as absolute and uncompromisable and who deem life of value only
for truth's sake.

The best soldiers the nation has had from Washington to
our own day have been Christian men. The Civil War produced no general of more remarkable power than Stonewall
Jackson, and Col. Henderson, his biographer, tells us of him
that "his religion entered into every action of his life." . . .
We need the Stonewalls today and it is religion that can make
them for us.

Motives of pride and anger and indignation may last
through an hour, but nothing but an immovable and unselfish
moral purpose will endure all things. "Blessed be God," said
President Lincoln to a Christian delegation in a dark hour of
the Civil War, "Blessed be God who in an hour like this
giveth us the Churches." The Christian Church is the custo-
dian of the forces which wear down and outlast death. The
merely materialist energies and motives and purposes will go
down in the time of the last testing. Like John Brown's body,
they will simply molder under us. But John Brown's soul?
Through night and death it will go marching on, and the
fountains of life which fed that soul then will feed our souls

now until this war is won. We need in our nation now the sense of religion-nourished duty which sustained our fathers in the two great past crises of our history and which alone can sustain us now, a sense of duty which no power on earth or under the earth can relax until our work is done.

It is hard to forgive the moral madness beyond belief which brought on the war, its enormous wrong, its pitiful suffering. It is hard to see how God Himself can forgive. But He can forgive, and His Spirit and His Spirit alone can enable men to forgive. . . .

It is part of our ancient blindness to assume that national interests must conflict. . . . We are sick of this idea and are ready for another long step onward in the way of human progress. We have our opportunity through the war to effect an organization of the nations which would bring them under a just and mutually helpful order, as binds in closer bonds the widely varied interests of our American Union.[92]

During the General Assembly of the Presbyterian Church in 1927, when Robert Speer was Moderator, pressure was exerted to induce him to endorse a statement in behalf of the Church in favor of the pacifist position. He resisted this pressure and stated that he thought it would be a mistake for the Church to endorse such an attitude as a policy: "There are occasions in history when criminal nations emerge and these nations must be restrained."

In the last book in which Robert Speer had a part, *The Crisis Decade*, published in 1951, for which Dr. Speer wrote the concluding chapter, "Basic Problems Challenging Foreign Missions," he spoke of the passing of the Second World War "with right result":

The first element in our present situation, though not the central and basic element, has been, of course, the tragedy of two World Wars. It is first in our thought, but it is not the central issue. The central and controlling issue is the Christian conception of the meaning of Jesus Christ to human life and destiny. The second war has passed, and it has passed with right result. If Nazi Germany had prevailed, it would have been the end of Christian missions, of the Christian Church, and of Christian liberty wherever German domination should extend. In Italian territory, there might have been a remnant of liberty for Roman Catholic missions. As Abyssinia showed, there would be none for Protestant. In Japan, Christianity and Christian Missions would have been subservient to the State. By the goodness of God and through the sacrifice of thousands of young men and women this tragic outcome of the war has been averted. But the war has left immense problems for Foreign Missions and the Church.[93]

XI. Two Deep Convictions

1. His Belief in the Virgin Birth of Christ

2. His Belief in the Equality of Women in the Church

BY EMMA BAILEY SPEER

1. His Belief in the Virgin Birth of Christ

The fairest thing we can experience is the mysterious. It's the fundamental emotion which stands at the cradle of pure art and science. He who knows it not, can no longer wonder, no longer feel amazement, is as good as dead, a snuffed-out candle.[94]

To Robert Speer the world was increasingly full of mystery. He studied St. Paul's sense of it and his use of the word, and more than once said, "When I get to Heaven, I'll take a long look at the Lord, and then I'll ask St. Paul what he meant by some of the things he said." Mystery for him was hidden in the commonplace, and he tried to take none of God's gifts for granted. There was mystery in pain, in suffering, in beauty, in happiness and human love, and in that last enemy, death. But the greatest of all mysteries and miracles was in the Love that is the nature of God, in His patience with us all, and supremely in His incarnation, His willingness to enter this human scene at a point of time and space, to bear all the limitations and humiliations of our humanity and to be truly the Son of Man while never failing to be the true Son of God.

Of course it is beyond human understanding, and yet we can believe, as one great thinker has said, "because it *is* impossible." At a time when many young men were being swept along with the "receding tide of faith" that Matthew Arnold saw on Dover Beach, Robert Speer was building his foundations for himself on the New Testament and found confirmation of them in books like Liddon's *Divinity of Our Lord*, Uhlman's *Sinlessness of Jesus*, and in Horace Bushnell's *Nature and the Supernatural*," especially the chapter, "The Character of Jesus, Forbidding His Possible Classification with Men." In Brother Lawrence's *Practice of the Presence of God*, "The Best Rule for a Holy Life," he found incentive to study in the Bible the nature of the God whose presence we should practice, and in Edersheim's *Life and Times of Jesus the Messiah* he found profound insight into the Jewish background of the Lord's life.

His travels and weeks of illness in Asia, before the turn of the century gave Robert Speer time to absorb the real feeling of a country little changed from the days of Abraham. With the tomb of Esther and Mordecai within walking distance, those weeks in Persia made clear to him the value of tradition. These values are not so clear to men who study records from the remote vantage point of a library in Europe.[95]

His Bible study and his wide reading increased his sense of the wonder and miracle of life even in small things, and he liked to recall the traditional saying of the Lord that Clement of Alexandria records, "He that wonders shall reign; he that reigns shall rest. Look with wonder at that which is before you."

To some, this sense of the ultimate miracle at the heart of all life can come in a flash, even on the barrenness of the Damascus road. To others it comes in the lifelong attitude of the transcendentalist, who sees eternity in a grain of sand, believing that "we live in a world of eternal and infinite mystery, invisible and inconceivable, yet most real and so interconnected with the visible universe that constant reference to it is the supreme necessity of the human spirit, the highest duty of man, and the indispensable condition of all that's best in the human genius.[96]

In a long article on the Virgin Birth, published first in the magazine, *The King's Business,* and later in *Some Living Issues* Robert Speer replies to questions at a time when the Virgin Birth was a subject of controversy, and gives his reasons for believing in this phase of miracle which he connects inescapably with the ultimate miracle of the Resurrection. He refers to the belief in the Virgin Birth as a part of the whole fabric of his belief and thought. His prayer in *Five Minutes a Day* (p. 324) gives thanks to the Father for "His only begotten Son who 'took our nature upon Him and was born of a Virgin,'" and in another place he writes he can "rejoice with great joy in the miracle of the Virgin Birth."

Anyone who believed wholeheartedly, as Robert Speer did, in the Virgin Birth of the Man, Christ Jesus, was therefore inevitably a believer in an equal place for woman in the Church and in society. Robert Speer tried in all his contacts with women and women's organizations to show the same spirit of consideration and insight that His Lord had shown.

He believed that women had equal rights, but not regardless of training, character or ability; character, ability, and training were to be taken into account in the service assigned to them. But they were not to be excluded from such service merely because they were women.

He believed that if the Saviour of the world had not been born of a woman without the mediation of a human father, women would have remained inferior to men, a mere segment of the race, a biological necessity for its preservation, instead of a normal half of it, a half that was worthy of the same dignity, the same respect and consideration that is due to each child of God. "Male and female created he them." In Cameroun in West Africa a Bulu Christian woman said, "Before the Words of God came into the forest, women were not considered to be 'people.'"

For God, the Creator and Source of all life, to become Incarnate is the greatest mystery and miracle in all history. He came in the fullness of time, and as the world was constituted, he had to come as a man and had to live a man's life; but everything in His acts and teaching shows that He gave to women a new place, with an understanding, tenderness, and consideration accorded to them in no other faith or creed. His teaching in this regard is very slowly working as a leaven throughout human society and has not yet been achieved universally even in "Christian" countries.

In one of his books[97] Robert Speer wrote fully and clearly of his belief in the Virgin Birth of Our Lord. A summary of his statement follows:

I believe in the Virgin Birth and the Resurrection because I believe that the Gospels are true and that they teach unmistakably that our Lord was born of a Virgin and rose from the dead.

It is sometimes said that the story of the Virgin Birth is in only two of the Gospels but it is in both of the Gospels that deal with Jesus' earthly life at all.

No one questions the teaching of Jesus because they are not in all the Gospels; the Sermon on the Mount is in only one Gospel; the Prodigal Son and the Good Samaritan are in only one Gospel. The Gospel of Mark does not mention the Virgin Birth but begins like a trumpet call—"The good news of Jesus Christ, the Son of God!" The voice from Heaven follows, "Thou art my beloved Son." Mark's Gospel is the only one that entirely omits Joseph; Mark speaks of Jesus only as Mary's Son, "the carpenter, the son of Mary."

It is objected that because neither John nor Paul refer to the Virgin Birth it cannot be fundamental. The present question is not how fundamental a truth is but whether it is *Truth.* Even if John and Paul did not refer to it, if this were the fact it would not prove that it were not true. Neither one of them refers to the Sermon on the Mount or to most of the events or sayings in the life of Jesus. Their silence would not disprove declarations of Matthew and Luke; but

are they silent? John's Gospel begins with the loftiest assertion of the pre-existence of Jesus as the Eternal Word.

John mentions Joseph twice and then quotes references to
Him by others in a way that would have been the common
usage; however, in each of these cases he at once supplies a
complete corrective of the natural popular supposition. Philip
says to Nathaniel, "We have found . . . Jesus of Nazareth,
the son of Joseph." But notice what follows when Nathaniel
comes to Jesus. "Rabbi, Thou art the Son of God." In the
second case, the Jews said, "Is this not Jesus, son of Joseph,
whose father and mother we know?" And immediately John
quotes some of Jesus's plainest words about the Divine Son-
ship, beginning at once with the reference to "the Father that
sent me."

In the Gospel of Luke, where there is the full story of
Jesus' Virgin Birth, there is the same kind of statement of the
popular view that John quotes, and in Luke 3:23, where Luke
calls Jesus "the Son (as was supposed) of Joseph," and again,
in Luke 4:22, where he quotes the popular word, "Is this not
Joseph's son?" obviously the quotation of such a popular no-
tion does not mean that he knew nothing of the Virgin Birth.

John constantly reports words of Jesus on His unique origin, "Ye know not whence I come," and John adds that the
Jews sought to kill Him because "he called God his own
father."

No language could be plainer than that used by Paul in
asserting God's unique Fatherhood of Jesus. He quotes at
Antioch the Second Psalm, "Thou art my Son, this day have
I begotten thee," and immediately connects His unique origin
with His unique end and the Resurrection. Both John, in the
prologue of his Gospel, and Paul, in the first chapter of Colos-
sians, deal with the pre-existence of Jesus in a way that makes
it utterly impossible to think of him as originating and ending
in the world as an ordinary human child. In one word, the
New Testament in certain books asserts unequivocally the
Virgin Birth of Our Lord, and in its other books either as-
sumes it or implies it or says nothing inconsistent with it.

Accordingly, if the New Testament's representations of Jesus are trustworthy, the Virgin Birth must be accepted as a fact as reliable as any other fact of the life or character of the Saviour.

I believe in the Virgin Birth because it has been the faith of the Church from the outset. Ignatius, early in the second century, speaks emphatically of it. Aristides of Athens, in his *Apology*, written about the year 130, is equally clear. Justin Martyr, in his first *Apology*, between A.D. 140 and 150, is unmistakable in both the belief that Christ should be born of a Virgin, that He should die and rise again, and "should both be and be called 'the Son of God' "; and so one could quote Irenæus, 190; Tertullian, 200; Clement, 190; Origen, 230.

The Doctrine of the Virgin Birth is natural, right, and congruous. Jesus was unique, as Bushnell clearly demonstrated; His character forbids His possible classification with men. That such a Life should be as different in its origin and its end as it was in its spirit, principle and manifestation, is more natural, right and congruous than that it should have had a naturalistic ending and beginning—His life was a *supernatural life!* I believe it harmonizes best with this fact about it, that it began and ended supernaturally.

Furthermore, the work that Christ came to do and the place which He came to fill in humanity called for this unique and miraculous origin. It is sometimes said that the Virgin Birth is not essential to the deity of Our Lord; but that depends upon our conception of His deity and of the saving work that He came to do. He was the Saviour that he was and is, not only because of His character, but also because of the whole fact of His being, which included the supernatural uniqueness of His origin and personality.

The Bible nowhere declares that knowledge of the Virgin Birth of Christ is essential to salvation and there is much preaching of the Gospel in the New Testament that makes no mention of it. But this is true also of other facts in the life of our Lord. The Virgin Birth is a fact which is part of the Gospel record and is part of the whole meaning and significance of the Gospel. It is as essential an element in the Gospels of Matthew and Luke as the accounts of the Sermon on the Mount in those same Gospels. If the Gospels are trustworthy in their account of Jesus' teaching, they are equally trustworthy in their representation of the convictions of their writers with regard to the manner of Jesus' birth.

Lastly, I believe in the Virgin Birth of Christ because the alternative view is intolerable.

For many of the same reasons for believing in the Virgin Birth, I believe also in the Resurrection; it is the natural and appropriate ending of such a life as Christ's. His life began in miracle and ended in miracle because He was and *is* the Son of God.

2. His Belief in the Equality of Women in the Church

Robert Speer's position on the place of women in the Church and his reasons are given in full in his volume, *Some Living Issues*. These are briefly summarized here:

In going over his study of "The Place of Women in the Church" in the light of 1953 one realizes how greatly conditions have changed. Two world wars brought women responsibilities in many areas and in the service of the Church that they had not had previously. More and more women are receiving ordination today and there is a much wider understanding of the need for women as well as their ability and willingness to serve.

There is nothing in the Bible to warrant a discrimination against women, or their exclusion as a sex in the work of God in His Church.

No one can read the Gospels and the Book of Acts and find there any evidence of the subjugation or subordination of women. They were in the company of the Disciples; they shared in the work and friendship of Christ; they were present at the giving of the Great Command; women were among the creatures to be evangelized and were assuredly counted among the Evangelists. The remarkable fact about the Gospels and the Acts is that they take for granted the place and part of women; all the ideals and obligations and privileges and endowments of the Gospels are for "mankind," for men and women alike. There are no sex discriminations or distinctions whatsoever. Christ laid down no rules for women as separate from men. In other religions there is special teaching about women. Only in the religion of Christ is this special teaching absent. There is not one set of virtues for women and another for men. And in Galatians 3:28, there is the great charter of Human Equality:

"There is neither Jew nor Greek, there is neither bond nor free, there is neither male nor female: for ye are all one in Christ Jesus."

It should be noted that this comprehensive assertion of absolute equality in Christ and in His Body, the Church, is from St. Paul, who is sometimes supposed to have held and taught the doctrine of sex inequality and of the subordination of women to man. Paul no more taught this than he taught slavery. He recognized certain existing social usages but he proclaimed no principle of sex inequality in the Gospel, nor in Christ, nor in His Church. His whole conception of the Gospel and the Christian life takes in all alike on the one basis of obligation and privilege. Make a list of the great universals in Paul's letters, the "alls" and the "ones" and see how comprehensive they are! All divisions of race and color and nationality and sex fade away and disappear in the family of the One Father and of the Church of the One Lord and Saviour who died for all and in whom all live.

This principle is conceded by many who still hold that there are diversities of functions between men and women and that women ought not to be admitted into ecclesiastical office. There are indeed differences of function but do they include or involve this discrimination? If the New Testament teaching is not against the freedom and right of women to render any service they can in the Church, then the only

questions are, first: Are women capable of service in an
ecclesiastical office; and, second: even if they are, is it advis-
able that they should be eligible? As to the first question it
is certainly indisputable that there are some women who are
far more capable to discharge efficiently the duties of the
Christian ministry and other Christian offices than some of
the men in these positions. . . .

The only specialization of function and activity in the
church is according to capacity and not according to sex.
This is a fundamental principle of life; service does not rest
on sex. It's true that only women are mothers and only men
are fathers, but not all women are mothers and not all men
fathers. Statements of function in the church or state that are
identified with sex are contrary to the facts of life.

It would be strange and anomalous to deny to women
equality in the church, which is the very fountain of the
principle of equality. It is Christ who has made woman free
and equal. Is she to be allowed this freedom and equality
elsewhere and denied it in the Church, where freedom and
equality had their origin?

The Christian Churches on the foreign mission field are
apprehending the measure of the Gospel in this better than
we. . . . God shuts no doors to His daughters which He
opens to His sons.

In the International Missionary Council in Jerusalem in
1928 the following resolution was unanimously carried, although the published report tucks it away in a small-type
footnote: "That the principle and ideals which this Council
has adopted in the report on racial relationships with regard
to equal rights for races it declares and maintains also with
regard to the equal rights of men and women in and between
all races."

The Church needs today all that women can bring into
it. If there are women who, as elders, evangelists, or as ordained ministers, can serve the Church better than the men
to whom otherwise the Church would be confined, the
Church ought to be free to command their service. There
will be such women. Probably there will not be as many as

the Church needs. The fear that if the whole work of the Church is opened to women they will crowd out men so that men will withdraw from the work and leave it to women, is a groundless fear. There will be a great gain in making men and women equal. The door will be fully open to all that women can give and do. And the reproach of the past, that the Church alone denies to women the principle of Christianity which has gone out from the Church over all the rest of life, will be once and for all removed. We shall have done *right*, and that is all that we need to do.

But some still say that it is inexpedient or premature. It is not inexpedient to do what is right. And it is scarcely premature to do late what through the influence of Christ has been already done in realm after realm of life, and what only now we are coming so tardily to do in Christ's own Body, the Church.[98]

This view of Robert Speer's expressed twenty-five years ago was prophetic of the action of the General Assembly of the Presbyterian Church of the U.S.A., taken in May, 1955, approving of the submission to the Presbyteries for their action the ordination of women by the Church.

XII. His Methods of Work

Humility is not stooping lower than yourself; it is measuring yourself always with Jesus Christ.

—PHILLIPS BROOKS.

Men succeed not because they use successful methods. They use these methods simply because they open themselves to the energy of the Divine Will, which is ever seeking unhindered channels for its flow through human lives.

—R. E. SPEER: Foreword p. 7, *Studies of Missionary Leadership*, 1914.

ROBERT E. SPEER'S RECORD OF ACHIEVEMENT WAS PHENOMenal. How was he able to accomplish all that he did? What were his methods? What were his habits of study and work? What is the explanation of his prodigious accomplishment?

Such a man cannot be explained wholly in terms of heredity or environment. The simplest answer is that he was a man of exceptional talents, with a sense of mission and complete dedication to a world cause; in a true sense, and especially in religious service, he was "a man sent from God." We can thank God for him, follow his leadership, try to learn from him, and be blessed by his spirit, but we cannot really explain him. Yet such men have certain methods, certain attitudes that become habits of work, and these methods and habits we can analyze and describe.

Among some general principles of Robert Speer in his work, I would name first his disciplined use of time, particularly fragments of time often wasted and unused. For many years, he was one of the vast army of commuters who had to spend nearly two hours in traveling between home and office. I have often watched the stream of travelers on commuters' trains; the great majority of them follow a fixed procedure. In the morning they read the morning paper, and talk with fellow commuters; in the evening, they talk with fellow commuters, and read the evening paper. The diurnal journey is not distinguished by mental productivity.

Robert Speer followed a different course. When he boarded the train, his bag of papers and books was with him; out of the battered brown bag came papers and reports from the office, or a book. He plunged at once into their perusal, and concentrated on his reading to the exclusion of all conversation with fellow passengers, as many of them discovered. I have seen him intent on a book while standing up and clinging to a strap in a train in the Hudson Tube. A friend told me how even on a summer vacation, a ten-minute period before meals was used for writing, ten minutes that others less thrifty in time-saving would usually spend in less productive ways. The summer vacation month was used, not only for fishing, tennis and gardening, but for writing another book.

In the ways indicated in the two preceding pages time was saved and "the unforgiving minute was filled with sixty seconds worth of distance run."

A missionary relates the origin of an impressive address given before the Baltimore Presbytery on September 11, 1941, on the subject of Paul's use of the titles of Christ. Delivered on the day after Robert Speer's seventy-fourth birthday, without notes of any sort, the impact of the address was deepened by the fact that it was given extemporaneously from the Greek New Testament, and particularly when Dr. Speer told of the source of the material with which he was so profoundly familiar. It seems that during the days of his early work among students, as a man of about thirty, he was traveling by train through the Allegheny Mountains. A severe winter blizzard soon stalled the train and the tracks were completely covered. Being near a small village, the passengers took refuge there until the way was at last opened some twenty-four hours later. While the largest part of the company killed the weary hours of delay by verbose complaint, games of cards, or restless sleep, Robert seized the opportunity to accomplish something he had longed to do. He put those twenty-four hours into an intensive study of Paul's writings, in the Greek, especially Paul's use of the titles of Christ. It was there that his address of forty or so years later had its genesis, and it was on that occasion he laid the basis for his later wider studies of the subject.[99]

As has been indicated in an earlier chapter, Robert Speer was an outstanding athlete at Princeton, where he played for four years on the University football team. Some years after his graduation, a friend who knew his athletic record, invited him to a football game. Robert Speer declined. He said that he had gone to a game after his graduation and after he had entered foreign mission service, and had become so absorbed in the game and so stirred emotionally by it that for several days afterwards he could not concentrate on his work. Thereupon he decided not to go to any future games, and declined his friend's invitation to watch the game in the sport which he loved and in which in college days he had excelled.

Even in his home Robert Speer put his work ahead of social amenities or conversation. Most men leave their work when they leave their office. Not so with Dr. Speer. He took his work home with him; promptly after the evening meal the papers would come out of the portfolio, and he would retire to his study and turn to his work. This habit of saving time, even at a loss of personal contact, was formed early in his life—apparently during his college days. A Princeton classmate tells how other members of the class would be seen after meals lounging around, "bickering" with one another, while Robert Speer always made for his room and his work. It requires real discipline of will thus to bind

> ". . . the free
> And holiday-rejoicing spirit down
> To that dry drudgery at the desk's dead wood,"

as Charles Lamb has put it. But as Robert Speer said, the only way he could keep his desk clear was to work in the evening, in addition to working during the day. His capacity to keep his desk cleared and to keep ahead of his work was won through a rigid exclusion of social and personal relationships.

A third method, as John Mackay has indicated in the Foreword, was that of continually filling his mind with information and sources of inspiration in regard to the tasks before him. Constant reading was for him both a duty and a joy. In an early book he wrote, "The young man's chief pleasure will come from reading." He set before himself the reading of at least two books a week, and found both pleasure and strength in that reading. He read carefully the denominational papers, and no one was better informed on the contents of the religious press of his own church.

A fourth characteristic of Robert Speer's work was his neatness and his attention to detail. The question reported to have been asked a great sculptor is applicable to Robert Speer: "Why do you pay so much attention to trifles?" "Because trifles make perfection and perfection is no trifle." Robert Speer gave his full attention to apparent trifles in his work. His scrapbooks and diaries were neatly kept and filed. This work was not done for him by a personal secretary or file clerk, but was done by Robert Speer himself. A visit to "Iona," the barn that housed his personal library at Rockledge, Lakeville, Connecticut, is revealing. There in orderly rows on the shelves of the library are his scrapbooks with clippings neatly pasted in, from his second year at Andover, 1883-1884, to the last year of his life, 1947. There are his diaries and his notebooks kept during deputation trips overseas. His neatness and orderliness were the product and the indication of a neat and orderly mind, in which first things were put first, and thus his desk was cleared for action on the essential and primary phases of his work.

A fifth principle was to keep his thought and work on a level above that of petty and irrelevant arguments and animosities. Speaking to a missionary group one day, he said the greatest elements in missionary life were love and patience. A revealing sentence is contained in one of his books in which he advised a man who is in perplexity as to the seeming unreality of the religious life. "Do not do wrong, thus avoiding remorse; will to love, thus winning peace." There were many situations in Dr. Speer's nearly half century of service in which he could have easily and understandably dropped below the level of these principles. But one of the secrets of his power and influence was his steadfast adherence to the ideals expressed in these words, the ideals of love and patience, that made serene and radiant his own life and work.

Robert Speer carried his brown bag of papers and reports to his home, but he did not convey to his dinner table the battles of the day in the office and the Church.* His self-control and mastery of his spirit and of his tongue were extraordinary. During the long ordeal of the attacks made upon him by the extremists in the Church his wife reports that not once did he bring home an account of those criticisms or of the barrage of his assailants. Someone has said that a man is master of his unspoken words; Robert Speer demonstrated that mastery. St. James wrote: "Let every man be swift to hear, slow to speak, slow to wrath," and again: "If any man

---

* Mrs. Speer has repeatedly said that not once in his forty-six years of work with the Foreign Board did she ever hear him criticize his colleagues.

stumbleth not in word, the same is a perfect man and able to bridle the whole body." Robert E. Speer carried out in word and in deed these admonitions of the brother of the Lord.

We have, in Robert Speer's own words, precise and detailed statements of the methods he tried to follow in his work. His ability in public speech, and his freedom and power in that speech, without the help of manuscript or notes, are well-known. In 1909 he made an address on the topic, "How to Speak Effectively without Notes." [100] He made certain practical suggestions, based on his own personal experience. In regard to the form of the address he stated four essentials: "To have a definite aim; to state the subject in the form of a definite proposition; to arrange the propositions according to their relative strength and so work up to the climax; to make each point clear and not stay on it too long." As to the manner of speaking, he suggested: "Keep your eyes on the audience to which you are speaking; never waste thought on a gesture; talk straight ahead; eliminate all slang; and the shorter the words used, the better.

"Often I have tried to rearrange statements so as to make numbers of syllables a multiple of five, having noted that this gave the speech a special cadence of rhythmical vigor."

Four final suggestions were:

We ought to read a great many books, good books, and fewer newspapers. To read the newspapers too much debauches the mind, and breaks its power to keep long on any one line of thought. Especially we must know the Bible and store it in our minds. We must be morally earnest in our lives in order to be morally earnest in our public speech. Do not imitate anybody else; do not try to adapt yourself too much to the personality of the audience to which you are speaking, that is, we should speak our convictions with kindness and tact and real love, without compromise, without any toning down. Finally, our hearts must be in it. There must be warmth and tenderness and love and self-forgetfulness.

Robert Speer in an address called attention to certain principles of Archbishop Benson which one felt he had tried to carry out in his own life and work:

We had hanging up in our office for years four little rules of Archbishop Benson's. Almost everyone noticed them. One day a man came through who read them and he felt sure they must be only a fragment from something more and took pains to get the prayers of Archbishop Benson from which these four little rules in our office were taken. Let me quote a few of them that we may ask ourselves whether our lives have been yielded to live under the eye of Christ and under His law of love.

"Not to be dilatory in commencing the day's main work."

"Not to murmur at multitude of business or shortness of time, but to buy up time all around."

"Not to groan when the letters are brought in; not even a murmur."

"Not to magnify undertaken duties by seeming to suffer under them, but to treat all as liberties and gladnesses."

"Not to call attention to crowded work or petty fatigues, or trivial experiences."

"Before censuring anyone, obtain from God a real love for them. Be sure that you know, and that you allow all allowances which can be made. Otherwise how ineffective, how perhaps unintelligible, or perhaps provocative, your best meant censure may be."

"Oh! how well doth it make for peace to be silent about others, not to believe everything without discernment, and not to go on easily telling things."

"Not to seek praise, gratitude, or respect, or regard from superiors or equals on account of age or past service."

"Not to feel any uneasiness when my advice or opinion is not asked or is set aside."

"Never to let oneself be placed in favorable contrast with another."

"To make no remarks from answers to which self-satisfaction is highest; talking of self; seeming singular; hungering for conversation to turn on oneself."

"To seek no favor, no compassion: to deserve, not ask for tenderness."

"To bear blame rather than share or transmit it."

"To endure often, if one's innocence cannot be established without shame to another."

"When credit for my own design or execution is given to another, not to be disturbed, but to give thanks." [101]

Carrying out these high principles would involve tension and effort on the part of any man. There was such tension in the work and in the bearing of Robert Speer. But those who think that he was not capable of relaxation, of enjoying or telling a good joke, or of taking part, on occasion, in slapstick comedy, or of living days and nights in the open and in the woods and along the trout streams, did not know Robert Speer.

Underlying all the standards and objectives described in this chapter, there is, I believe, a deeper current of life and power. What E. S. Martin wrote in an article some years ago was true of Robert Speer: he had a vitality that came, "not merely from vittles, but from a living relationship with the energy that drives the stars."

XIII. Interdenominational Service

ROBERT E. SPEER WAS A STAUNCH PRESBYTERIAN; BUT HE ALSO was an active and influential spokesman and supporter of interdenominational service; and he believed the two spheres of service did not conflict but supplemented and enriched each other.

In this attitude he was in line and in accord with the official actions of the Presbyterian Foreign Board and of the General Assembly of the Presbyterian Church in the U.S.A. On May 15, 1900, the Presbyterian Foreign Board took action in regard to interdenominational co-operation and the General Assembly of that year approved this action: "In the view of the Board, the object of the foreign missionary enterprise is not to perpetuate on the mission field the denominational distinctions of Christendom, but to build up on scriptural lines, and according to scriptural principles and methods, the Kingdom of our Lord Jesus Christ. Where Church union cannot be obtained, the Board and Missions will seek such divisions of territory as will leave as large districts as possible to the exclusive care and development of separate agencies."

Robert Speer believed in interdenominational co-operation on a sound Christian basis; but he was stalwart in his criticism and opposition to those interdenominational movements which he thought unwise or that did not have a true Christian spirit and objective or those that were extravagantly launched and carried forward. One of these movements was the Inter-Church World Movement, which was organized immediately after the First World War. The Methodist Centenary had been successful in securing large gifts for the Church and for foreign missions; co-operative war funds had secured immense amounts during the war; it was argued that the Churches, if they combined, could surpass the success of the Methodist Centenary and of the secular war funds. Thus the Inter-Church World Movement was projected in 1919. The Movement took a ten-year lease on the large Greenhut Building in New York City. The work was developed on a grandiose scale, with surveys by a large force of "fact-finders" and "appraisers" to bring back reports; the whole Movement was to come to a climax in a great financial canvas and appeal in the spring of 1920 for a total of many millions. Robert Speer did not approve of the extravagance and many details of the Movement, although he did accept chairmanship of the committee which was appealing for volunteers for church and foreign mission service. It was expected by the leaders of the Movement that the individual churches would receive large gifts designated for them from their supporting church constituencies, and that the overhead expense of the Movement would be borne by so-called "friendly citizens."

Meetings were held in the East and in other areas, with special presentations of the Movement in which well-known individuals participated and spoke, including John D. Rockefeller, Jr., Governor Millikin, of Maine, and others. All went well, apparently, until the actual financial appeal was made. The gifts for denominational causes were substantial from members of the various churches; but the "friendly citizens" who had been looked to for contributions to defray the overhead cost of the Movement did not register heavily, with the result that the Movement ended up with a deficit of approximately three million dollars.

John R. Mott, who had been one of the leading spokesmen and advocates of the Movement, went to Europe for long-standing engagements there, and Robert Speer and other foreign missions leaders faced the situation before their own church bodies. I remember when Robert Speer spoke to the General Assembly of the Presbyterian Church, which met in 1920 in Philadelphia. James M. Speers, a vice-president of the Foreign Board, had been active in the Movement; John Willis Baer, who was Moderator that year, called for a statement from Mr. Speers. Mr. Speers spoke briefly and then asked if Robert Speer were in the audience and if he would come to the platform and speak. Dr. Speer had just arrived from New York and appeared on the platform carrying his hat and overcoat. When he arose he said:

I protested earnestly against being asked to speak to the Assembly on this subject. I am not a commissioner of the Assembly and I do not think my views would be of interest or value to this audience. *I do not believe in the Inter-Church World Movement as it is at present organized.* Its emphasis has been on the organization instead of upon Christ, the true leader of any such foreign missionary cause. Its expense has been extravagant and impossible. The campaign for funds has been carried on like that of a secular organization, a company trying to sell its stock to possible buyers. On the other hand, I do not approve the suggested action before the Assembly of complete withdrawal from the Movement. Such an action and similar actions by other denominations will demonstrate the fact that Protestant organizations, and especially those interested in foreign missions, cannot co-operate successfully; the Roman Catholic Church will take note of this failure of the Protestants to unite in behalf of foreign missions. I would favor a radical reduction in the overhead expenses of the Movement and would support a motion referring the whole question to the Executive Committee of the General Assembly to work out along the lines as indicated.[102]

The General Assembly did not adopt Dr. Speer's suggestion but voted to withdraw from the Inter-Church Movement and to pay off its share of the indebtedness for the Movement through annual increases in the contribution to the various Boards of the Church. After some years, the debt was paid

off. There were a number of references to Dr. Speer's mag-
nanimity and his stout-hearted attempt to salvage the organization which had continually flouted his advice and had so
harshly criticized him for his suggestions in regard to keeping
the Movement within practicable financial bounds.

Robert Speer was a courageous and stalwart foe of injustice
and a champion of freedom, and through the co-operative
Christian organizations to which he belonged he exerted his
powerful influence in support of efforts toward Christian
unity, justice, and freedom.

In 1923 the Federal Council of Churches took a strong position, together with organizations representing the Roman
Catholic and Hebrew agencies, protesting against the twelve-
hour day in the steel industry. Robert Speer was President of
the Federal Council at that time. F. Ernest Johnson, Research
Secretary, Commission on the Church and Social Service,
Federal Council of Churches, wrote of Dr. Speer's part in this
battle:

Following the refusal by the steel industry to do anything
about the twelve-hour day, some of us went to work on the
draft of a three-faith statement which the Federal Council's
Department of the Church and Social Service might pro-
mulgate together with corresponding Catholic and Jewish
agencies. Speer was President of the Federal Council. The
subject was a hot one and it was a fine opportunity for con-
ventional caution to manifest itself at the administrative level.
But not Speer. He said, "I will sign that myself if you wish
it." He had social vision and the courage to back it up. He
was a stalwart, if I ever knew one.[103]

John H. Reisner, Executive Secretary of Agricultural Missions, Inc., has written of Robert Speer's part in securing in
1922 a million dollars from unexpended China Famine Relief
Funds, $675,000 for the University of Nanking, and $225,000
for Yenching, and $100,000 for the Committee of Reference

and Counsel of the Foreign Missions Conference of North America:

Dr. Speer's relationship to securing the million dollars for Nanking and Yenching from the Committee of One Hundred for China Famine Relief was very real. I wrote out a tentative statement dealing with the use of left-over Famine funds for the prevention of famines in China through scientific agriculture and forestry. I sent the statement to him, asking him to read it and then to discuss it with me. Several weeks later I had a brief note, saying that the statement had been forwarded to Mr. Thomas Lamont.

One can only conjecture that he spoke to Mr. Lamont personally and the fact that Dr. Speer was interested provided Mr. Lamont and others with the necessary assurance that the money would be wisely used. There was a period when this proposal, along with others from China, was discussed by the Committee of One Hundred, and the final result was that Nanking received $675,000, Yenching $225,000, and the Committee of Reference and Counsel for the Foreign Missions Conference of North America was assigned $100,000. Yenching and Nanking shared $50,000 later on in the ratio of one to three.[104]

An incident which Robert Speer recalled from a conversation with a friend from the University of Alabama, Professor Lang, throws a revealing light on Dr. Speer's conception of the solution of international problems. Professor Lang had attended in 1909 a lecture at the University of Edinburgh by the Hon. Arthur Balfour on "The Moral Values Which Unite the Nations." Mr. Balfour spoke of the different ties that bind together the peoples of the world, common knowledge, common commercial interests, the intercourse of diplomatic relationships, and the bonds of human friendship. At the close of the lecture, a Japanese student in the university stood up and called out: "But, Mr. Balfour, what about Jesus Christ?"

Professor Lang said that one could have heard a pin drop in the hall. Everybody felt at once the justice of the rebuke. The leading statesmen of the greatest Christian empire of the world have been dealing with the different ties that are to unite mankind and had omitted the one fundamental and essential bond. And everyone felt, too, the dramatic element in the situation, that the reminder of his forgetfulness had come to him from a Japanese student from a far away, non-Christian land. "What about Jesus Christ?"

There is one great affirmation of St. Paul which concerns the field of thought with which Mr. Balfour was dealing, "The head of every man is Christ." In other words, the solution of the international problem is just the same as the solution of every problem: nothing else than Jesus Christ.

Francis J. McConnell, former President of DePauw University, President of the Federal Council of Churches, and Bishop of the Methodist Church, who accompanied Robert Speer to the Congress on Christian Work in Montevideo in March 1925, has written:

The first impressions I remember of Dr. Robert E. Speer were those of strength; all kinds of strength. He did not become an especially familiar figure to me until 1912, after I had come into the Bishopric of the Methodist Church. Thereafter, for several years, I was often in relation with him through my activities in Latin America, especially for administrative work in Mexico, for which I had such supervision as was possible during the revolutionary years from 1913 to 1924. In addition I attended the Jerusalem Missionary Conference in 1928 and the World Missionary Conference held at Lausanne.

Anyone who attends missionary conferences learns that there are different kinds of strength at such gatherings: one the type that carries force by "throwing its weight about." This type of strength is expressed by loudness of voice, emphasis of gesture, impatience of anything like criticism. Dr. Speer's strength was not of that sort, but came out of the

range and exactness of knowledge from prolonged patience
in listening, out of keen feeling of perspective, out of aware-
ness of the different values of missionary proposals.

Dr. Speer almost unerringly saw what could or could not
be done in an actual situation arising unexpectedly. I recall
that once there was a debate in this country as to the worth
of "social" activities on foreign fields. Some of the more conservative workers could not see the significance of such plans.
Dr. Speer declared that if such plans were necessary, indispensable in some cases, they should be employed at the
earliest possible moment. For example, in performing practical
tasks in a mission center, he said there was no wisdom in
holding to out-of-date machines or methods if later ones
were economically available.

Again, Dr. Speer never was to be charged with disparaging
or discounting the work of women as missionaries. Any of
us who have seen missions at work on the foreign field have
observed how easy it is for men workers, in building a program for utterance or action, especially at a convention for
discussion, to assume wholly unconsciously, perhaps, that
the really superior qualities belong to the men. If Dr. Speer
ever yielded to that feeling, I never knew of it.

It was the practice of Dr. Speer to remember, or at least
not to forget, the solid social gains won by the Church in its
years of progress. I recall that at a missionary conference at
Montevideo he took his stand against some activities of a
somewhat political cast which seemed to criticize a national
policy of the United States. As I listened to the discussion I
felt that Dr. Speer was too free in his praise of his own country. I thought he should have been more charitable to the
Latin Americans. Looking back at the discussion, after a
quarter of a century, I am now quite certain that his point of
view was more intelligent than mine.

It is easy for an admirer of a character like Dr. Speer's
to be charmed by the sweep of his imagination and the
thoroughly expert grasp of even the details of his knowledge.
It would be easily possible to miss the fineness of his humor,
clean and lofty as it was, and the soundness of piety, espe-

cially in his devotion and helpfulness to his fellow workers in the missionary task. No matter how long I may live, I am sure that I can never forget the glimpses I have had of fellow feeling for his comrades, of his reliance upon practice in prayer, of his personal loyalty to specially urgent duties which he always approached with an attitude of personal responsibility. If it can be said that the most Christian result of missionary effort is the convert himself, it can also be said that of equal Christian worth is the spiritual miracle of the missionary himself; and I will remember always the noble miracle of the character and life of Robert Speer.[105]

Walton W. Rankin, formerly on the Editorial Staff of the Cleveland *Plain-Dealer*, now editor of *Monday Morning*, a magazine which goes to over 8,000 ministers in the Presbyterian Church, worked with Robert Speer in many interchurch groups. Dr. Rankin spoke of the same quality in Robert Speer which Bishop McConnell described:

"Out of the strong came forth sweetness" (Judges 14:14). Dr. Speer had great strength of intellect, character, and purpose. His strength was more evident than his sweetness but his sweetness was nonetheless very real. It lay in the inward exaltation of his soul which issued from time to time in his writings and which could be caught from his preaching. When the Sicilian martyrs were led to trial before the Roman authorities in Carthage they bravely upheld their loyalty to Christ, saying they were "persuaded that neither death nor life" was "able to separate them from the love of God in Christ Jesus the Lord." Nothing mattered except to be loyal to Him and when the sentence of death was pronounced, the leader of the martyrs said, "We give thanks unto God." Another of the martyrs said, "Today we are witnesses in heaven." Of such is the spiritual center of Christendom, and Dr. Speer has his assured place among those who from age to age have this spirit in them.[106]

Samuel McCrea Cavert, former Secretary of the Federal Council of Churches and of the National Council of Churches of Christ in North America, has written of Robert E. Speer as an "Apostle of Christian Unity":

Dr. Speer's concern for Christian unity had a much deeper rootage than any interest in efficient organization or immediate practical objectives. He thought of unity in a more fundamental sense; for him it was not something which we achieve so much as something that we receive. For Dr. Speer unity was something *given*, given in what God has done for us through Christ. His basic position was not that Christians *ought* to be one but that they *are* one by virtue of their common relation to Christ and that they should make this oneness *manifest* to the world. This stands out clearly in his reflections on his experience as Chairman of the General War-time Commission of the Churches during the First World War. He said:

"What is needed is not so much to create a unity as to provide external forms for the expression of the unity we already have. . . . We may learn a clear lesson from the family. Unity prevails there far more fully than in any other part of our social experience. . . . Why may we not work far more boldly and extensively with this principle? The whole Church is a family and ought to be conceived as such. We should refuse to recognize division and exclusiveness as anything else than a vain and impossible denial of facts that cannot be altered by refusing to recognize them." *

Another of Dr. Speer's great convictions was that the larger unity of the future will be secured only as we act, concretely and positively, upon such unity as we already have. He was an eager advocate of church union, but insisted that co-operation, more than union, was the key word for our time. He was always urging that unless we obediently follow the light which our Lord has already given us we cannot expect fuller light to break upon our path. His was

* *Christian Unity: Its Principles and Possibilities*. By the Committee on the War and the Religious Outlook. Association Press.

not the theoretical or academic mind, so focussed on an ultimate union that it neglects the measure of unity that is
practicable now. He was therefore a consistent and never-
failing supporter of every movement that led the Churches
to work together in a spirit of conscious fellowship in
Christ. On this point he once said:

> "The pathway of advance lies through the field of action
> and embodied service. . . . Here we find ground for hope
> as we look ahead. . . . For great tasks confront us before
> which we shall be relatively impotent if we cannot deal
> with them in co-operation. . . . We shall never be able
> to solve them along our old lines of division and separa-
> tion. They are indivisible tasks."

Still another reason why Dr. Speer threw the ardor of
his great soul into the interdenominational movement was
that he saw Christian unity as a necessary precondition of the
effective witness of the Church in the tremendous social issues
of our time. He knew that the Churches could not bring the
healing and reconciling power of Christ to bear upon our
economic and interracial and international life unless they
could demonstrate that power in their own relations with
one another. He saw plainly and felt deeply, that the spec-
tacle of divisiveness or contentiousness, either within a denomination or within the Church as a whole, undermines the
testimony of the Church to its Lord as the one destined to
bring all mankind into its true status as one family under God.

Seeing Christian unity thus as inseparable from God's
revelation of Himself in Christ, Dr. Speer never thought of
any organization for unity as an end in itself. It was only a
means of serving Him whom all the Churches recognize as
their common Lord. During his four years as President of
the Federal Council of the Churches of Christ in America,
from 1920 to 1924, he constantly insisted that it always be
thought of as "the servant of the Churches." The best legacy
he left to the Federal Council was the clarity of his vision at
this point. He wanted to see it judged, not by the extent of
its activities, still less by the size of its budget or its public

prestige, but by the degree to which it helped to bring about an atmosphere of mutual appreciation and trustful interdependence among Christians of our different denominational families. In a well-remembered address to the Council in 1925, protesting against the emphasis on such party terms as "fundamentalist," "modernist," "conservative," and "liberal," Dr. Speer spoke these ringing words, disclosing his own catholicity of spirit and setting a standard for us all:

"We have to quit this business of partisanship, to quit calling each other by factional names. . . . The truth of God is greater than any one party can claim or any one title but Christian can cover. What we need is the New Testament conception of the fullness of the truth and of its communicability to the whole body alone. Only the whole body of Christ is competent to know and experience the whole faith of Christ. . . . For my part I want no label but Christian and mean to try to call no brother Christian by any other name."

For the unity of the Churches, as in all the other interests of his life, Dr. Speer's one controlling principle was the sufficiency of Christ. None of us who had the blessed privilege of working with him could ever miss his emphasis on this decisive point. How often have we heard him quote Frederick Myers' poem, "St. Paul," as voicing his own conviction as to the significance of Christ for all of life:

"Christ! I am Christ's! and let the name suffice you,
Aye, for me too He greatly hath sufficed:
Lo, with no winning words would I entice you,
Paul has no honor and no friend but Christ. . . .
Yea, through life, death, through sorrow and through sinning,
He shall suffice me, for He hath sufficed;
Christ is the end, for Christ was the beginning;
Christ the beginning, for the end is Christ." [107]

The issues involved in the question of co-operation aroused much feeling throughout the Church and were discussed with heat as well as with light. At a meeting of the International Missionary Conference, held at Oxford, England, in 1923, Robert Speer read a paper which attempted to deal with the basic topic, "Is Identity of Doctrinal Opinion Necessary to Continued Missionary Co-operation?" In that paper Robert Speer gave a clear statement of his own doctrinal position and convictions.

The problem proposed is real and difficult. It is real. Already in several fields organizations have been formed, such as the Bible Union in China, to unite those who believe that on doctrinal grounds they should separate themselves from others and to oppose co-operation and union except on the basis of agreement in the convictions laid down in the constitutions of these organizations. And in other fields where no formal organizations have been set up the problem is none the less real as to what basis of doctrinal agreement, if any, is essential. In former days the doctrinal views of foreign missionaries were so far uniform and accordant, so it is said, that it could be assumed that common action was possible, so far as doctrinal opinion was concerned, without risk of friction or conflict. But now the rift between conservative and modernist opinion is said to be so wide and so widely prevalent on the mission field, that the question of more co-operation or of the continuance of old co-operation is an open and real issue.

The problem is also difficult. It is made difficult by our human frailties, by the confusion of prejudice with conviction, by partisan temper, by mutual misapprehensions, by careless and unguarded speech, by the inadequacy of language in the sphere of truth which is beyond language. But apart from all elements of personal difficulty, the problem is perplexing as a problem of principle, or indeed rather as a double problem of principle: How much doctrinal agreement is necessary to Christian fellowship, or what are the limits of tolerance; and how much doctrinal agreement is necessary to common organic action, or what are the limits of co-operation?

Before attempting to answer those questions, the writer of this paper ought perhaps, in order to avoid all misunderstanding, to state his own point of view. He accepts the whole of Christianity as set forth in the New Testament. He believes unqualifiedly every article of the Apostles' Creed. No language is adequate to state his conception of Christ. He believes that He is more and greater than any words can ever express, "the Word made flesh," God incarnate, reconciling the world to Himself, the only Saviour, our Lord and our God. He believes in the truthfulness of the record of Christ's life, including His miracles, and rejoices with great joy in the miracle of the Virgin Birth and of the real resurrection of Christ and of His future, personal advent. He believes that it is God alone who through Christ saves men, not by their characters, nor by any works of righteousness which they can do, but by His own grace through the death and life of His dear Son. As to the Bible, he accepts the doctrine of the Westminster Confession and regards its authority as supreme, not in faith only but also in the practice, conduct, and relations of men. I am afraid this may seem to many very antiquated and unmodern, and the writer must be prepared to accept whatever limitations of value in the modern mind such views set upon his judgment as to the doctrinal limits of tolerance and the doctrinal basis of co-operation.

What can any one do here but state his own conviction? The conviction of the writer of this paper is that in our co-operative missionary undertakings and associations identity of opinion on the whole body of Christian doctrine is not requisite; that in many matters a diversity of view which assures a fuller apprehension and presentation of the truth than any one individual or group of individuals can achieve is desirable, is indeed the very *raison d'être* both of our individualism and of our fellowships; but that one thing only is essential, and that is that we should hold a fundamentally unitary faith in and about our Lord Jesus Christ as He is set forth in the New Testament. There is room for the full freedom of the Spirit, and the New Testament itself declares that "the letter killeth"; but the picture of Christ in the New Testament is not letter but life. St. Paul knew no fundamental issue but the issue of Christ. He is the one and only foundation, the sufficient and indispensable condition. "Other foundation can no man lay than that is laid, which is Jesus Christ." And the possession of Christian spirit is the essential and sufficient credential. "If any man have not the spirit of Christ, he is none of his." If we are really at one in the acceptance of this New Testament conception and valuation of Christ, we have an adequate intellectual basis for our co-operative missionary undertakings and associations. Different forms of these undertakings, like literature societies and theological schools, will still involve special problems. Shall they present all types of Biblical criticism? Shall they describe and defend diverse theological points of view? One may hold earnestly his own convictions on these issues which exist among us, and may desire to see his convictions prevail, and yet as long as other men hold with him the New Testament view of Christ, he ought to be willing to allow, within the associations which he supports, the presentation of convictions which in all probability are as defective as his own are likely to be, in the patient hope of some larger and richer comprehension of the truth.

No doubt there are those who will demand more than this and others who would require less as the essential basis of our continued co-operative relationships. But I can find no more or no less than is suggested here to have been laid down as requisite in the New Testament nor as warranted in the teaching of the Spirit in the corporate experience of the Church.

The end that we seek is the persuasion of all men to the truth, above all, to the truth of the pre-eminence of Christ, in whom dwelleth all the fullness of the Godhead bodily. We may be sure that the path to this end is not the way of alienation and judgment and expulsion, but the way of gentleness and meekness and love, of the calm and reasonable statement of the grounds on which we hold what appears to us to be the truth. In this purpose we best help others and best pass on ourselves into the fuller apprehension by keeping wide and kind the bounds of Christian fellowship, by preserving the unity of the Spirit in the bond of peace, and by doing together as much of the service of the Kingdom of Christ as we can. (See note.)[108]

NOTE: In the volume, *Christian Realities*, published in 1930, Robert Speer developed the other side of this question of tolerance: "When did Jesus ignore disagreements and when did He emphasize these and even go to the extent of denouncing the men and courses which met His disapproval?"

XIV. His Service in Behalf
of Latin America

If religion has nothing to do with morality . . . we can leave South America alone. But if, as we believe, religion is nothing but a living morality, the morality of a true and loving fellowship with a Heavenly Father, a righteousness alive in Christ, if true religion and undefiled is this, that a man should visit the fatherless and the widow in their affliction and keep himself unspotted—then we are no Christians if we do not carry such a religion to South America.[109]

ROBERT E. SPEER WAS THE SENIOR SECRETARY OF THE PRESBYterian Foreign Board for the major portion of his service with that Board. Accordingly, he had responsibility for the administrative and promotional work for the Board as a whole. But he also served as Administrative and Promotional Secretary for specific Missions and areas. He carried the portfolios of the Secretary for two Missions in Persia, three Missions in India, two Missions in China, and for the Syria Mission in the Near East. He was also Chairman of the Committee on Co-operation in Latin America from 1916 until his retirement in 1937.

The Committee on Co-operation in Latin America had grown out of the co-operative work in that area of which the chief spokesman and promotor was Samuel Guy Inman, who began his service in Latin America as a missionary of the Disciples of Christ in Northern Mexico in 1906, and became Secretary of the Committee on Co-operation in 1913.

Robert Speer and Guy Inman differed sharply in temperament, background and training, but they complemented each other in their work and made an extraordinarily able and effective team in the service of Latin America and of the cause of Christ in that area.

Robert Speer had played four years as a linesman on a Princeton University football team; he was tall, stalwart and calm in bearing and in speech. Guy Inman, weighing only 135 pounds, was quarterback on the Texas Christian University eleven, and one year was elected as quarterback for a regional Texan team. He was diminutive in stature but fiery and courageous in temperament and speech; to use a football metaphor, in the Latin American work, Inman called the signals, and Robert Speer opened the holes in the line for the ball carriers and often himself carried the ball on tackle-around plays; and the two men played a hard, clean, fierce game in behalf of Latin America and the Church of Christ there.

Robert Speer said once of Guy Inman: "Latin America has no better friend and there is no one better informed about Latin America than Dr. Inman." Guy Inman wrote of Robert Speer: "He is more like Christ than any man I know." With such mutual appreciation and trust, the two men worked together in harmony and with success in their service of the Committee on Co-operation with Latin America and the continental cause which it represented.

John A. Mackay has written of Robert Speer's action which was one of the decisive factors in bringing Latin America into the sphere of Protestant missionary service after the Missionary Conference at Edinburgh in 1910 had excluded Latin America from the agenda of the meeting:

Speer, the Missionary Statesman, was profoundly dissatisfied when that first great ecumenical gathering had refused to consider the validity of countries where the Roman Church dominated as legitimate spheres of action for Protestant missionary activity. Shortly thereafter he visited the South Amer-

ican countries and wrote, as a result of his six-months'
journey, one of the most illuminating and incisive studies of
that great area that had appeared to date. I have no hesitation
in saying that it was his statesmanlike insight into those countries as a legitimate sphere of evangelical activity which led
to their incorporation within the orbit of the world-wide
activity of the Christian Church. It can be regarded as a
tribute to his memory that the next world gathering of the
International Missionary Council, which at one time excluded
representatives of the South American countries, will be held
in Rio de Janeiro.[110]

Guy Inman has written of the protest meeting in Edinburgh
in June, 1910, when the proposal was made of including Latin
America in the sphere of Evangelical Service. An informal
luncheon was organized by several missionaries from Latin
America, and at the luncheon, which was attended by about
sixty individuals, a Mexican missionary arose and explained
that the luncheon had been held to discuss the restoration of
Latin America to its rightful place in the missionary program
of the Protestant Church. Among those who supported the
suggestion were Bishop John W. Hamilton, of the Methodist
Episcopal Church, veteran Latin American missionaries like
John W. Butler of Mexico, and H. C. Tucker of Brazil.
Robert Speer was present and strongly endorsed the proposal.
A second luncheon was arranged, at which it was decided to
name a small committee to study the question of holding a
special conference at which the service of Latin America by
the Protestant Churches would be considered. Robert E.
Speer was elected Chairman of the Committee in charge, and
Samuel Guy Inman was chosen as Secretary.

Guy Inman has written of Dr. Speer's championing missionary service in Latin America.

Following a long trip in 1909 to Colombia, Brazil, Venezuela, Chile and other republics, he returned to the United
States with a thrilling appeal for the need of Christ in these

countries. His address at the Rochester Student Volunteer Movement in 1910 describing the appeal of Latin America for the simple Gospel of Christ thrilled the youth of North America and led the Mission Boards to plan new programs of service for their neighbors to the South.

Published in 1912, his book, *South American Problems*, the mission study book of the year, was a masterpiece in presenting the social, educational and religious conditions of the southern continent. Nothing in English, or in any other language, had before presented such a clear account of the condition of those lands, showing on the one hand the enormous opportunities for development and at the same time the surprising backwardness in education, in moral and scientific development and in religious freedom. Up to that time no publication on the subject had been so thoroughly documented with Latin Americans themselves quoted as authorities.[111]

Acting on the sentiment of the Edinburgh luncheon conferences, Dr. Speer presented the matter of Latin American missions to the Conference on Foreign Missions of North America in 1912 and he was made the Chairman of a Committee on Latin American Missions, other members being Bishop William Oldham of the Methodist Episcopal Board, Dr. E. C. Cook of the Southern Methodist Board, Dr. Frank Brown of the World's Sunday School Association, and Dr. S. H. Chester of the Southern Presbyterian Board. This Committee began periodic meetings and discussed the ways and means of holding an interdenominational conference on mission work in these fields. A circular letter was issued in January, 1914, to the Christian workers in Latin America, asking their advice concerning the matter of a conference. This first communication with the Latin American workers was delivered in person to many of them by Guy Inman, who spent nine months on a trip through the West Indies and South America for the Disciples of Christ.

The missionaries, national ministers and educators were

enthusiastic about a conference, which was reported to the New York Committee by Guy Inman. In the meantime, under Dr. Speer's driving power, the Committee had been enlarged to twenty-eight members on the principle that each Board that was willing to co-operate should name its own representative to speak officially for his organization.

It was this principle which Dr. Speer insisted must be the basis of the Latin American organization that won the confidence of the mission boards.

The Committee on Co-operation decided to accept Dr. Inman's report recommending that a conference be held in Panama within the next two years, and Dr. Speer took a train to Atlanta, where the Disciples were holding their national convention, to ask them to release their Mexican missionary to organize the conference. There was some opposition to Dr. Inman's leaving his own denominational work for the service of an interdenominational organization. Robert Speer met this opposition with his customary patience, persuasiveness, and wisdom. "Of course you cannot refuse such a request," said the man who himself was giving so much of his energy to interdenominational activities, "because you yourselves owe so much to the work of individuals of other denominations and church groups. I have been going over the songs you are singing here. Almost all of them were written by members of other Christian denominations. The Bible which you are using here was printed by an interdenominational agency. In fact, are you not indebted to other than your own church members for the very translation of the Book of Books?"

Robert Speer's persuasive arguments won the day, and within six weeks Dr. Inman was working in the new office of the Committee on Co-operation in Latin America at 156 Fifth Avenue, located next door to the office of Robert E. Speer. Dr. Inman describes the securing of the first gifts for the work of the newly-formed committee:

The Committee needed funds with which to carry on the extensive preparations for the Conference (in Latin America, called "Congress"), to be held at Panama in 1916, recalling Simon Bolivar's Panama Congress of 1826. "Put on your hat and coat," said the Chairman one morning, "and we will go down to Wall Street and see if some of our friends will help us." The first man we called on was a Presbyterian layman, James H. Post, president of a number of large West Indies sugar companies. The Chairman, of course, did the talking. I was overawed. Would Mr. Post be the treasurer of our new committee, which, of course, was interested in Cuba, just as was Mr. Post? "Impossible! Impossible!" He was already treasurer of nearly fifty church and charity organizations. He would, however, give us a thousand dollars! Our next call was on Arthur Curtiss James, also a Presbyterian layman, a key figure in some of America's largest railroads, with a whole floor of offices in a big skyscraper. He thought the Committee was a fine idea. No! He could not be treasurer, but he would give us twenty-five hundred dollars to help start the good work. In the outer office, we met Mr. James' manager, Mr. Carmen. He, too, was sorry, but it was impossible for him to be our treasurer. However, he would give us five hundred dollars. One more call, another failure to get a treasurer, and another contribution of a thousand dollars. Thus, as a result of the morning's work, we had received a number of expressions of interest and good will, and had collected promises of $5,000.

During the years that followed, when I had to assume more responsibility for constantly increasing budgets, the Chairman never refused the use of his name with his intimate friends, to whom he was constantly appealing for the work of his own board. His attitude differed sharply from that of most of the other Committee members, who were willing to sign a general appeal, but who guarded carefully the large contributors in their own organizations.

The reports of eight commissions in preparation for the Congress on Christian Work in Latin America in 1916 represented careful inquiry and were printed in proof sheets and sent to the delegates for study before the conference. They were the basis of the two-weeks' debate at Panama in February of 1916. More than 300 selected delegates were enrolled. For the first time the Latin American scene was thoroughly examined and a program of co-operative activities was planned.

Robert Speer, as Chairman of the Committee on Co-operation, presided over all the open meetings during the two weeks. Differences of opinion between conservatives and liberals, Latins and Anglo-Saxons, and other opposing groups, made the task a difficult one. The universal confidence in the Chairman's fairness and profound devotion to Christ was a great aid. Each evening some outstanding Christian leaders from Latin America, Europe or the United States gave an address. That of the Chairman was one never to be forgotten. For more than an hour he spoke with rare eloquence and spiritual power, quoting passages from some of the world's great literature and applying the principles of Christ to the solution of world problems. When asked if the address was written and committed to memory, he removed from his vest pocket a loose-leaf notebook and displayed a single page of notes. I traveled with him later for weeks around Latin America, when he spoke no less than three or four times a day. Not once did one discover a repetition or see him resort to manuscript.

Because of his crowded program it was naturally difficult to secure Robert Speer's attention and his approval of a written report. The Report of the Committee on Co-operation, which was prepared annually, was signed by both the Chairman and Secretary. The Report, which the Secretary had written and to which he had given much time and thought, usually totalled thirty or forty pages. In order to meet the printer's deadline, it was necessary on some occasions to catch Dr. Speer as he mounted the train at Englewood, N. J., his home, for the trip to New York by railroad and ferry, or later by the tube. Despite the interruptions of the trip, Robert Speer would go through the report, clarify certain expressions, modify or delete overstatements, soften other assertions here, insert more punch there, so that, after more editorial struggles, the report was ready for the Annual Meeting of the Committee and for the press.

The Committee authorized the Executive Secretary, with the aid of the Boards and Christian laymen who desired to co-operate, to assume responsibility for the publishing of *La Nueva Democracia,* a monthly magazine in Spanish, aiming to reach the educators, government officials, writers and intellectuals of Latin America with the Christian message and to act as a forum for the Christian solution of world problems. Under the editorship of a remarkable Spanish Evangelical, a graduate of the University of Madrid, formerly President of an important Roman Catholic school in Spain, Dr. Juan Orts Gonzales, with the Executive Secretary as Director, the magazine sailed out on an uncharted sea. This unique venture soon challenged the attention of leading Latin Americans who dared write for a Protestant organ. This publication developed a spiritual fellowship of individuals usually not connected with any ecclesiastical organization but deeply interested in a spiritual quest. Thus the interpretation of the Christian message to all who sought Truth and Light became one of the most important activities of the Committee.

Some people thought that the Chairman of the Committee who so definitely believed in the direct evangelistic approach would not approve of the idea of an open forum where many different viewpoints were presented. But they were mistaken. He stood squarely for giving the magazine every opportunity for this unique search for the inner Light by those who had abandoned the old church. Dr. Orts Gonzales was a tower of strength to the Committee, and became one of the most beloved men among the Evangelicals of Spanish speaking worlds. His death in 1941 was a tragic loss. He was succeeded by a brilliant young Mexican Congregationalist and Yale graduate, Dr. Alberto Rembao, who still holds the position of editor of *La Democracia.*[112]

Guy Inman was criticized in certain quarters for spending too much time on political issues and too little time on the work of the mission boards themselves. One of the critics went directly to Dr. Speer. Robert Speer stated that he believed in carefully and prayerfully selecting the best man available for a position and then giving him freedom to work out his own program.

Dr. Inman wrote:

When the American petroleum owners in Mexico in 1914 started the campaign for United States intervention in that country, the Secretary of the Committee on Co-operation publicly opposed that movement. The battle became warm and turbulent. Dr. Speer said nothing about the Secretary's action. When the Secretary showed the Chairman the draft of a letter he had written intended as a public reply to a vitriolic attack made by the petroleum group, the Chairman read the letter and said: "If I were in your place, I would not answer. But if you are going to answer, give them all you've got!"

One morning in the fall of 1919 the New York newspapers carried a front-page story that the Secretary of the Committee on Co-operation in Latin America had been discharged for political activities in connection with the question of intervention in Mexico. The truth was that the Committee was meeting that morning to consider what was to be done about the testimony the Secretary had given before the Senate Committee investigating the question. Dr. Speer asked each member to express his opinion. Two members representing large mission boards said that the Secretary's political activities had lost their boards several million dollars in contributions from the oil magnates, and some action was necessary. The last man to speak was Bishop Francis J. McConnell, who seldom came to the meetings, as his residence was in Denver. I learned afterwards that Robert Speer had telegraphed the Bishop that his presence was needed. Bishop McConnell, who had administered the Methodist Episcopal work in Mexico during the Revolution there, said that he thought there were two questions involved. One was whether a man in an official position should speak his convictions or, if he should report only the position of his organization. As for the men under his jurisdiction, the Bishop said he always told them to express their convictions, to be men rather than machines. The second question was in regard to Mexico. In that matter, he regarded Dr. Inman, the Secretary of the Committee, as one hundred per cent correct.

Dr. Speer had another method of meeting critics which I witnessed one day when a man came into his office and attempted to discredit another Christian worker. Dr. Speer allowed the visitor to talk for twenty-five minutes without interruption. The visitor waited for a rebuttal, but Dr. Speer attempted none. Tremendously embarrassed, the accuser left the room without Dr. Speer's having said a word.

Never was Dr. Speer seen in a happier vein than when he headed a pilgrimage of North American Protestant leaders to South America for the meetings of the Congress on Christian work in South America, held in Montevideo, Uruguay, in the spring of 1925. A group of some fifty delegates sailed from New York on the *Southern Cross* on February 28, 1925, spent a week in Rio de Janeiro, two weeks in Montevideo, ten days in Buenos Aires, crossed the Andes to Chile, all remaining in Santiago for a reception by President Alessandri of Chile and a visit with the noted poet Gabriela Mistral, returning, after a trip up the west coast, by Panama Canal to New York. Everywhere Evangelical Churches, schools and social centers welcomed the delegates and Robert Speer and others made public addresses. Never before had the citizens of South America seen such a distinguished group of North American Christians and the press and the public gave them a royal welcome.

"The conference at Montevideo differed from the congress held in Panama nine years before, in that it was directed largely by South Americans. The presiding officer, Erasmo Braga, a well-known Brazilian educator, Secretary of the Committee on Co-operation in Brazil, and a former Moderator of the Presbyterian Church in Brazil, personified the new

type of leadership the Protestant Church was furnishing
South America. A man with fluent command of the four
languages used at the Congress, Spanish, Portuguese, English
and French, a man of deep conviction and spiritual power,
Dr. Braga declared at the close of the Montevideo meetings:
"When we came here, we all started to crowd up to the
front, carrying our ecclesiastical baggage. But as we gained
a clear view of Christ and tried to draw closer to Him we
dropped the baggage which separated us; then as we drew
closer to each other we came closer to Christ." [113]

Robert Speer was Chairman of the Business Committee
which was responsible for the organization and functioning of
the Congress. Under his leadership, the Committee worked
long hours and cleared all detail promptly and efficiently. Dr.
Speer never appeared on the platform, but did his work in-
conspicuously and never missed an hour of the Congress. A
two-volume report of the Congress was published under his
editorship, entitled: "Christian work in South America,"
which was the most complete and fairest summary of the subject which had been published up to that year. The wide
scope of the program set before the Committee on Co-operation by the Montevideo Congress seems in retrospect to have
been a forerunner of the Point Four Program adopted a
quarter of a century later by the United Nations.

Fred C. MacMillan, President of the Central Iowa Fuel
Company of DesMoines, Iowa, a layman and an influential
member of the United Presbyterian Church, wrote of his
impressions of Robert Speer at the Montevideo Congress:

The first Sabbath on shipboard, Dr. Speer was asked to
preach. One of the passengers was the head of a large business
concern in the United States, with extensive interests in
South America, with whom I had talked. He was not a
professing Christian and had little patience with foreign missionaries. I invited him to go with me to the service, which,
after considerable reluctance, he consented to do. The sub-

ject of the sermon was "The Risen Christ and the Church's
Mission to Witness to His Resurrection." My guest was
greatly impressed. Later he met Dr. Speer, with whom he
had some earnest conversations. My friend's hostile attitude
changed to one of interest and deep concern. Before leaving
the ship he thanked me for taking him to the service Sabbath
morning and for introducing him to the speaker.

On the long voyage from New York to Montevideo Dr.
Speer had little time to himself. He took part in various games
with passengers, but other than this diversion, his hours were
largely filled by those wanting conferences or seeking to en-
gage him in conversation. One marveled at his patience and
his poise. He never appeared annoyed or perturbed. His "day
was guarded," when, every morning, as his custom was, he
went apart to a quiet place for a period alone with his Bible
and for prayer.

It has been said if you would know a person you should
travel with him and share the weariness and inconvenience of
a long journey. The trip to Montevideo on the Atlantic,
through the Argentine and over the Andes, to Santiago, on
the Pacific, and to the North visiting the several Missions,
many not easily accessible, conferring with the missionaries,
was a thrilling, although a wearying, way. Dr. Speer's untiring energy and enthusiasm, his unfailing kindness and consideration marked our fellowship through the long and
eventful days.[114]

In addition to a full schedule of speaking appointments,
interviews and consultations on Mission policy, Robert E.
Speer always found time during his deputation trips to the
field to write "travel letters" for the constituency at home.
These letters gave a more informal picture of the work on
the field than it was possible to provide in administrative reports. One of these letters was the description that he wrote
of a Sunday in Chile in the capital city of Santiago. His keen-
ness of observation and his energy are revealed in this letter:

Long before the sun had climbed over the mountains, which rose 17,000 feet along the eastern side of the Great Chilean Valley, I woke to look out from my window over the city, over the chrome-colored tower of San Augustinas Church with its ancient bell, to the verdure-clad, rocky hill of Santa Lucia and on beyond to the great wall of the Andes. In the early morning, before the smoke and dust, less in any case on Sunday, had risen to dim the air with haze, the huge, purple-brown mountains rising to the snow peaks of La Chapa and Las Amarillos stood forth sharp and clear, always and yet never the same. It was just time for early Mass and I walked up to San Augustinas, where a *novena* had begun and joined the little company in the great old church.

An old flower woman was selling flowers at the door. The altar was as sadly gaudy as most of these South American church altars are. It was full of angels and tinsel and the center of it was covered with flimsy pink netting drapery, which perhaps hid the crucifix. At any rate, even the image of Christ was hidden and the one conspicuous figure was the Virgin and the Child Jesus at the top of the altar over all else. Perhaps a dozen men and thirty or forty women and children were present, most of them faithful old women who came hurrying in and hurried out again. The service over, I climbed to the top of the little rocky hill of Santa Lucia from which, in 1541, Pedro Valdivia, with his band of 150 Spanish soldiers, threw himself down on the Indian warriors surrounding him and decided the fate of Chile. For many years the hill was only a place of refuge, with provision on one side for the burial of the foreign Protestant dead for whom there was no admission to consecrated ground. When in the seventies Vicuna Mackenna transformed the hill into one of the most beautiful adornments of the city, these out-cast bodies were removed and a tablet was set up which we copied one day as we were clambering about. It was in Spanish and read: *A la memoria de los expatriados del cielo y de la tierra que en este sitio yacieron sepultados durante medio siglo,* 1820-1870.

To the Memory
Of Those
Exiles from Heaven
and Earth
Who in this Place
Lay Buried
For Half a Century
1820-1870

From Santa Lucia I came down to the near-by church or basilica of La Merced, one of the most popular and fashionable churches of the city. Again it was Mary in full figure and crown who stood over the altar, but on one side was one of the terrible representations of the suffering Saviour on the cross, bleeding and torn, which make the heart sick with their gross realism.

From the Plaza de Armas it was a comfortable walk over to the Alameda, the great, broad street that runs through the city from Santa Lucia to the Alameda Station. At the southern end not far from Santa Lucia is the old pink church of the Franciscans, built in the sixteenth century, where the principal figure on the altar is the little bedecked doll, a foot or two long, which was Pedro Valdivia's Virgin and bequeathed by him to the Church. On one side of the church in a glass case is a seated figure of the Saviour, thong-tied, thorn-crowned, bleeding, and terrible, and neither here nor in any other church in South America, except the Church of the Passionist Fathers in Buenos Aires, have we ever seen any symbol or representation of the resurrection or the risen Lord. Not even in the great Easter service in the cathedral in Buenos Aires did we hear any real utterance of the triumph and joy of the resurrection day.

At Calle Nataniel, the corner of the Young Men's Christian Association, we turned down to the red brick church with its bright rooms where the English-Speaking Union congregation worships. It is a church with a good and useful history. True Christian men of the British and American communities have here for two generations expressed and nourished their faith. The names of some of these men upon whose uprightness and honor the good names of these communities have been built were on tablets about the walls; but I sat down under a new bronze tablet with a purple wreath over it, inscribed in perpetual honor of those lads of the church "who responded to the call of their country and of humanity, served as valiant soldiers in the Great European war, and perished gloriously on the field of battle that others might inherit and enjoy true liberty."

Sitting under the inspiration of that memorial we listened to a good, true sermon by Mr. Wheeler, one of the secretaries of the Presbyterian Board of Foreign Missions, who also was visiting Chile, on Jesus Christ as the Saviour who died and lives again and is the Lord of our lives. We sang "Jesus, Son of Righteousness, Brightest Beam of Love Divine" and "O Jesus, I Have Promised to Serve Thee to the End," and then came out into the beautiful Chilean autumn sun. There surely is need of these union churches. It is appalling to see what a purely external and environmental thing the Christian religion is to many who come out of these countries from our churches at home. It is easier to lose them than it is to win new Christians from the people of these other lands.

In the evening, as the mountains were glowing pink and purple in the sunset, I walked back to the cathedral, but it was silent and dark. La Merced was open but there was no service. At San Augustinas, however, a really good service was just beginning. There was good music, in some of which the people joined, a long responsive litany, a reading from the Scriptures, and the sermon, short and earnest, and a hundred poor and simple folk who had come in got good from it if that came to them which came to me. Then the lights went out, and I sat alone in the dim old church, wondering how the good of all this could be preserved and its lack supplied and its errors be set right and its power be multiplied. How can the Church which bears His name really become Christ's true church? And God's quest be met? For "they that worship him must worship in spirit and truth. . . . For such doth the Father seek to be his worshippers." Nowhere are our evangelical Missions engaged in a more legitimate task than here.[115]

XV. Moderator of the Presbyterian Church in the U.S.A.

THE MODERATOR OF THE PRESBYTERIAN CHURCH IN THE U.S.A. is elected annually; he is the presiding officer at the annual meeting of the General Assembly. During the year that he holds office the Moderator usually travels widely throughout the Church, speaking at church gatherings and serving as official spokesman of the Church. The Stated Clerk of the General Assembly is the permanent officer of that body, elected not for definite periods of service, but for an indefinite term until his successor is selected.

For a number of years friends of Robert Speer tried to persuade him to allow his name to be presented as a candidate for the Moderatorship. His service to the Church by written and spoken word and his wide-ranging appointments throughout the country and overseas had made him familiar with the work of the Church both at home and abroad. He had been the chief spokesman for the foreign missionary cause during his generation. But until the year 1927 he had always refused to accede to the request that he be considered as a candidate for Moderator.

The years preceding 1927 had been turbulent. The Church needed a recognized leader, with steady hand and head, courage, undoubted allegiance to the historic faith, with an irenic spirit, whose faith in Christ was unquestioned and indisputable, one who could unite liberals and conservatives in the unity of the spirit, in the bonds of peace; one who would represent the historic devotion of the Church to its missionary principles and ideals.

Robert Speer's associates realized that his senior colleague, Arthur J. Brown, would be needed at 156 Fifth Avenue, and in the work of the Foreign Board, if Robert Speer were to be drafted for the field service and speaking engagements and burdens of the Moderatorship. The staff in the Board also knew that Dr. Brown was due to retire in 1929; therefore Robert Speer's colleagues in the Executive Council of the Foreign Board urged him to allow his name to be presented at a meeting of the General Assembly for election to the Moderatorship. In 1927, two years before Arthur Brown's retirement, Robert Speer finally acceded to this request. His name was endorsed by his Presbytery in New Jersey; he was nominated at the meeting of the General Assembly in San Francisco in May, 1927, and, after a token vote for a candidate presented to the Assembly by a California Presbytery, Robert Speer was elected Moderator by acclamation.

Stuart Nye Hutchison, for twenty-six years pastor of the East Liberty Presbyterian Church in Pittsburgh, Pennsylvania, who was Moderator in 1942-43, has written of Robert Speer's service as Moderator:

When Robert Speer was elected Moderator of the General Assembly he was literally called to the helm in the storm. The Church was in danger of being split asunder by the strife between the so-called Liberals and Fundamentalists. During the meetings of the Assembly and all through his moderatorial year he sounded a clarion call to the Church to forget the inconsequential things that divided it and to remember Jesus Christ.

This was the message the Church most needed and we thanked God that Robert E. Speer lived to see his hopes and prayers answered in a united church, moving to the fulfilment of the Divine purpose.

In the East Liberty Church of Pittsburgh is a wonderful

stained glass window depicting the men who have contributed their leadership to the Presbyterian Church in America. Among them are two elders chosen from the great host
who have served the Church. They are Stonewall Jackson and
Robert E. Speer. Mr. Speer is standing with his hand upon
a globe and his eyes looking off into the distance, and to
everyone who passes he seems to be saying, "Remember
Jesus Christ." [116]

T. F. Smiley of Tulsa, Oklahoma, retired newspaperman,
and for many years an elder, first in the Knoxville Presbyterian Church, Pittsburgh, and later in the First Presbyterian
Church, Tulsa, wrote of an incident at a meeting of the General Assembly in San Francisco in 1927:

Among all the tributes paid to Dr. Speer, the one that
impressed me most came from a sophisticated, slightly cynical
newspaperman from Chicago. This was at the time of the
1927 Presbyterian General Assembly meeting in San Francisco, which I was covering as a reporter from Pittsburgh.
This Chicago man was blunt of speech and intolerant of
sham, with an unexpurgated vocabulary.

The evening of the day Dr. Speer was elected Moderator,
I went as usual to the Western Union Telegraph office to
file my story. There I met a Detroit reporter who had come
for a similar purpose. He and I were chatting when the
Chicago man appeared. I noted the subdued manner of the
latter as he joined us. "I have just been interviewing Dr.
Speer in his hotel room," he said. "Fellows, it was like sitting
at the right hand of God."

Coming from a man who was always quick to detect any
sign of pretense, that statement, bearing the marks of complete sincerity, struck me as indicating in a peculiarly poignant way the Christ-like impact of Dr. Speer's character upon
others. [117]

A similar tribute came from another layman, a decade later.
W. E. Hervey, M.D., of New Alexandria, Pennsylvania, in

1939 had made the largest annuity gift received by the Presbyterian Foreign Board. Robert Speer went to Dr. Hervey's simple home to thank him for his gift. After their visit together Dr. Hervey wrote: "Dr Speer has been here and I have beheld the Power and the Glory." [118]

Stanley Armstrong Hunter, pastor of St. John's Presbyterian Church, Berkeley, California, has written of Robert Speer's favorite hymns and of an incident in 1927 when he was elected Moderator:

Journeying across San Francisco Bay with Robert Speer on the ferryboat three days before the opening of the Presbyterian General Assembly in 1927, I ventured to ask him what his favorite hymns were. The six which he gave me reveal his religious life. He spoke first of Oliver Wendell Holmes:

> "Lord of all being, throned afar,
> Thy glory flames from sun and star;
> Centre and soul of every sphere,
> Yet to each loving heart how dear!"

The setting sun was painting the western sky over Golden Gate with lovely coloring, so it was natural that he suggested Henry Twell's "At Even Ere the Sun Was Set."

Next he referred to John Ellerton's hymn, "The Day Thou Gavest, Lord, Is Ended." He told me of that arduous journey through Persia (1921-22) when his wagon was snowbound and he had to wait for over a day and a night in a miserable Persian khan. He pieced together this hymn, line by line, and rejoiced that he was able at last to complete it.

Another favorite hymn, he said, was "O Zion, Haste, Thy Mission High Fulfilling," of Mary Ann Thomson. This is one of the best modern hymns of missions and stewardship, with a ringing appeal to the Church.

Lastly he mentioned Faber's "Faith of Our Fathers." The first hymn was written in 1848, the second in 1868, the next two in 1870, and the last in 1849, so that all these five may be considered modern hymns. Some years later he wrote in my hymnal in which many friends have indicated their favorite hymns,

"None Other Lamb," by Christina G. Rossetti.[119]

At the meeting of the General Assembly of the Presbyterian Church, held in San Francisco in May, 1927, Robert Speer, the newly elected Moderator, made the address on foreign missions, "The Old, Ever New, Call of Christ." He said, in part:

The same grave issues within the Christian Church and as between the Christian Church and the world, which are disclosed in the Book of Acts for Western Asia 1900 years ago are alive in the Church of Eastern Asia today.

We are facing these great issues at the beginning of the last decade of the century of our foreign missionary work. Of the great history of the ninety years that are past I can remember nearly one-half. Indeed, my own life and the life of Dr. John C. Lowrie span the whole of these ninety years. Dr. Lowrie was one of the first missionaries of the old Western Foreign Missionary Society, out of which our present Board of Foreign Missions sprang in 1837. Compelled by ill health to lay down his work in India, he joined his father, the Hon. Walter Lowrie, in the secretaryship of the Board, and it was to succeed him, in 1891, that I came into the Board's service. Dr. Lowrie survived for several years and sought to pass over the resources of his experience and memory, and I look back with gratitude to that contact with the very beginnings of our foreign missionary work and to all the wonderful progress of the decades. In my lifetime the number of our foreign missionaries has grown from 155 to 1606; the number of our communicants on the foreign field from 1616 to 224,370, not counting some independent churches which have been set off for their own life and work; and our foreign missionary receipts from living sources alone, excluding legacies and other such income, have increased from $241,788 to between four and five million dollars. One thanks God for what his own eyes have seen, and his own ears have heard and his own hands have handled of the Word of Life.

Speaking of China in the period 1926-27, which included the Nanking Incident of March 23-24, 1927, when all foreigners were driven from Nanking, he continued:

But again it is said, Has not the Chinese Church itself broken down and is it not glad to see the missionary go? Unequivocally, no. No doubt there will be Chinese Christians who will break amid the storm of persecution and revolution, but there are others who will stand fast and hold all that has been won and wait eagerly for the return of their missionary fellow workers. Here is an extract from a letter of the Principal of the Taoyuen Orphanage in Hunan, in the worst disturbed and most disorganized Province in China, written to the Second Presbyterian Church in Pittsburgh, which has supported Mr. Jenkins as its missionary who, with other foreigners, was obliged to leave the interior stations. I will quote Liu Hsia Seng's quaint English letter:

"There were twenty people baptized while Mr. Jenkin's farewell. We ask them 'don't you afraid the anti-Christian movement?' They answered 'Those who kills our body and not our souls we don't afraid at all.' These new Christians come to church every week.

"There are sixty boys in this orphanage. Now we have Mr. Chou Moh Wha, a graduate of Peking University leather department, is now starting a Tanning trade here. We hope to send you some samples by and by.

"Kindly pray for us and remember our work here. If possible, please let us have your kind advice that we need your help and your prayer."

Let me quote, too, what some of the schoolboys in the University of Nanking have written to their missionary teachers in Shanghai:

"It is shocking news to all of us that you have gone through the hard experiences of life in the tragedy at Nanking. I am very much ashamed that my own people did treat you, my unfailing friends, in this inhuman way. How much I wish to have a part in rescuing you from danger. We are happy to tears that you have got out of it safely. God will rest your heart in His Love."

"Dr. Williams' death is a great shock to all of us—that such an honored, endeared Vice-President should meet his end this way! His blood I know will stir up many young people to tread fearlessly for Jesus Christ, the way which Dr. Williams unflinchingly went through."

"The way of love is tediously long, but victorious eventually. We all believe that the love of Christ will finally win out. God will preserve every drop of sweat which you shed for His work. Do not feel discouraged, please."

"What can I say that will in the smallest degree express my sorrow and regret? The terrible things of Dr. Williams' death and your departure occurred, and I was so shocked that I could not realize what was happening. But I know that you feel as I feel, that the departure is but for a while, and that in a future more peaceful state you will come back to Nanking again—I do hope so!"

"In last Friday's issue of the *China Times* there was an account of an interview of the reporters with Miss Faith Williams, daughter of the late Dr. J. E. Williams. In that report Miss Williams said she wishes to return to the Orient to work. That certainly would win the hearts of the Chinese people—the few soldiers that took part in the Nanking affair are excepted!"

It would be a shameful thing for us to fear and falter when these Chinese Christians stand steadfast and are not afraid.

Experiences like these must not intimidate or stampede the Christian Church. It would be a false and silly thing to sing of the faith of the fathers and their dungeons and their chains and their martyrdoms and our happiness to share in their experiences and to walk in their steps, and then in the safety and comfort of our easy and indulgent lives to abandon the missionary enterprise in China because of such a transient storm as this which has brought no peril to us at home, and to the great body of our missionaries only such inconvenience and discomfort as men and women must be forever prepared for in the way of duty. The whole Christian movement in China will take on new power after these days. Have we not witnessed in the generations past the Indian mutiny, the Taiping rebellion, the Boxer uprising, and hindrance and outbursts in many other lands and lived to see the missionary enterprise come back afterwards with unshaken purpose and deathless faithfulness? China's future is hopeless without Christianity and she will some day see this.

In Mrs. Williams' last letters before the tragedy she had written:

"We all keep quiet, but there is a great anxiety in our hearts—not for our own lives so much as for the innocent, helpless people whom we love so dearly.

> 'Blindfolded and alone we stand
> With unknown thresholds on each hand,
> The darkness deepens as we grope,
> Afraid to fear, afraid to hope;
> Yet this one thing we learn to know—
> Each day more surely as we go,
> That doors are open, ways are made,
> Burdens lifted or are laid,
> By some great law unseen and still,
> Unfathomed purpose to fulfill.'

"Spring has come and the sky is blue. The violets are blooming, sweet and fragrant under the South Wall, and my bulbs tucked away last November are full of buds. We trust God, and go on with our work. China is worth all we can do for her!"

And we may be sure that John Williams was ready and glad to give whatever he had for China, that China might live. And we are not Christian men if we cannot hear the call of his brave spirit today, and if we do not fix our purpose in new and iron resolve to carry forward what these began. Just four weeks ago I stood again on the spot where at Gettysburg Abraham Lincoln spoke his simple but undying words. We stand under memories as great and holy as those.

It is for us here today to dedicate our lives to the work to which these who have fallen had dedicated theirs, and to pledge to them and to Jesus Christ, who first died for us all, a new and complete devotion. . . .

The missionary enterprise never has been built on human applause or the world's wealth, or on any foundations whatsoever save the one Foundation of Jesus Christ. He began the missionary enterprise with no great organization, with no human supports, with no financial resources. Foxes had holes and the birds of the air had nests, but He had not where to lay His head. "Though He was on an equality with God," I quote the great words from the Epistle to the Philippians as Dr. Warfield taught us to translate them, "He counted not equality with God a prize to be jealously retained, but He emptied Himself and took upon Him the form of a servant, and was made in the likeness of men and being found in fashion as a man, He humbled Himself and became obedient unto death, even the death of the cross." It was the way the Master went. John Williams trod it. Shall not the servant tread it still? Who is the disciple that he should be above his Master or the servant that he should be above his Lord? Beyond all these other calls of which I have been speaking this morning let us be still and hear again the old, ever new, call of Christ: "If any man will come after me let him deny himself and take up his cross and follow me." And today may it be with us, as of old it was with those men who first heard that call by the waters of Galilee, and who straightway, straightway, rose up and left all and followed Him.[120] *

* The moderatorial sermon preached by Robert E. Speer at the General Assembly held the following year in Tulsa, Oklahoma, May 24, 1928, "Returning to Jerusalem to Jesus" was an eloquent and moving address, which the General Assembly ordered to be printed for the whole Church.

XVI. Stormy Years

Our lives would be very different if all the energy now wasted in anxiety, foreboding, retrospection, self-condemnation, and the ceaseless treadmill of puzzling about the right and wrong of other people's actions and conditions were to be spent in quietly realizing the truth of the Presence of the Living Christ.

—A. M. CURTIS: *Meditation and Health*

We cannot live by "yes" alone any more than we can live by bread alone. It is not enough to be a "yea-sayer." We must face the fierce and stubborn opposite, the everlasting No, and we must learn to endure strippings which winnow away everything but the central seed.

—RUFUS M. JONES: *Fundamental Ends of Life*

DURING THE FIRST THIRTY-FIVE YEARS OF ROBERT SPEER'S service as Secretary of the Presbyterian Foreign Board many trying and difficult problems emerged; but the most painful and cruel tests of his character and faith came during the last decade of his service. This chapter will describe four of these problems and tests.

First was the necessity of solving the problem of the right relationship between a "foreign" organization, subsidized in large part from abroad, and manned and controlled chiefly by "foreigners," and the native church, composed of individuals living on a much lower scale than that of the "foreigners," poor in property and in financial resources, and dependent in the initial stages of missionary contact largely upon the financial aid of the "foreign" group. On the solution of this problem depended the successful outcome of the establishment of a truly native, indigenous church. This was a vital issue all along the missionary and church frontier in the various countries in which Presbyterian missionaries were at work, but it was most acute in 1926 in China.

Secondly, Robert Speer had to meet harsh criticism and attacks on his leadership and on his faith in Christ which were launched and supported by a small group of critics, of enemies, and of rivals in the Presbyterian Church and in his own theological *alma mater*, Princeton Theological Seminary. The Biblical prophecy was fulfilled: "A man's foes shall be those of his own household." The General Assembly acted on these criticisms and attacks, and supported the Foreign Board and Robert Speer at the meeting of the Assembly in 1933.

Thirdly, the work of Presbyterian foreign missions and the whole missionary enterprise, in both of which Robert Speer had had such an outstanding part, were criticized and attacked in the Laymen's Inquiry on Foreign Missions, Rethinking Missions for which field surveys were conducted in 1930-31, the Report being published in 1932. The General Assembly acted on this Laymen's Report in 1933.

Finally, in 1934 Robert Speer's older son, Elliott, Headmaster of Mount Hermon School at Northfield, Massachusetts, was murdered by an assassin, who was never apprehended or punished.

The force and violence and pain and suffering of these onslaughts on Robert Speer's equanimity and courage were agonizing and cumulative, and only a man of his character and faith in Christ could have endured and come through this quadruple ordeal with calmness and steadiness and unembittered spirit.

The first problem, that of the right relationship between

Missions and Church, did not touch him so closely personally as the three problems that followed, but it did challenge
the fundamental principles of mission administration to which
Robert Speer had given his life. The problem is not easy; its
solution is most difficult; at times it appears insuperable.
Only with love, patience, wisdom, and the grace of Christ
can such a problem be solved. How can an organization,
foreign in origin, highly subsidized, with impressive property and equipment far beyond the reach and financial resources of the national members, with foreigners in control
—how can this organization, related to a church and land
which to the people in the new churches seem unlimited in
resources, with standards of living vastly higher than those
of the people to whom the missionaries go, plant and build
up and help to expand a truly indigenous church that will
live on its own resources, blessed by God in Christ, and
be worthy and able to develop as an independent church,
autonomous, self-supporting, self-propagating, and self-governing, and truly free from foreign subsidy and control?
How can such a church be launched and built up?

This is the problem that every foreign missionary and
every missionary board faces. No one saw more clearly than
Robert Speer the factors involved in this problem, and no
one has stated more clearly the true solution or tried more
patiently and wisely and bravely to help mission and native
church achieve a solution.

One of the earliest Presbyterian missionaries in China had
seen the problem and worked out principles to meet it. This
missionary was John L. Nevius of Shantung, who served in
that province from 1854 to 1893. The gist of his solution
was to plant the Church, subsidize it for a brief period,
during which it needed assistance, and then gradually, but
steadily, reduce the current subsidies from abroad. The missionaries were to withdraw from membership in the local
churches and presbyteries until, with indigenous personnel

and support, the Church could stand squarely on its own feet. This plan obviously ran counter to the natural inclinations of both Christian nationals and foreign missionaries. Once having had foreign support and the aid of apparently un-limited funds from abroad, the native church naturally wanted to continue this relationship, without enduring the pain and effort and almost insuperable difficulties of forging its own way. Some missionaries also did not wish to give up positions of influence and leadership, nor did they wish to leave the lands which had become their own dear home.

As the churches in different lands grew, different Missions worked out varying ways of solving this stubborn problem. The Brazil Plan was one of the most successful of the suggested solutions; this plan placed on the foreign missionaries the responsibility for pioneer service on the frontier, the breaking of the road and opening up of new areas, and helping to organize new churches; the native Christians followed up the front line, organizing churches behind the front, developing schools, hospitals, literary work. In this plan the missionaries are the "Commandos" of the church; they are "the paratroopers," who drop into enemy territory; their supporters follow up and consolidate the new region and maintain the lines back of the front.

The Brazil Plan worked most successfully in Brazil, where, in 1925, the native Presbyterian Church, which had been founded in 1860, was contributing over US$200,000 and was receiving less than US$10,000 in aid from the Foreign Board in the United States. This plan depended to a certain extent on the area in which it was carried out. This area included a wide, new country, sparsely inhabited, with the frontier pushing westward, and large cities springing up on the coast and near the coast.

But the principle of the Brazil Plan was sound, and modifications of the plan were put into effect in Chile and in other countries. In northern Mexico, in accordance with the

Cincinnati Plan, worked out in 1914, the Presbyterian Mission withdrew from the north to Mexico City, the Federal District, and to the southern portion of Mexico. The Frontier Presbytery in Mexico, composed of national pastors, continued in northern Mexico, refusing to join a proposed Union Church, and gained in vitality and strength after the financial support from the United States was withdrawn. The Cincinnati Plan was unpopular at first among the Mexican Presbyterians, who protested because its principles were not fully explained before it was put into effect. But this plan has been a means of new strength and vitality in the national churches, and Robert Speer was one of the main protagonists for that plan.

In Argentina, in 1925, I remember vividly how Robert Speer's face brightened with true joy when we met certain native evangelists who were working without mission subsidy and were paying their own way with the aid of Argentinian members of the church. "This is like the early church," Robert Speer exclaimed, citing St. Paul's example of self-support so that he would not be a burden on the early church.

This plan of self-support by the native church was challenged directly in China in 1926 and 1927, when a deputation of the Presbyterian Foreign Board headed by Robert Speer was visiting the field. The definition of a true native church had for years included the adjectives "self-supporting, self-propagating, self-governing." The Chinese in 1926 made a determined effort to secure approval of their self-government, but with support from abroad. In other words, they wished to delete the adjective "self-supporting." Robert Speer saw the issue and met it squarely. He said: "A self-governing church *must* be self-supporting." He affirmed strongly that it was a contradiction in terms to divorce the two adjectives and the realities for which they stood. This was not a popular position for him to take, and he met

strong and determined opposition by the Chinese church
and by some of the missionaries. He put the issue bluntly:
"You cannot *give* a church independence! The church must
seize independence, must grasp it; we should go out on the
field, stirring up the spirit of revolution and revolt in the
Chinese church!"

Robert Speer and Arthur J. Brown, his colleague in the
Board, composed and put into effect a definition of the task
and purpose of foreign missions, which includes this principle and that is destined to stand throughout the years:

The supreme and controlling aim of foreign missions is to
make the Lord Jesus Christ known to all men as their Divine
Saviour and to persuade them to become His disciples; to
gather these disciples into Christian churches which shall be
self-propagating, self-supporting, and self-governing; to co-
operate, so long as may be necessary, with these churches in
the evangelizing of their countrymen and in bringing to bear
on all human life the spirit and principles of Christ.

We deem all methods and forms of missionary service legitimate in so far as they contribute to the realization of this
end." [121]

Here are four steps: proclamation, persuasion, organization, co-operation. The young church is developing through
these four stages in various fields around the world. The
Gospel message has been spoken and the Christian Church
has been planted and organized throughout almost the whole
world; true progress has been made toward the goal where
all men shall have had the opportunity to hear of Christ;
true advance has been made along the way toward "that
far-off divine event toward which the whole creation moves";
and no one had a more formative and influential share in
stating and helping to put into effect principles and goals
of that advance than Robert E. Speer.

It was during the latter years of his service with the Presbyterian Foreign Board that Robert Speer became the target

for attack by certain conservatives in the Presbyterian Church, who impugned his ability as a representative of the Foreign Board and of the Church and attacked the reality and orthodoxy of his belief in Christ. These were blows aimed directly at his heart.

The critics also attacked the orthodoxy of the Presbyterian missionaries.

A colleague in the Presbyterian Foreign Board secretarial staff, George T. Scott, described this controversy:

Probably the most acute public distress that affected Mr. Speer was caused by the abortive but vehement attempt of belligerent Presbyterian Fundamentalists to remove leaders of Princeton Theological Seminary, to convict the Foreign Board of malfeasance in appointing allegedly unorthodox missionaries, and later to divide our denomination. A few extremist missionaries abetted the foment. Feeling was intense; relations were strained. Mr. Speer was disturbed to the depths and challenged by the subtle peril; all of his great intellectual and spiritual capacities were freely given toward wise procedures and Christian attitudes. Through raking fire by open opponents and unseen snipers, he and others marched straight forward to victory with much less loss to the church than had been threatened. The experience was exhausting to Robert Speer but his accustomed vigor was restored by his phenomenal recuperative ability.[122]

To a veteran missionary in China, Robert Speer wrote:

I wish we could get up such a glow and fervor and onrush of evangelical and evangelistic conviction and action that we would be swept clear past issues like the present ones so that men who want to dispute over these things could stay behind and do so, while the rest of us could march ahead, more than making up by new conquests for all the defections and losses of those who stay behind.[123]

In the General Letter to the Missions #51, written July 24, 1933, there is a description of the meeting of the General Assembly at Columbus, Ohio, held May 25-29, 1933, which dealt with the meeting of the Assembly and its actions concerning the Board of Foreign Missions, with special reference to the criticism of the Board on doctrinal grounds:

Of course, you will be keenly interested in the actions of the General Assembly regarding our own Board. You must have observed in recent months that the Foreign Board has been singled out for attack by brethren who declared it had lost the confidence of the Church and should be reconstructed entirely. Secretaries and members of the Board and missionaries on the field, policies and methods, relationships and institutions, were all included. A pamphlet of 110 pages sharply condemnatory of the Board was issued some months ago and sent widely throughout the Church and directly to each commissioner to this General Assembly. It was in support of an Overture which appears in full later in this letter.

It was impossible to determine how widespread this influence had become and it seemed wise for the Foreign Missions Committee (forty-four members beside Dr. Herbert Booth Smith as chairman) to invite all who wished to lay charges or criticisms against the Board or the work to come before it and speak freely. The author of the overture and pamphlet referred to, Dr. Machen, was not a member of the General Assembly, but he asked the privilege of appearing. He spoke at length and laid the pamphlet before the Committee with some additional remarks. To the surprise of all, only three others appeared and these followed much the same line as that laid down in the pamphlet. The Committee invited all officers and members of the Board at the Assembly to attend its meetings, except in certain executive sessions, and many inquiries were made of them regarding the matters complained of. The whole matter was thoroughly discussed. The result was an extended report giving the Board and the missionary force unqualified commendation and support. It dismissed the charges against the work and its administration, with some measure of rebuke for those who had brought them. This report was submitted by forty-three of the Com-

mittee, led by the chairman, and was adopted with so great
a vote by the General Assembly that no division was even
suggested. Two members of the Committee submitted a minority report declaring the Board and its work unworthy of
confidence and proposing a group of new members in place
of the re-election of any of the outgoing class. This minority
report was submitted to the General Assembly but was re-
jected by a very large vote.

The report of the Standing Committee on Foreign Missions
at this Assembly contained an estimate of the Board of Foreign Missions:

The General Assembly is convinced that the work of Dr.
Robert E. Speer, our senior secretary and his associates, and
also the work of the missionaries in the various foreign fields
as a whole deserve the whole-hearted, unequivocal, enthusiastic and affectionate commendation of the Church at large.
We know that Dr. Speer stands absolutely true to the historic
doctrinal position of the Presbyterian Church, and we would
be remiss if we did not testify to our recognition that his entire life bears testimony to his supreme effort to extend the
Gospel to humanity across the world.

The Assembly also expresses its thorough confidence in the
members of the Board of Foreign Missions and its belief that
they have steadfastly endeavored and are endeavoring, by
every means within their power, to support the secretaries
and the missionaries of the Board in the Gospel enterprise.

The Laymen's Inquiry of Foreign Missions was launched
in 1930-31, appraisers were sent to the field to make a study
and report, and the report itself was made public in 1932.
This was the third of the trying problems and attacks with
which Robert Speer had to deal during the closing years
of his foreign mission service.

George T. Scott wrote of the Inquiry:

Mr. Speer had doubts about the general wisdom of the
project; yet at the request of his friend John D. Rockefeller,
Jr., who financed it, he tried to assist in the selection of personnel and in other ways. The hope of the sponsor and of

the organizers was an objective, independent study by Christian laymen of Missions in eastern and southern Asia with a resulting report that might include suggestions for improvement in the work and specifically that would encourage larger financial support by laymen. The assignment of authors for several of the sections seemed infelicitous; some of the writers had insufficient experience in Missions to broadcast sweeping judgments pro or con after brief visits to a relatively few centers of a vast and complex enterprise. While some criticisms were pertinent and formative, little was suggested that the Boards had not been working toward, and that little was obscured by the confused reaction to the Report. The Presbyterian Board, with the largest work in the area surveyed, studied the Report and was nonplussed; its vice-president was a leading organizer; a beloved former Board member was a surveyor, the sponsor and the surveyors were friends of Board members and officers, and the Missions were highly hopeful of increased appropriations. All Boards were invited as guests to a hotel conference for the presentation of the Report. What a dilemma! Mr. Speer felt profoundly that the Report presented an unfair picture of Missions and that it proposed a faulty religious basis and some unwise, impractical projects. It was hard and painful for him to declare his position in public but he stated it fearlessly and forcefully to the Board and in a widely-read pamphlet, "Rethinking Missions Examined." Nothing short of complete commitment to truth and duty as he saw them would have constrained him to oppose so strongly close friends of many years. His penetrating analysis of the Inquiry served to weaken its general impact. Although some recommendations were adopted in the course of time, on the whole the Inquiry failed in its hoped-for effectiveness. Dr. Speer regretted the failure with a troubled mind and a sad heart.[124] He wrote to a friend in China: "The report has disappointed our hopes and fulfilled our fears." [125]

John A. Mackay, President of Princeton Theological Seminary, and for some years President of the Presbyterian Foreign Board, summarized this battle of the Laymen's Inquiry thus:

No one in the last missionary generation succeeded as Dr. Speer did in formulating the ultimate issues and principles involved in this great enterprise. It was his clear insight into these principles that led him to take issue with that famous inquiry known as "Rethinking Missions—A Laymen's Inquiry After One Hundred Years." Dr. Speer wrote a critique of that report entitled "Rethinking Missions Examined—An Attempt at a Just Review of the Report of the Appraisal Commission of the Laymen's Foreign Missions Inquiry." There was one issue in particular which he met head on. That report, strangely enough, although written on the edge, so to speak, of the rumbling volcano which was to burst forth and disrupt contemporary society, did not suggest anywhere that Communism was becoming a major issue. No mention was made of the cataclysm that was to break forth. There was no sense in that report of the oncoming tragedy. It went on record rather as believing that all religions had something to offer to an eventual religious synthesis, and that now it was time to look forward to "The New Testament of every existing faith." Christianity was, of course, the highest religion to date, but beyond Christianity, when merged and fused with what was best in the other religions, the "New Testament of every existing faith" would be written. Dr. Speer saw the issue and repudiated the doctrine. He did so violently, in a notable piece of polemic, in which, as in everything else, he was nothing but a Christian gentleman. What happened afterwards? The greatest revolutionary era in the world's history began, and some of those religions, which were supposed to flower and to contribute to "The New Testament of every existing faith" are in full and complete disintegration.[126]

Archbishop William Temple wrote from London to Robert Speer concerning "Rethinking Missions":

I do not think that "Rethinking Missions" has attracted very much attention in England, but it is a most important symptom. I should regard it as alarming if it were not so manifestly out of date. It is Liberalism of the Harnack school and period. What is quite clear—at least in Europe—is that the coming generation will have to be divided into those who avowedly have no religion at all, and those who start from acceptance of a Divine Self-Revelation.

There is no future at all for the Christianized pantheistic humanism of Hocking and his friends. Hocking is such a charming person, and I have learnt much from his philosophy, but at the crucial point, like Royce, he takes the turning which leads to the denial of all positive religion, and can put in its place only a vague religiousness, which, being without serious effect on conduct, is quite unable to maintain itself in the pressures of the contemporary world.[127]

Galen Fisher, General Director of the Fact Finding Technical Staff of the Laymen's Missionary Inquiry, carried out in 1930 and 1931, wrote of Robert Speer's relation to that organization and its report:

Speer was a mystic rather than a theologian. I never heard him indulge in theological speculation or the preaching of abstract dogma. The deep strain of mysticism in him found expression in his prayers, as well as in his apt quotation from memory of choice religious poetry. Like John R. Mott, Speer based his faith on experimental verification, and bore testimony to it with magnetic eloquence. He was pained by the humanistic teaching of certain liberal thinkers, but so far as I know, he never resorted to bitter denunciation of them. Possibly, the nearest he came to doing that was in his criticism of "Re-Thinking Missions." His critique was published in the thin volume, "Re-Thinking Missions Examined."

The Laymen's Inquiry was divided into two distinct parts: the Fact-finding in India, Burma, China and Japan; and the Appraisal. It happened that I was General Director of the Fact-finding process, which was done by three technical staffs during 1930 and 1931. Their extensive findings were printed for the use of the Appraisal Commission, which visited the same countries during 1931 and 1932, and issued its conclusions in "Re-Thinking Missions," in November, 1932. The fact-finding volumes were a compilation of objective data which the Director of the Missionary Research Library, Dr. Charles H. Fahs, declared to be "the most valuable and extensive data on foreign missions ever assembled." If, perchance, the Fact-finders had been asked to make an appraisal, they would have deduced it from their data, and theological principles would have received little attention, except in connection with the training of Christian workers. Of the three Parts of "Re-Thinking Missions," only Part II, on "Aspects of Mission Work," leans heavily on the fact-finding data, whereas Part III, on "Administration and Home Base," leans but slightly, and Part I, on "General Principles," including the theological basis of missions, leans hardly at all on them.

There are many sound observations in Part I, but Speer was justified, in my opinion, in taking exception to the syncretism apparently advocated in it, that is, the blending of Christianity with non-Christian religions, and the omission of Christ's death and resurrection from the essentials of the faith. Yet, in spite of his intense opposition to these views, he maintained a charitable attitude toward their advocates.[128]

"Re-Thinking Missions" was the subject of actions by the Presbyterian Board of Foreign Missions in 1933 and by the General Assembly that same spring.

On December 19, 1932, chapters of the Laymen's Inquiry Report were referred to appropriate committees of the Foreign Board and also to the Missions of the Board.

On March 20, 1933, the following two actions were taken:

The sub-committee on Policy and Methods, appointed to consider the first four chapters of the Report of the Appraisal Committee of the Laymen's Missionary Inquiry, having carefully studied these chapters, would report:

(1) That these chapters do not conform to the fundamental aim of foreign missions as expressed in the Manual of the Board (quoted on page 250):

(2) That the Board affirms its loyalty to the standards of the Presbyterian Church and maintains the absolute finality, sufficiency, and universality of the Gospel of Christ.

This report was unanimously adopted.

Another action of the Board had to do with an inquiry from a Pittsburgh church:

The President of the Board presented a communication from the Session of the First Presbyterian Church of Pittsburgh, under date of March 16, 1933, in which certain information was requested at the hands of the Board. President Erdman was authorized to answer the communication in the name of the Board, thanking the Session of the Church for its assurance of interest in and loyalty to the missionary work of the Presbyterian Church and advising the Session, in answer to its inquiries, that the Board was not in any way responsible for the Report of the Laymen's Inquiry in Foreign Missions and that at its earliest opportunity, after the release of the Report of the Laymen's Inquiry, the Board had formally reaffirmed its unbroken allegiance to the evangelical standards of the Church, had set forth its position with regard to the Report and had given widespread publicity to such action. And, further, that the Board had committed to certain of its Standing Committees various sections of the Report of the Laymen's Inquiry for detailed consideration and that, at a subsequent meeting of the Board, the Committee on Policy and Methods (composed in part of the Chairmen of the various Standing Committees) had presented to the Board a report to the effect that Chapters 1 to 4 in the Report of the Laymen's Inquiry were not in accord with the standards and purpose of the Board, as set forth in its historic aim as expressed in the Manual, and that the Board reaffirmed its loyalty to the standards of the Church and its maintenance of the absolute finality, sufficiency and universality of the Gospel of Christ, which report of its Committee on Policy and Methods was unanimously adopted by the Board.

The Standing Committee on Foreign Missions at the 1933 Assembly presented a report on the "Commission of Appraisal" of the "Laymen's Inquiry After One Hundred Years":

The General Assembly recognizes the profound interest in the foreign missions enterprise which is evidenced in the painstaking and far-reaching inquiry, the results of which are stated in the volume entitled "Re-Thinking Missions." The practical suggestions incorporated in the volume have been considered by the Board of Foreign Missions. The General Assembly is content to leave the application of these suggestions with the Board. The Assembly does, however, definitely repudiate any and all theological statements and implications in that volume which are not in essential agreement with the doctrinal position of the Church. The Assembly cannot see its way clear to approve a complete, centralized administration of Protestant Foreign Mission work.[129]

Toward the end of service with the Board, Dr. Speer once remarked: "Whatever can be said of my life and work, at least I have stayed put." What he meant was that having put his hand to the plow of Foreign Mission service, he never turned back. He plowed that furrow for forty-six years, often amid hostile criticism and opposition, both from without the Board organization and from within. Five times he was offered the presidency of an outstanding university. Other influential positions in the interdenominational organizations were offered to him. At times he had to exert his great force of will to hold himself to his task. Outsiders never knew of his weariness and load of care.

When the *Christian Century* printed characteristic sermons from twenty-five outstanding preachers of the Church and each man was asked to send in his choice among his sermons, Dr. Speer sent a sermon with a text from Galatians 2:20:

"I have been crucified with Christ; and it is no longer I that live, but Christ liveth in me; and that life which I now live in the flesh, I live in faith, the faith which is in the Son of God, who loved me, and gave himself up for me." [130]

At the close of his forty-six years of service with the Presbyterian Board of Foreign Missions, Robert Speer gave a radio address in which he stated with clarity and power the service and contribution to welfare rendered by foreign missions during the century since that movement had been launched. This address summarized his own experiences in his nearly half-century of service and his convictions concerning the supreme relevance and validity of that cause. He said:

For a century and more the Christian Churches of America have carried on their work of world service and world evangelization. During these three generations they have sent out more than 50,000 American missionaries and have contributed more than a billion dollars to support them and their ministry to humanity. These missionaries have been among our choicest men and women. They and their children hold proportionately the highest place in any roll of the greatest servants of the world in modern history. For a generation or more the most powerful appeal to our best student life has been the missionary appeal. The movement has gone in advance of exploration and commerce. It has been the greatest single contribution that America has made to the cause of true human progress, to international and interracial good will, and to the building of a world Christian community across all the lines of division and distrust between the peoples.

These are bold claims, but they are supported by the most competent and unimpeachable witnesses. I will cite only four of them. First, General Smuts of South Africa, one of the three or four greatest statesmen of our time: "It is difficult to conceive what Africa would have been without the civilizing effects of Christian missions. . . . Missionary enterprise, with its universal Christian message and its vast educative and civilizing effort, is and remains the greatest and most powerful influence for good in Africa."

Second, Lord Halifax, who as Lord Irwin was one of the greatest viceroys of India: "For many years administrators have been under no delusion regarding the greatness of the debt they owe to the splendid work of missions. As one had an opportunity of seeing that work as I was able to see it in India—up and down, under every sort of condition, in crowded cities, jungles or mountains, everywhere devoted men and women, priests, sisters, nurses, doctors, educators, everything going forward under the influence of the Christian faith—one would have no kind of doubt as to the contribution they are making to the work of civilization."

Third, Sir William Mackworth Young, Lieutenant Governor of the Punjab: "As a business man speaking to business men, I am prepared to say that the work which has been done by missionary agency in India exceeds in importance all that has been done (and much has been done) by the British Government in India since its commencement. Let me take the Province which I know best. I ask myself what has been the most potent influence which has been working among the people since annexation fifty-four years ago, and to that question I feel there is but one answer—Christianity as set forth in the lives and teaching of Christian missionaries. I do not underestimate the forces which have been brought to bear on the races in the Punjab by our beneficent rule, by British justice and enlightenment; but I am convinced that the effect on native character produced by the self-denying labors of missionaries is far greater. The Punjab bears on its historical roll the names of many Christian statesmen who have honored God by their lives and endeared themselves to the people by their faithful work; but I venture to say that if they could speak to us from the great unseen, there is not one of them who would not proclaim that the work done by men like French, Clark, Newton, and Forman, who went in and out among the people for a whole generation or more, and who preached by their lives the nobility of self-sacrifice, and the lesson of love to God and man, is a higher and nobler work, and more far-reaching in its consequences."

The fourth witness is the late Frederick W. Stevens, of the Law School of the University of Michigan, who was the American representative on what was known as the "Consortium," which sought to protect China in a crucial time against financial corruption and exploitation. Mr. Stevens went to China unsympathetic with the missionary enterprise. Before he left China he declared: "I have come to believe that America's greatest contribution to China, greater even than America's political friendship, is the work of the American missionaries in China. This statement may indicate the importance I attach to the need of moral regeneration which must precede any great political or industrial improvement. In all China there is not a single organization, on a scale of importance, that aims at moral improvement or that is calculated to bring it about, that is not traceable in its origin to the Christian missionaries."

And what have been the fruitages of this movement? The first is the widespread and far-reaching evangelism of the century. The Gospel has been preached to millions of people, and hundreds of thousands of them have accepted it and have been gathered into living Christian churches. There are tens of thousands of such churches in the missions of our American churches, with millions of living members and an army of native preachers and teachers. And these churches are not dependent upon the American Church. They are independent national units of the one universal Christian community.

This century of direct evangelism has also been a century of rich human service. Missions have been the pioneer and leader in modern medicine in Asia and Africa with their hospitals and dispensaries. They introduced vaccination and the care of lepers in Siam; the education of the deaf and dumb in Japan and of the blind in China; modern surgery in two continents.

They laid the foundations for medical and nursing education in many lands. They have healed the sick, opened the eyes of the blind, visited the prisoner and clothed the naked, not in the name of charity only, but in the name of Christ.

This century has been one of illumination and emancipation through the school. The great universities and national systems of education and the education of women in Asia owe their origin to missionaries. There are millions of Bible readers today who would not have been but for our missions. For generations mission presses did the printing of school books and of all Bibles.

The movement that has justified such testimonies as these to its influence and that has done work such as this is not a transitory movement. The necessities which called for it and the motives which have sustained it have not been outgrown. No words can exaggerate the gravity of the religious situation throughout the world. In the January issue of the magazine *El Neshra wal-Bustan,* one of the leading educators in the Near East analyzes the contemporary time: "Many states," he says, "that are struggling for national revival after the war are holding religion as secondary to patriotism. Other lands are so confusing medieval rites with true spirituality that they are publicly denouncing religion as a harmful influence. The radio and cinema have introduced the modes of the most materialistic cities of the West into localities of the East which are unprepared for such innovations. Scientific ideas have so unsettled the minds of school children in Asia that they know not what to believe and are unwilling to be guided by leaders of the older generation." And all political, economic, social and moral problems, as well as the educational, appear to us to have taken on today, especially in Asia, an acute and crucial form.

When again and again the missionary enterprise has met its crisis in the past, it has seemed to be overshadowed in its service by the mass of human indifference or opposition. It has had to meet criticism and hostility. Public opinion in influential quarters blamed it for the Indian Mutiny, the Taiping Rebellion and the Boxer Movement. Such charges were simply screens for the real guilt of other forces. The missionary movement has been an upheaving power but its work has been a work of consolidation, of constructive and creative human service. We are still too close to it to judge it justly and the temper of this ephemeral day is not favorable to a wide and true measurement of spiritual forces, but a future day will return to the judgment of an earlier and wiser time as expressed by the geographer Meinicke: "It is scarcely possible to deny the extraordinary importance of the missionary efforts of our time; they are yet really in their infancy; yet it is certain that they will wholly transform the nature and the relations of the un-Christian peoples and will thereby produce one of the most magnificent and most colossal revolutions that human history contains." If such a prophecy sounds wild today, how much wilder must be deemed the daring confidence of St. Paul as he wrote in prison, with his martyrdom not far away, of a time that was surely coming when the name of Jesus would be above every name and when every tongue should confess that Jesus Christ is Lord.

We hold this bold faith with regard to Christianity because of our conviction with regard to its fundamental nature, as that conviction has been represented in the foreign missionary movement of the past century. The movement sprang from, and rests upon, the view of Christianity held by St. Paul and embodied in the New Testament and inspiring the whole expansive movement of our Faith for nineteen centuries. That view is that Christianity is something distinctive and unique. It is generally and essentially different from what we speak of as the world religions. It is indeed not a religion at all in the dictionary definition or popular conception of religion. Religion is man's search for God, man's effort to answer the irrepressible questions of the soul. But Christianity is God's search for man, God's answer to these questions for man. Man may dispute this view and this claim in its behalf. But this is the view and claim which produced and has sustained this movement throughout the century.

The Christian Church believes that the Gospel is good news of deeds done by God in history for the salvation of man. As my friend Visser 't Hooft has said in his little book, *None Other Gods:* "Our business is to relate what God has done for the world, and not merely to present ideas about God. This means that the real difference between the Christian witness and other religions, or other absolutist truths, is not in this or that concept but in the fact of God in Jesus Christ. . . . Christian witness is essentially to present the news that God has spoken in Christ, that this fact is the central event both of time and eternity, and that it concerns every human being."

This Christian message of a sovereign and loving God who has come to men in Christ and who is at work in the world with a purpose of righteousness, to make men good and brotherly and to bring all humanity together in good will and unity, is the world's one message of hope. It is the doom of tyranny and human absolutism. It is the one road to peace. When we talk today of a world community, the one expression which we find of it and the one promise of its realization are in the brotherhood of which the missionary enterprise has laid the foundations in the Christian Churches which it has founded in every land. Within and through this world Christian community, already begun, the supreme achievement of this movement of the century that is past has been the lifting up of Christ in the midst of human society, the presentation of His Kingdom as the supreme law and order of the world. This has been the duty and the joy of the missionary enterprise for a hundred years now past. So long as the faith of Christ endures, and that faith will outlast time, it will continue to be the holy duty and the triumphant joy of Christians.

For every consideration that was valid a century ago and to which our fathers responded when they established this movement is valid today. The Gospel is unchanged. Jesus Christ is the same yesterday, today, and forever. The good in the world has grown, but so also has the evil. The morning comes but also the night. But the night need not come. There can be a dawn that will endure. There is a morning star and there is a Sun of righteousness. It is our business and our privilege to prepare for them. It is to this that we are all summoned afresh today.

XVII. His Strength in Adversity

A generation which wishes for a religion without tears must find it difficult to adjust its beliefs to the teaching of the New Testament and to the facts of life. . . . Bereavement is the sharpest challenge to our trust in God; if faith can overcome this, there is no mountain which it cannot remove. And faith can overcome.

—W. R. INGE: *Personal Religion and the Life of Devotion*

> The hook of love
> Caught me, long since,
> And when strength failed
> And pain beset me,
> Then, on that "hook" I felt
> The Tug of God.
>
> —MEISTER ECKHART

ROBERT SPEER KNEW WHAT IT WAS TO WALK THROUGH THE "Valley of the Shadow of Death." His mother had died when he was a little boy; a baby sister had died in infancy, and his father died in the prime of his manhood, when Robert Speer was just entering on his own life work. When, then, his little daughter died in her fourth year, death was not an unknown enemy. In this experience, he met the double mystery of deep sorrow and unanswered prayer. But he never for a moment felt that "God would extinguish in the dark tomb what He had litten in the dark womb." He knew that life was immortal and love was eternal, and he took at His word the Lord's saying, that those who had gone on ahead were with Him and that He Himself was always with His servants and, therefore, there is no separation in death. He told Mrs. Speer that he had a very clear consciousness of Eleanor's loving presence when he was away from home on long journeys.

The greatest test of Robert Speer's Christian faith and character was the death of his older son Elliott, who was killed by an unknown person at Mount Hermon, Mass., on the evening of September 14, 1934, two years after Elliott had taken up the Headmastership of Mount Hermon School.

In an unpublished memoir of his son, Dr. Speer described the tragedy:

As Elliott rose from his chair and turned to take down a book from the shelves behind him, the quiet of the campus was broken by the shot of an unknown assassin, lurking in the dark, just outside the window, who had been waiting for Elliott to rise and who fired at his back as he turned, the buckshot and heavy slug with which the gun was charged tearing through Elliott's arm and right lung and heart. He stood for an instant behind his chair in a pool of his blood which flecked also the paper on his desk and the book in his hand, and then walked across the room to the hall, a stream of blood marking his course, and fell in the hall. His father-in-law, Henry H. Welles, had hurried to him from the room across the hall and his wife from the floor above, and asked, "Elliott, what was it?" "I don't know," Elliott replied, "but put a tourniquet on my arm and send for Dr. McCastline." The doctor, although five miles away, was there in fifteen minutes, but Elliott had already lost consciousness and in the few minutes the freed spirit was gone to the "Church of the First Born," and to the infinite liberty and light of God. The murderer and his motive are still an unsolved enigma, a part of that awful "mystery of iniquity" which is ever at war with the righteous and loving will of God, which slew even the Son of God and which has no pity for the sons of men.[131]

Cleland B. MacAfee, a Secretary of the Presbyterian For-. eign Board, in behalf of the Board and Council, wrote to Robert Speer, and Dr. Speer replied:

My dear Cleland:

Your loving messages from Mrs. MacAfee and yourself and from the staff and from so many of our associates in the Board and in the offices have been a great comfort to us in this amazing experience. It has been so utterly beyond all understanding and so irreparable that there has been nothing to do except to be quiet and to go on steadily doing moment by moment what needed to be done, remembering the dear things of the past and readjusting life and plans for the future. One's only and adequate light is to think of what God allowed to happen in the life of His Own dear Son and to be sure that even out of the deepest evil He can bring good.

We are all at peace and trying to do all things in a Christian way for Christ's sake and our own sake and for the sake of the children.

As to understanding it, one is absolutely baffled and can only and simply trust to infinite wisdom and love.

Please thank the many dear friends who have sent their loving sympathy. I shall thank them individually later as there is opportunity.

We are all here at Lakeville now but shall probably go up to Mount Hermon later in the week.

Ever affectionately,

(Signed) Robert [132]

The Teheran Station of the American Presbyterian Mission in Persia (now Iran) sent a message of sympathy to which Robert Speer replied:

We have received the cablegram from the Station with its message of loving sympathy with us in our tragedy. We have as yet no light on our Mount Hermon mystery. The police are working diligently. One of the Massachusetts State men was here today and I had a three-hour talk with him, but I cannot see that they have made any real headway. Perhaps they have and I am mistaken. They have, of course, eliminated a great many possibilities but I cannot see that they have found as yet any possible clue.

I am enclosing herewith a copy of the little note that Mrs. Speer and I are sending out to our friends in acknowledgment of the loving letters that have come pouring in from all over the world.[133]

To two trusted members of the Mission, who had written to him about the tragedy, Dr. Speer replied:

Your loving letters of October 8th have just come and I am writing at once to thank you for them and for all the comfort and strength which they bring. I want to add this very special expression of our gratitude to you. Every memory of Elliott is very dear to us, and William's reference to his visit with his choir to the hospital in 1924 is just of a piece of so much that we are hearing now from many to whom he went with his love and joy and good cheer. There is to be a Memorial Service at Mount Hermon on November 11th, and I have been preparing a memorial address. The difficulty has been to select out of the great mass of tributes that have come a few for which there will be time at that service. Men and women in widely separated places have written to tell what he had been to them or done for them.

It has been amazing to see how far his influence had gone and with what confident expectations so many were looking to him for the leadership into which God was already bringing him in the cause of Christian Education and in the work of Christ's Church.

We have the youngest of his three children with us now, and she is as dear, as loving as she can be, going to school for a few hours each morning, but being with Mrs. Speer through the afternoon. It is terrible to see how devastating such a wicked deed as this can be, tearing our human life apart, carrying anguish far and wide. No one but a mad man, no matter how bad he could be, could deliberately do such an evil and destructive deed.

I do not believe for a moment that wrongs like this are a

part of the will of God. They must grieve God far more than they can grieve man, but our comfort is that God's love sets to work to do all that the love of God can do to atone for such evil. All this one reads in the Cross where the murder of God's Son has been made, through God's love, the redemption of mankind.

I hope that you are all well, including the new little one, and that God's blessing may be on the work in a new and richer measure than ever before.

Ever affectionately,
Robert E. Speer[134]

Robert and Mrs. Speer sent a printed letter to the many friends who had written them.

Elliott Speer

All Saints' Day, 1898, Englewood, N.J.
September 14, 1934, Mount Hermon, Mass.

"E'en as he trod that day to God, so walked he from his birth
In simpleness and gentleness and honor and clean mirth."

Thanks be to God who giveth us the victory through our Lord Jesus Christ.

The disciple is not above his Master, nor the servant above his Lord. It is enough for the disciple that he be as his Master and the servant as his Lord.

If we walk in the light, as He is in the light, we have fellowship one with another, and the blood of Jesus Christ His Son cleanseth us from all sin.

If God be for us, who can be against us? . . .

Who shall separate us from the love of Christ? . . .

Nay, in all these things we are more than conquerors through Him that loved us. For we are persuaded that neither death nor life, nor things present, nor things to come, nor height, nor depth . . . shall be able to separate us from the love of God which is in Christ Jesus our Lord.

"O Almighty God, who has knit together Thine elect in one communion and fellowship, in the mystical body of Thy

Son Christ our Lord; grant us grace so to follow Thy blessed saints in all virtuous and godly living, that we may come to those unspeakable joys which Thou hast prepared for those who unfeignedly love Thee; through the same Thy Son, Jesus Christ our Lord. Amen."

(Collect for All Saints' Day)

We seem to give him back to Thee, dear God, who gavest him to us. Yet as Thou didst not lose him in giving, so we have not lost him by his return. Not as the world gives, givest Thou, O Lover of Souls! What Thou givest, Thou takest not away, for what is Thine is ours always, if we are Thine. And Life is eternal and Love is immortal; and Death is only an horizon; and an horizon is nothing save the limit of one's sight.

Lift us up, strong Son of God, that we may see farther. Cleanse our eyes that we may see more clearly; draw us closer to thyself, that so we may know ourselves nearer to our beloved who are with Thee, and while Thou dost prepare a place for us, prepare us for that happy place, that where they are and Thou art we too may be. Amen.

The love and prayers and sympathy of our friends are a ceaseless direct help both now and for the years to come. We are grateful for them beyond words. This strong tide of human love helps us to realize "the nearness of the Love Divine." We walk in the light that streams from the Cross, that evidence in time of the meaning and power of Infinite Love, that revelation of the heart of God and His perfect forgiveness and holiness. We are more conscious, hour by hour, of the whole world's need, of those who sorrow without hope, of those who sorrow without sympathy. The way of love is the only way out of darkness into light, the only way forward through time into eternity.

A friend sent to Robert and Mrs. Speer a quotation from a book by W. R. Inge, Dean of St. Paul's Cathedral. Mrs.

Speer wrote of the comfort that came to her and to Dr. Speer from reading the book.

When we were traveling through the Valley of the Shadow, a friend sent a copy of Dean Inge's *Personal Religion and the Life of Devotion*. The book meant a great deal to us, but the most valuable part was the chapter on bereavement, written after the death of his lovely eleven-year-old daughter. We read and reread it and it was one of the messages that helped Rob most.[135]

The quotation follows:

"A generation which wishes for a religion without tears must find it difficult to adjust its beliefs to the teaching of the New Testament and of the facts of life. . . .

"I think that those who have had to bear sorrow will agree with me that bereavement is the deepest initiation into the mysteries of human life, an initiation more searching and profound than even happy love. Love remembered and consecrated by grief belongs more clearly than the happy intercourse of friends to the eternal world; it has proved itself stronger than death. Bereavement is the sharpest challenge to our trust in God; if faith can overcome this there is no mountain which it cannot remove. And faith can overcome it. It brings the eternal world nearer to us, and makes it seem more real. Pure affection so remembered and so consecrated carries us beyond the bourne of time and place altogether. It transports us into a pure air, where all that has been, is, and will be, lives together, in its true being, meaning and value, before the throne of God. . . .

"There is no wilfulness of self-deception in this confidence. It is God Himself, Who is Love, from Whom we learn so to believe and so hope." [136]

A friend of the Speer family was Charles Ernest Scott, who, with his wife, went to China in 1906, and served there for thirty-nine years as a Presbyterian missionary. Their five children and their wives and husbands all went as missionaries to China, and their eldest daughter Betty, and her husband, the Rev. John Stam, were martyred by the Chinese Communists on December 8, 1934, three months after Elliott Speer's death. They wrote of Dr. Speer's sympathy and understanding.

When our John and Betty were taken from us, when hundreds of letters and editorials and messages poured in upon us, among all the messages came the words of Dr. Speer, like the balm of Gilead, bringing healing to an open, savage wound. He, as a noble Christian, really trusting God, in the midst of his own tragedy at Mount Hermon School, understood poignant bereavement, how to measure it, how to stand up to it, how (as the magnificent Greek language, with its clean-cut distinction and fine differentiation so accurately puts it), how to "sympathize," "suffer with" us.

Many throughout the Christian world shared with us this tragedy. Even the dailies of Berlin and Vienna, in large front-page headlines, announced later, on receiving the news of the saving of the tiny two-months-old Helen Priscilla through the life-risking of brave and faithful Chinese Christian friends, *Das Kind noch lebt* ("The baby still lives").

Dr. Speer's letters received from half-way around the world were a special comfort to our hearts, because he understood. Treasured all these years, here is part of those discerning letters: "We can only rejoice that our children are now beyond all pain and anguish of our mortal life, in the midst of the love and the light and the joy of God. You will have a sacred charge now in the little one, just as we feel we have in Elliott's three little girls." [137]

Again later: "I know how far transcending all words this experience has been for you and all your family; and one only wonders with awe and thanksgiving as to what God's great purpose may be with regard to little Helen Priscilla's life and service. He must have some great purpose for her as she starts out so manifestly under His direct care, and with such a halo of suffering about her dear head. May God's blessing be upon her and may His grace make up to her all that she has lost." [138]

Howard L. Rubendall, who was chosen Headmaster of Mount Hermon School after Elliott's death, wrote of the Memorial Address given by Elliott's father:

Dr. Speer gave the address at the Memorial Service. The address itself was a masterpiece in the expression of Christian love and hope. That Robert E. Speer could do what he did in that service was to the people here on the Hill one of the greatest affirmations of Christian faith they had witnessed or ever expect to witness. This was indeed strength in adversity.[139]

On Sunday, November 11, 1934, friends of Elliott Speer gathered at Mount Hermon to do honor to his memory. His favorite hymns were sung: "This Is My Father's World," by Maltbie D. Babcock: "Oh, Love That Will Not Let Me Go," by George Matheson; "He Who Would Valiant Be," by John Bunyan; "Ten Thousand Times Ten Thousand," by Henry Alford.

Robert Speer, who was presented by President Wilfred W. Fry, made the address in behalf of his son. He said in part:

We are gathered here today to remember the life and character of Elliott Speer, who was for these past two years Headmaster of this school, to recall some of his ideals for life and education, especially here at Mount Hermon, and to remind ourselves of our own duty as friends and members of this school for today and for the days to come.

As one of those who knew and loved him best I am to try to tell you simply the outline of his bright, brief life. . . .

I would recall an experience one evening during his childhood when he brought me a card which had been given him by a carpenter working on a neighbor's barn, and asked me for a pencil that he might sign it if I were willing. I have that card still. On one side is a bit of verse about God's wanting boys, all kinds of boys, to fight for truth and purity, and on the other side were this question and declaration: "Are you willing to be God's boy? If so, sign your name to this Covenant and daily ask God to help you keep it: 'I receive Jesus as my Saviour and I will try hard to do what I think He would like to have me do.' " Could he sign it? he asked. I said, "Yes." And the eight-year-old lad's signature is under the Covenant.

The memories of these childhood years are all pure and fragrant to us, full of happy joy, of a radiant, generous boyhood.

"I like to think again today," writes an older man, "of Elliott's face as I saw him twenty-one years ago, so pure and so full of promise. I have thought of him these years as going on from strength to strength. At about the age that Jesus died, he, too, has died—cut off in the midst of his days, living purely and unselfishly, just as a boy."

At the age of fourteen he entered the second year at Phillips Academy at Andover. I took him up to Andover and with fear and trembling we saw his little boat put out to sea. But the character had already set in honor, in courage, and faith. . . . Mr. Thomas W. Lamont writes: "If there were ever a person in the whole world whose fine and wonderful life from his earliest years commanded admiration and love, it was Elliott. He and my Tom grew up together. Youth's testimony of youth is generally the soundest, and I can almost remember the tones in which Tommy would speak of Elliott and of his marvelous qualities of mind and character."

Mr. Allan V. Heely of the Phillips Andover faculty, and later Headmaster of Lawrenceville, who was in the Academy at Andover at the same time with Elliott, bears witness to what he was in those schoolboy days: "I first met Elliott in 1913, when he was fifteen years old. He was a tall, slender boy, erect in carriage, vivacious of manner. His smile was frequent and it had his spirit back of it. At Andover he was a busy and useful citizen; always a ready speaker, he was president of Philo, the old debating club, and was a Draper prize speaker. He helped edit the school paper; was on the student and athletic councils; and Senior year he was President of the Society of Inquiry, the School's religious organization."

From Andover he went in the Fall of 1916 to Princeton, where, as at Andover, he did his class work conscientiously and efficiently; but he was no unusual student and this was only a part of the full life which he was ever living. He was one of the leaders in the religious life of the college, a member of the lighter rowing squad and of the editorial board of *The Princetonian*, and one of the mainsprings in any good movement in the life of the University. . . .

The fever of the wartime was in the veins of youth in those times, and it was hard for boys to hold steady. Elliott was too young to go into the camps, but he must be in it in some way, and on May 5, 1917, he sailed with a group of students to help in the work of the British Army YMCA. How well I remember that dark, chill day and the crowd of lads on the pier. A group of them were singing and I can feel the tremors of that song still:

> "And it holds, my anchor holds;
> Blow your wildest, then, O gale.
> On my bark so small and frail;
> By His grace I shall not fail,
> For my anchor holds, my anchor holds."

We have the war-censored diary which Elliott kept and sent home at intervals and all of his letters, and they tell the story of the tragic experience through which the faith and idealism of our young men had to pass. And they tell the story of the lesser perils to men's bodies. . . .

He came back from Europe in July, 1918, and though the year had given him some deep convictions regarding the wickedness and futility of war, which, carefully held and carefully expressed, were to deepen with the years, he was seeking to enlist in Naval aviation when the war came to an end.* Many a man found himself shaken to his depths by

---

* After Elliott's return from Europe he served in the fall of 1918 in the Englewood Hospital as a volunteer orderly during the influenza epidemic.

what he had seen and experienced in those years, and I remember lovingly the full month that Elliott and I spent by ourselves in a little cabin belonging to a trapper friend of ours on a Northern lake, where we found our way back to the steadiness of the eternal things and felt the anchor of spiritual faith and purpose, and lay fast hold again upon the Rock.

Elliott's broken class was graduated piecemeal a year or less late, and he took his diploma at Princeton in February, 1921, instead of June, 1920. It was of God's great goodness that life took on its fullness for him at once, as he was married, on March 12, 1921, to Miss Charlotte Rose Welles, a graduate of Vassar and a sister of one of his classmates and dearest friends. It had been clear to him for some time that his work was to be in the ministry or in the foreign mission field, and he and his wife sailed on March 26, 1921, to Scotland, where he took three terms and the equivalent of two years' work in the Theological College of the United Free Church. His notebooks show the thorough piece of work which he did and his wide range of the best reading. He returned to America in the spring of 1922 and worked until the autumn of 1924 on the staff of the Old First Presbyterian Church of New York City, in charge of Bethlehem Chapel in Greenwich Village, largely among the Italians. . . .

After two years of this work in downtown New York, he went in September, 1924, to Lafayette College as chaplain and head of the Bible Department. . . .

Dr. John MacCracken, who as President of the college brought Elliott to Lafayette, wrote of him:

"From the day that the college heard that deep voice of his fill the college chapel without hesitation or tremor, it recognized him as a valiant man, sincere, unafraid, teaching with the authority which belongs to one whose doctrine is also his life. . . . He belonged to an automobile age, accustomed to move forward quickly and certainly, with little expectation or thought of obstacles. The reaction of the students was described by one sophomore in his diary, 'He's a prince.' "

During his first year at Lafayette, Elliott was ordained by the Presbytery of Jersey City. . . . In June, 1926, Elliott began his connection with Northfield, where for five years, until 1931, he was President of the Board of Trustees in association with and in succession to Mr. W. R. Moody. While he shrank from the heavy responsibilities, he bravely accepted the call to share in the Northfield work. It did not prove to be an easy task. There were many and tangled problems and he would be the first to recognize that he may have made his mistakes. But he meant to think and do only right; he sought nothing for himself; he was concerned simply and alone for the welfare of the schools and the true maintenance of the great tradition and ideal of the Founder and his successors. And through all the difficulties he made his brave and patient way, burning his own smoke, speaking only healing words and trying to effect the transition which each generation must make constructively, high-mindedly, and in unswerving fidelity to the obligation of the future to the past and also to the obligation of the past to the future. As he wrote to one who thought that there might be danger of unwarranted change: "If you think that Hermon is swinging away from her traditional teaching I must simply register my sincere disagreement. I cannot claim by experience to know all about her past. I am, however, tremendously interested in the future, and believe that it can only be successful if it holds fast to all that is essential in the great inheritance from D. L. Moody."

The work of these years in the equipment and development of the schools was crowned by a special effort to raise an Endowment Fund of $3,000,000. Into this effort he threw all his indomitable faith and courage at a time when the acute financial conditions were halting all educational philanthropy.

As Elliott worked, he became convinced that the Presidency of the Board of Trustees no longer required a salaried officer and he resigned to accept the Headmastership of Mount Hermon in succession to Dr. Cutler. He wanted to be working directly with and for boys. It seemed to him that he needed another year of special preparation for his new post, and accordingly, with the consent of the Trustees, he returned to Scotland and put in a thorough year in the University of Edinburgh, working on his thesis, "The Influence on

the Formation of Character of Certain Religious Doctrines—
a Pedagogical Estimate."

Elliott returned to Mount Hermon and was installed as
Headmaster on Sunday, October 30, 1932.

Some of you will be asking, Was he then a perfect figure?
Were there no defects of character or limitations of capacity
and personality? He would have been the first to laugh in
amusement at such a thought. He never took himself too seriously, and he wanted no one else to do so.

Dr. Boyd Edwards, Headmaster of the Mercersburg
School, wrote: "We loved Elliott and honored him with all
our hearts for his quality, his spirit, his influence and his
promise. . . ."

Dr. Henry Sloane Coffin wrote: "As I have seen him in recent years, I came to admire the wisdom, the utter selflessness,
the manifest faith in God with which he approached his questions. One loved him for his charm, his humor, his gaiety of
spirit, and there was this maturing man of large dimensions
looking out at you under the youthful face and figure. I con-
fidently expected Elliott to become one of the great leaders in
the cause of Christ in his generation."

We have no words to measure our loss—our loss in the
family circle where he was a ceaseless joy, the loss of the
schools and the Nation and the Church. His going lays on us
all a holier duty to keep the sacred trust of the great tradition;
to seek the light of God on our present tasks in a changing
world, to see that no harm comes to these schools into whose
foundations have been built such priceless lives, to make sure
that the future shall bring all it was in Elliott Speer's clear
vision and brave will.

As for him, it is enough to remember Dean Weigle's words
—"One of the strongest proofs of life beyond death is the
impossibility that a personality as radiant and as full of
promise as he should cease to exist," and to recall the verses
of Thomas Curtis Clark, which I found among his papers.
They are called "The Journey." Never did Elliott dream of
my quoting them on an occasion such as this.

"When Death, the angel of our higher dreams,
　　Shall come, far ranging from the hills of light,
　　He will not catch me unaware; for I
　　Shall be as now communing with the dawn.
　　For I shall make all haste to follow him
　　Along the valley, up the misty slope,
　　Where life lets go and Life at last is born;
　　There I shall find the dreams that I have lost
　　On toilsome earth, and they will guide me on,
　　Beyond the mists unto the farthest height.
　　I shall not grieve except to pity those
　　Who cannot hear the songs that I shall hear."

And I will add this, too, which he had found on a piece of birch bark in a friend's cabin in Canada:

"Be like a bird
　　That halting in its flight
　　Awhile, on bough too low,
　　Feels itself sinking and yet sings,
　　Knowing she hath wings."

To this he had added the three words:

"Death, Immortality, Life."

God rest his dear and radiant soul! [140]

The loss of his son deepened Robert Speer's sympathy for others who had faced similar bereavements, and the letter he wrote in November, 1945, to a friend whose son had died, revealed this deeper insight and understanding:

A note from —— tells me of the great sorrow and loss that have come to you in ——'s going, and I write at once to send you both deepest love and sympathy from Mrs. Speer and me. . . . We know well just what this sorrow means to you, though the mystery of it is beyond our understanding. One can only be quiet and trustful and lean on the Everlasting Love and God's wise purpose. May He bless and keep and comfort you.[141]

In a chapter written for a book during the summer before his death, Dr. Speer summed up his Christian philosophy of life, with its tragedy and the concomitant healing comfort and triumphant power of Christ:

Let me say only a concluding word about the real nature of this life that we are trying to live and this work that we are seeking to do. It is a conflict in which we are engaged, a conflict ever changing and unchanging. We are passing beyond the easy conception of the last generation or two with regard to the automatic self-progression of humanity. As our friend, Dr. Adolph Keller, wrote from Geneva, as he surveyed the European scene: "We are coming back to the first Christian conception of the world. The world is not plastic material to be easily molded by Christian influence. There is a hostile, demonic element. The Church has to fight stubbornly against principalities and powers for its faith and liberty, for the conversion of peoples and the spread of the gospel."

This was Paul's view. "For we wrestle," said he, "not against flesh and blood but against principalities, against powers, against the rulers of the darkness of this world, against spiritual wickedness in high places." If any of us have lived such placid lives that we do not realize this, if we still think life is a bright and happy unfolding of its own latent nature and possibilities of good, I hope we may be spared those deep tragedies through which others of us have had to pass which have taught us the truth of Paul's interpretation.

We do believe as our hymn declares:

"God is working His purpose out
    As year succeeds to year:
God is working His purpose out,
And the time is drawing near;
Nearer, nearer draws the time,
The time that shall surely be,
When the earth shall be filled with the glory of God
    As the waters cover the sea."

We believe this. If Paul could believe it and declare it in his letter to the Philippian Christians, written from jail, from discouragement, from loneliness, from the treachery of fellow Christians, surely we can believe it and declare it today.

But God's purpose will be accomplished only at the end of a great struggle, a struggle that cost the life of the Son of God, a struggle that is calling today for everything within us, that is demanding of us more than all that Jawaharlal Nehru is giving to his nationalism, all that Edward Wilson gave to Antarctic exploration, that David Livingstone gave to those dark journeys which lifted the somber fringes of the night and let light in upon Africa, all that hundreds of thousands of our young men and the young men of other nations gave with full devotion in the dark and tragic years just behind us; all that Jesus asked and is asking still: "If any man will come after me, let him deny himself and take up his cross and follow me." This is the summons that is unchanged and unchanging. We consider the times, as Ignatius bade, but we look to Him who is above time.[142]

XVIII. His Active Retirement

THE GENERAL ASSEMBLY OF THE PRESBYTERIAN CHURCH IN the U.S.A. had set the age limit for retirement for the men secretaries and officers of the Church Boards at seventy, and on September 10, 1937, his seventieth birthday, Robert E. Speer gave up the work of Secretary of the Board that he had carried for forty-six years.

At its meeting in May, 1937, the General Assembly, through the adoption of a resolution framed by the Foreign Missions Committee of the Assembly, had taken action about Robert Speer's coming retirement. The action of the Committee and of the General Assembly was, in part, as follows:

Dr. Speer has been one of the most successful of recruiting agents, for his name has exercised a magic influence on the youth of our colleges; his eloquence has compelled both the church and the world to give serious heed to the missionary appeal, while his wise and sober judgment has won for him recognition as one of the leading missionary statesmen of the age. We are glad to think that after his retirement the Presbyterian Church may still look to him for counsel and guidance when difficult problems arise in the sphere where he is a master. We assure him today of the appreciation and affection of the Presbyterian Church. His name is enshrined in our hearts and our earnest prayer goes up to our Heavenly Father that he may be long spared to us in health and strength.[143]

This resolution of the General Assembly was adopted as a resolution of the Board of Foreign Missions at its meeting, June 14, 1937.

The individual Missions of the Board recorded their love and gratitude for Robert Speer by formal resolutions and by letters from individual members. From Beirut, Syria, came such a message from the hearts and minds of the members of the Syrian Mission, transmitted by James H. Nicol, Secretary of that Mission:

It is impossible for me to carry out the instruction of the Mission in any perfunctory or official way. The associations and memories of over forty years are too intimate and too profoundly significant to permit me to face their official termination without a deep sense of personal loss. I well remember the day in Toronto thirty-five years ago, when you were talking to the Presbyterian students about the call to the foreign field. I was peacefully enjoying it for the sake of others who might be concerned, but it was no particular concern of mine, for was I not called to stay in America? Then you pointed most impolitely straight at me and the other students, and said: "You are sitting there saying that you haven't been called. Well, then, in the name of God, I call you now." It was just the word I needed at the time, and the happiness and sense of fulfillment that my life has had for thirty-two years is due in large measure to your moving word. Just how many others of the past student generation owe their life fulfillment to a similar call no one will ever know, but as the Assembly report so truly says, "His name has exercised a magic influence on the youth of our colleges." And of course we know that a human name exerts such magic influence only when it gets its power from that Name which is above every name, even the name of Jesus Christ our Lord.

Since the withdrawal of Dr. White you have been our own Secretary. It has been my privilege throughout the period to be the corresponding Secretary for the Mission. On behalf of the Mission, therefore, I wish to express our gratitude for your patience with our weaknesses and foibles, your almost uncanny understanding of our problems, your sympathy and helpfulness at all times.

In all of our affectionate remembrances and good wishes we associate with you your wife, who in her turn has been an inspiration to the young women of her time, and a constant friend to us all.

May the Lord bless you and keep you both, and give us the benefit of your friendship and help for many years to come.

Your friends and colleagues in the Syria Mission,

(Signed) James H. Nicol, Secretary[144]

Other Missions took similar action and many letters and telegrams and cables came from friends and admirers all over the world.

Robert Speer deeply appreciated the kindness that prompted these messages, but his genuine humility and his shyness and reserve led him to try to forestall, or avoid, such public statements of approbation and praise. His attitude was that of the Scotsman who asserted, "Praise to the face is open disgrace," and he did his best to stifle or turn aside such expressions of admiration and gratitude. Thus, when the editor of a missionary magazine had planned to print a sketch of the life and work of Robert Speer "with appropriate recognition of the unique place he has so long occupied in the esteem and affection of his brethren of all denominations," the editor published, instead, a paragraph of a letter from Robert Speer asking that he desist from that purpose:

I appreciate deeply what you have in mind, but earnestly hope that you will not go forward with it. I am doing my utmost to keep everything of a biographical and personal character out of these closing months of my official connection with our Board. . . . In whatever you write, will you not make it just as impersonal as possible? Let the cause fill the whole picture, and let us water-carriers and wood hewers who have sought to serve it be in our proper place out of sight.[145]

Despite Robert Speer's feeling about publicity and praise, he did submit to attending a Board dinner held in September,

1937. Many messages were received from other Foreign Mission Boards and other Boards of the Presbyterian Church and from other churches and mission organizations.

The wish that after his retirement Robert Speer would be available for advice and counsel, "when difficult problems arise in the sphere where he is a master" was not fulfilled. Robert Speer met his retirement with the same decision and forthrightness that he had brought to other phases of his service. "When Dr. Speer retired, he really retired," as one of his friends commented. With his retirement from his official relation to the Foreign Board went also the severance of his official relations with many other organizations related to Foreign Missions. Robert Speer resisted the temptation to give advice and to maintain an active part in the work of the Foreign Board after his official severance of relations, and to all requests for his opinion on problems as they arose he declined to be drawn into that arena again. This was one of the wisest decisions that he made, and later was appreciated and admired by those who had witnessed the difficulties and tensions and dissatisfaction that often arose when an "elder statesman" attempted to re-enter the arena of his earlier achievements and influence decisions and policies of his successors in positions of responsibility.

Thus, after his retirement, one of the younger secretaries put through a long distance call to Lakeville and asked him how to deal with and solve a difficult problem. Dr. Speer replied: "We are having a lovely winter up here, with lots of snow." One of his favorite observations was: "Those who express the judgments must bear the responsibility."

William P. Schell, a colleague in the Foreign Board, wrote:

For a man of his national and international usefulness and tireless energy, it must have been even more of a strain for Dr. Speer to retire at seventy than for most men and women facing a similar situation. He questioned, as did many others, the fairness of compelling Board Secretaries to retire at seventy, while allowing pastors to retain their active pastorates until eighty or ninety. For a time there was some agitation in the Church to ask the General Assembly to make an exception to the rule and to allow him to serve after seventy, but he would have none of it. One day he observed: "The rule is a good one and should be enforced." [146]

Mrs. Speer has written of the years in Lakeville, Conn:

When conditions changed at Diamond Pond, where we had had so many happy summers, and the children grew older, we began looking for a place nearer to New York where we could spend free week ends and eventually make our home.

Learning that our son William, who was a student at the Hotchkiss School, was in the Infirmary with a mild attack of measles, I went up to see him and at the station took a jitney with a pleasant fellow traveler. Asked if she, too, were going to the school, she said, "Nothing so pleasant; I'm going to sell our house that I dearly love, but it is too far from my husband's business to come here for summers." It was a heavenly May day; the jitney drove up to the house and I lost my heart at once. That evening I told Mr. Speer that I would have bought a house that morning if I had had the loose change in my pocket. Negotiations were begun and in two weeks the house was ours, and has been a true family center and home ever since. It has been described as a "small house with a large view," and the beauty of the setting never loses its charm for the family or our guests. Before long, Mr. Speer had done more exploring on foot of the woods and hills around us than any resident of Lakeville that we ever discovered, and he soon had the history of Litchfield County and its distinguished sons by heart.

The Hotchkiss School, where Mr. Speer had been a speaker for many years, was a natural anchorage. New York was not too far away but, happily, too far to commute, and Elliott's home was only a little over a hundred miles to the north through some of the most beautiful country in New England.

As 1937 approached, lists were made, in a carefully kept

notebook, of occupations for the years of retirement. These lists grew longer, until R.E.S. said he would have enough to do if he should live to be ninety. He was always gardening, with transplanting of trees and shrubs; he built stone walls, and did all manner of painting jobs and carpentry. An extra barn built before 1937 provided not only a place for visiting cars, but an extra guest room, a beautiful large study, given the name of "Iona," for St. Columba's Island off the west coast of Scotland, and an adequate little carpenter shop.

Iona was his place of refuge when the house overflowed with children and grandchildren. He could work there in the morning and systematically rested there in the afternoon. The carpenter shop was also a book bindery, where old books were repaired and a valuable collection of pamphlets was bound and indexed.

Iona was lined with books and was the fulfillment of a dream of many years, with real space for books of many kinds. I think he knew where every book was and could have found each one in the dark. Although it was a place of both work and rest, the grandchildren knew that they were welcome there after four o'clock of an afternoon, and he was always ready to tell them stories or to let them be busy with pencil and paper, or, best of all, to read to them from an illustrated copy of *Pilgrim's Progress*. Sometimes we had tea there, and now and then some special meeting was held there, with the books and curios showing his world-wide interests.

Although retirement was supposed to mean long stretches of quiet time at home, there were always two major outside interests: the work of the Seminars with George Irving, and the work of Princeton Seminary, where he was now President of the Board of Trustees. Along with this, there were many preaching engagements and in 1939 we visited our daughter, Constance Barbour, in England. This was my husband's first journey to be made without definite responsibility, a real holiday. When the bombs began to fall in Bristol, Constance came to us at Rockledge for three of the war years with her three children, and their presence gave endless joy. There was always a confident assurance that in the end victory would come. This was reinforced by the blessing we asked in unison at the table:

"Thine, O Lord, is the greatness and the power and the glory
    and the victory and the majesty,
For all that is in the Heaven and in the earth is Thine.
Thine is the kingdom, O Lord,
And Thou art exalted as Head above all."

When we really settled in at Rockledge, we found a household helper, Mrs. Alice Beard, who for eighteen years has been the cornerstone of our home, one of the finest characters among all our friends. After she went home at four o'clock, there was a division of labor: I prepared supper and my husband did the washing up. We recalled Christopher Morley's couplet: "The man who never in his life has washed the dishes with his wife, or polished up the silver plate, he still is largely celibate." But Robert Speer had never been "celibate" in any detachment from the technique of living that makes the basis for a comfortable home. In warm weather, meals were often out of doors on the porch—a lovely place, too, for our favorite relaxation, backgammon, which we took up as a part of the convalescence after ten weeks in the hospital in New York in the winter of 1943-4, and of which we kept a careful score for the next four years. Our daughter Margaret had come home from China on the second trip of the *Gripsholm*, but Constance had gone back to England with the children in the fall of 1943, and William was on the Seven Seas with the Navy.[147]

One day after Robert Speer had put in a strenuous week mending rock walls, weeding the garden, transplanting shrubs, and doing general handy-man work around the place, Mrs. Speer found on her desk the following:

Received from Mrs. R. E. Speer:

    Boundless patience.
    Infinite loving-kindness.
    Goodness beyond measure.
    Joyous companionship.

And the nicest and best home comfort and care.
In full payment for a week's hard labor

(Signed) Hired-man Robbie

E. Fay Campbell wrote of Robert Speer's retirement:

When George Irving retired from the Y.M.C.A. he joined his old friend, Dr. Robinson, in the Board of Christian Education of the Presbyterian Church U.S.A. Building on his years of evangelistic work in the Y.M.C.A., George conceived the idea of small seminars for ministers. "Faith and Life" was a term popular at the time because of the emerging World Council.

Those seminars took hold in a remarkable way. Two major reasons account for their success. In the first place, George was a great human and knew how to lead men. In the second place, he was able to persuade Dr. Speer to attend many of the seminars. Dr. Speer was so beloved in the Church that ministers, old and young, were eager to know in an intimate way this man of God. Speer and Irving were a great team. The story of their work together is told in *The Life of George Irving*.

I attended my only Seminar with them together in Concord, N. C. It was the first Seminar held for the ministers of our Church in North Carolina. All were Negroes. We met at Barber-Scotia College, one of the finest colleges we have in the Church. This was during the war. Irving, Speer and I met with a few leaders of the Seminar group prior to the meeting to discuss our plans and for prayer. As we were about to break, one of the ministers made a brief statement, expressing the gratitude of the men to Speer and Irving for being willing to take the time to be with them. He said that Speer's name had been known by all of them for years but that none of them ever expected to know him personally, this great Moderator, President of the Federal Council, etc., etc. Speer took it like a man. Then he very quietly and most graciously made a little speech too. It was as sincere a talk as I ever heard. He said it was a great honor for us to be in such a company of men who were serving the people. He said that he was an old man and would soon be gone to be with his Heavenly Father. He spoke about the different gifts that God had given to His children. He said that when we come to face God that no one will be thinking about who was Moderator of the General Assembly. There is only one question that really matters finally and that is: "Was I a good steward of the gifts that God gave me?"

Speer knew he was an able man and a powerful man. After Irving's death, I chaired a number of the Seminars with Dr. Speer as the only speaker. We traveled together for days. He told me stories of football games at Princeton. He told me of his almost perfect health record. We talked of the hundreds and hundreds of books that he had read. He was aware of his powers. But he never expected others to be just like him. He respected their gifts and their abilities. He had very little "small talk." He seldom told a joke. He kidded me about my pacifism now and then in a Seminar. He always respected my right to differ with him about the Christian attitude on war, but he did not like to corner me with a question. So long as I put Christ central in my talks and stressed the place of prayer and evangelism, he was happy. The Presbyterian Church will always have cause for gratitude of what Irving and Speer did with those Seminars.[148]

A note Robert Speer sent to Lewis Mudge, former Stated Clerk of the Assembly, a Princeton classmate and warm friend, who was gathering data for the *Princeton Alumni Weekly* on his classmates for the year 1944, when Speer was seventy-seven years of age, summarized the activity of the preceding year. Robert Speer wrote:

The year has been a busy one. I have been all over the country, in some thirty-six states, speaking at all kinds of gatherings—colleges, conferences, churches, dinners. I think I have made some 244 addresses, more even than when I was supposed to be in active service. One part of this work has been at a score of Faith and Life Seminars for our Presbyterian ministers with a dear friend, George Irving, whose death last summer has been one of my greatest sorrows. I have published one new book during the year, *Five Minutes a Day*, which, to my surprise, has far outdistanced all the others in its sale—some 35,000 copies in two months. I have had fine health and have kept up my side interests in carpentry, book-binding and gardening, though the severe winter a year ago destroyed almost all our roses.

Our son is in the Naval Reserve in charge of a gun crew and our son-in-law is a brigadier in the British Army, supervising hospitals in the Near East. Our younger daughter has returned to England with her three children and our older daughter came home from China on the *Gripsholm* after two years of internment by the Japanese.

In politics I am a divided Democrat, approving the President's foreign policy, and disapproving many of his policies in home affairs.[149]

The impression of Robert E. Speer's personality and spirit on a younger man who had heard of him through his father but had never met him was described by a pastor, Rev. Willard C. Mellin, who had known Robert Speer in his earlier years:

In Dr. Speer's eightieth year, in July, 1947, he delivered a series of lectures on the Gospel of St. John at the School of Religion held at Western Theological Seminary in Pittsburgh, Pennsylvania. The popular Sunday evening meeting was held in the Heinz Chapel of the University of Pittsburgh, with Dr. Speer as speaker. After the meeting, in the long summer twilight, I noticed Dr. Speer crossing the campus. I was with a young minister who had heard his father often speak of Dr. Speer, whom he had never met. I asked my friend, Ronald Seaton, if he would like to meet Dr. Speer. He eagerly assented, as all his life he had heard his father, Dr. Stuart Seaton, a missionary who had been assigned to Hainan Island, tell of Dr. Speer, but he had never seen him. Dr. Speer received Ronald with his usual courtesy and vigor and assured him that he knew well and highly esteemed his father of the Hainan Mission in China. For moments afterwards Ronald was in a state of rapture, as though he had been talking to God.[150]

Eugene Carson Blake, Stated Clerk of the General Assembly of the Presbyterian Church in the U.S.A., has written of Robert Speer, of the interdenominational range of his service, of his influence with young men, and the power and vitality of his service, which continued after his "retirement" and until the end of his life:

Robert E. Speer was one of the outstanding Christian churchmen of the last generation. His influence went far beyond his own denomination and his own nation. The qualities of his mind and spirit were evident from his early youth. Despite the fact that he had great influence as a young man, it is remarkable how that influence matured and grew through all the years to retirement and beyond. I heard of Robert Speer first through my mother, who remembered his tremendous vitality and influence from her youth in Kansas City, Missouri. My last personal contact with Robert Speer was at a Faith and Life Seminar at which he and I were leaders, perhaps fifty years after my mother's memories of him as a Christian leader began. At this time the vigor of his mind, the depth of his commitment and the persuasiveness of his personality were still in full evidence.[151]

XIX. His Entrance into Life

Think of
  Stepping on shore and finding it Heaven!
  Of taking hold of a hand and finding it God's hand,
  Of breathing a new air and finding it celestial air,
  Of feeling invigorated and finding it immortality,
  Of passing from storm and tempest to an unknown calm,
  Of waking up and finding it Home! [152]

FROM 1937 TO 1947 ROBERT E. SPEER CONTINUED IN HIS FAR-
ranging service of addresses and conferences and of writing
articles and books. He attended a gathering at 156 Fifth
Avenue, New York, on December 3, 1946, in honor of the
ninetieth birthday of his friend and colleague, Arthur J.
Brown, and took his part with wit and an appropriate message of love and fellowship; but friends noticed a pallor in
his face that was not usual and were concerned about his
health.

Eleven days after his eightieth birthday he wrote to a
former colleague in the Foreign Board:

I do thank you and Mrs. Trull for your cordial birthday
greeting. We had a happy family gathering here [Lakeville,
Connecticut], brightened by such good messages as yours.
Now I suppose that with firm resolve I should set out on
the second decade after Dr. Brown and then on the third
after Dr. Vail. You must come steadily along. [153]

At an October meeting of a Bible Class on the Gospel of St. John he was teaching in a Dutch Reformed Church in Poughkeepsie, New York, he fainted; but after a week's rest he resumed his schedule of appointments. In his diary for an October engagement he recorded speaking "in great misery." A substitute presided for him at a meeting of the Princeton Seminary Trustees, of which he was President. For a number of days he remained indoors and on October 24, he wrote: "Up but very weak." On October 28, he was down with bronchitis, but on the 29th his doctor allowed him to go to his Bible class and he addressed the class sitting down instead of standing, as was his custom. On November 5, he kept his last engagement with the class in Poughkeepsie. There he quoted from a favorite poem by Christina Rossetti, beginning, "None other Lamb, none other name," and ending, "Nor Heaven have I, nor place to lay my head, nor home but Thee."

On November 17 his family persuaded him to enter a hospital in Bryn Mawr for a physical check-up and examination. He would not admit that he was seriously ill, but spoke of being tired. His illness was diagnosed as leukemia. With characteristic courage, he fought against his adversaries, weakness and pain; in the evening of November 23 he "fell asleep."

The next day his family sent out word to his friends and to the Church that Robert Speer had "entered into Life." A service conducted by Robert Speer's life-long friend, Henry Sloane Coffin, and Rex S. Clements, pastor of the church, was held in the chapel in the Presbyterian Church in Bryn Mawr on November 25.

Burial was in the family plot in the cemetery in Englewood, New Jersey, close to the grave of his son Elliott beside the grave of his three-year-old daughter, Eleanor, where the small white cross bore the words: "And I beheld a new

Heaven and a new Earth." Henry Sloane Coffin conducted
the service.

On December 15, a memorial service was held in the First
Presbyterian Church in New York City, at which the speakers
were John A. Mackay, President of Princeton Theological
Seminary and former President of the Board of Foreign Mis-
sions; John R. Mott, former Chairman of the National and
International Committees of the Y.M.C.A.; Samuel McCrea
Cavert, Secretary of the Federal Council of Churches, and
Winn Fairfield, Secretary of the Foreign Missions' Confer-
ence.

Henry Sloane Coffin led in the prayer of thanksgiving
which was a sincere and true summary and tribute:

Father of lights, who kindlest holy souls to shine in their
generation, we bless Thy name for the glorious company of
apostles who have led Thy Church and by their message, life
and labor extended the reign of Christ in the earth.

More especially we praise Thee for the gift to the Church
of our time of this Thy servant whose stalwart faith and
abounding toil we have gratefully remembered together before Thee. We thank Thee for his vigor of body and force
of mind, the energy of will and the ardor of devotion with
which Thou didst endow him; for his charm which drew men
to him, for his grace of thought and speech with which he
drew them to his Master. We bless Thee for thousands of
young people in schools, colleges and conferences to whom
year after year he made life with Christ winsome; for hundreds whom he enlisted in the work of Thy Church, and for
scores of missionaries in many lands who were enriched and
fortified by his letters; for a wider circle to whom he minis-
tered through his books, facing them with Christ and opening to them the secret of fellowship with Him; for two
generations of church people who by the glowing influence
of his life have been fired to more fervent loyalty to Christ
and more zealous endeavor to bring a whole world in its
every realm under His sway.

We call to mind his lifelong study of the Scripture, his illumination of its pages from books he was ever reading, and the spiritual riches he brought from Thy Word to build up the faith and life of Thy ministers and people. We thank Thee for his vision of oneness of Thy Church, Christ's Body in the earth, and his eagerness to do away with barriers which hinder concord in Christ and the full sharing of His unsearchable riches. We offer Thee in thanksgiving the ties of friendship by which we in this company and many more around the world were bound to him and through him joined more firmly to his passionately adored Lord. We acknowledge Thy goodness to him in the reverent affection of multitudes and the honor in which he is held in all the churches.

Thou gavest him length of days and robust strength almost to the end, and he filled them with full measure of service. Now we rejoice that, set free for the larger offices of Thy heavenly kingdom, he has entered into the joy of the Lord, whom having not yet seen, he so dearly loved.

Raise up, we humbly pray Thee, men of like spiritual stature and flaming heart to lead Thy Church in the next generation. Let his memory abide to hallow and uplift to Thy presence us and all who knew and loved him, to render Heaven where he dwells with Thee more near, and to hold us inseparably to the Saviour in whom were the springs of his life and whom he now sees face to face. Amen.[154]

Arthur J. Brown, Secretary Emeritus of the Presbyterian Foreign Board, pronounced the Benediction.

Later, in answer to the hundreds of letters and messages that came flooding in from all over the world, a simple acknowledgement went out, in the Scotch fashion, reading as follows:

Robert Elliott Speer

September 10, 1867	Huntingdon, Pa.
November 23, 1947	Bryn Mawr, Pa.

I have fought a good fight, I have finished my course, I have kept the Faith.

Thanks be to God who giveth us the victory through our Lord Jesus Christ.

> "None other Lamb, none other Name,
> None other Hope in Heaven or Earth or Sea,
> None other Hiding Place from guilt and shame
> None beside Thee.

> "Lord, Thou art Life, though I be dead;
> Love's Fire Thou art, however cold I be;
> Nor heaven have I, nor place to lay my head,
> Nor home but Thee." [155]

Quoted by R.E.S., the last time he spoke in public, Poughkeepsie, N. Y., November 5, 1947.

O God, our Father, we who are children of time come to Thee who art above time. For us the days that are past are past beyond recall, and what we have written on life's page we may not erase. But our past is still present to Thee and Thou canst undo what is beyond our power to change. Thou canst restore the wasted years. And we bring them to Thee—all the time past of our lives. Take it into Thy molding Hands. What was amiss, do thou amend, what was faulty, do Thou fulfill. We bless Thee for forgiveness, but we ask for more, even that Thou shouldst annul the evil that we have done and accomplish the good in which we failed. We thank Thee that Thou art ever open to our cry, that none can come to Thee too late, that the door of the Father's house is never closed to any child that would come home. Father, we come bringing our marred lives for Thy remaking, our stained hands for Thy cleansing, our tired feet for Thy rest, our wearied hearts for Thy peace.

R.E.S.

After this it was noised abroad that Mr. Valiant for Truth was taken with a Summons by the same Post as the other, and had this for a Token that the Summons was true. That his Pitcher was broken at the Fountain. When he understood it, he called for his Friends and told them of it. Then said he, "I am going to my Father's, and though with great difficulty I am got hither, yet now I do not repent me of all the Trouble I have been at to arrive where I am. My Sword I give to Him that shall succeed me in my Pilgrimage and my Courage and Skill to Him that can get it. My Marks and Scars I carry with me to be a witness for me that I have fought His battles who now will be my Rewarder." When the day that he must go hence was come, many accompanied him to the Riverside, into which as he went, he said, "Death, Where is Thy Sting?" And as he went down deeper, he said, "Grave, Where Is Thy Victory?" So he passed over and all the trumpets sounded for him on the other side.

—John Bunyan: *Pilgrim's Progress*

The souls of the righteous are in the hands of God and there shall no torment touch them. In the sight of the unwise they seem to die; and their departure is taken for sorrow and their going from us to be utter destruction; but they are in peace. For, though they be chastised in the sight of men, yet is there hope full of immortality, and having been a little chastised they shall be greatly rewarded, for God proved them and found them worthy for Himself. As gold in a furnace hath He tried them and received them as a burnt offering. . . . They that put their trust in Him shall understand the truth; and such as be faithful in love shall abide with Him; for grace and mercy is to His Saints, and He doth care for His elect. . . . The righteous shall live forevermore; their reward also is with the Lord, and the care of them is with the Most High. Therefore, shall they receive a glorious Kingdom, and a . . . Crown from the Lord's Hand; for with His Right Hand shall he cover them and with His Arm shall He protect them.

—*The Wisdom of Solomon*

XX. Robert Speer as Seen by His Friends

FACILE PRINCEPS

He overtowered us all! Nobility
Of soul acquired by growth in heavenly grace;
Of ling'ring selfishness and pride, no trace;
Outstanding in his great ability
Of mind, adorned by great simplicities
Of character, outshining in his face.
In Christian life he held commanding place
Marked by his rare and sheer integrity!
Administrator, seer, with pen and voice
A champion of the Christian enterprise;
A leader, following his Lord of love;
In his rich ministry how we rejoice!
His soul, by grace, has won the heavenly prize.
He lives immortal, in the realms above! [156]

ROBERT E. SPEER'S FRIENDS WERE LEGION, AND INCLUDED IN-
dividuals of all vocations in this country and abroad. His
associates in the first days of the Student Volunteer Movement for Foreign Missions from 1886 were always peculiarly
dear to him. These associates included Dwight L. Moody
and Arthur T. Pierson of an earlier generation, and his contemporaries John Forman, Robert P. Wilder, John R. Mott,
J. Campbell White, Thomas H. P. Sailer, and Delevan L.
Pierson. In his administrative work from 1891 to 1937,
Robert Speer was most closely associated with the members,
officers and clerical staff of the Presbyterian Foreign Board,

all of whom esteemed him highly, many being warm and intimate friends. Inasmuch as the Board had such extensive and ramified enterprises and co-operated so fully in inter-denominational projects, the senior Secretary served on numerous interboard agencies with the representatives of practically all denominations.

Robert Speer was a member of an intimate group of friends who met once a year for prayer and fellowship in the home of Charles R. Erdman, of Princeton Theological Seminary, at Princeton. These meetings began in 1904, the first one being held in New York, and continued each year at Princeton until 1929, and later in the home of Samuel M. Zwemer, in New York. Members of the Quiet Day Circle of which Charles R. Erdman was host and leader, included Gilbert A. Beaver, Rockwell S. Brank, Marcus A. Brownson, Horace C. Coleman, Dwight H. Day, James B. Ely, Walter Erdman, Henry W. Frost, W. Henry Grant, Harry Wade Hicks, J. Stuart Holden, Philip E. Howard, David McConaughy, James McConaughy, Walter McDougall, William R. Moody, John R. Mott, Lewis S. Mudge, Delevan L. Pierson, T. H. P. Sailer, Robert E. Speer, J. Ross Stevenson, J. Timothy Stone, John H. Strong, Charles G. Trumbull, Fennell P. Turner, Charles R. Watson, J. Campbell White, Wilbert W. White, Robert P. Wilder and Samuel M. Zwemer.

Robert Speer was also a charter member of a prayer group which was formed by David McConaughy, who was the first American Y.M.C.A. Secretary to India and later was active in promoting stewardship among laymen. Each month, prayer notes were circulated by the Secretary, Delevan Pierson. Those notes were of two kinds, praise and requests for prayer. The group met once a year for what was called a Quiet Day. The group members shared experiences, spent unhurried time in prayer, and at luncheon would tell of the books they had read during the year. Robert Speer kept a full list of books he had read and he would comment on them briefly. "None of the rest of us was as methodical in keeping such a record, and we always looked forward to his list as the best part of that particular portion of the program." [157]

Luther A. Weigle, for twenty-one years Dean of the Divinity School, Yale University, former President of the Federal Council of Churches and President of the Board of Trustees, Yale-in-China Association, has written of Robert Speer:

My most vivid memories of Dr. Speer—save for some delightful visits with him and Mrs. Speer at their home in Lakeville—center about his participation in the Jerusalem Meeting of the International Missionary Council, March 24—April 8, 1928. He and Bishop William Temple, who was later to become Archbishop of Canterbury, were the co-chairmen of the Committee appointed to draft the statement on "The Christian Message," which was discussed, amended, and adopted by formal vote of the Council. Volume I of the *Jerusalem Reports* is devoted to the papers and discussions incident to this. Besides his part in drafting the statement, Dr. Speer was responsible for editing the record of the discussions, and his own words appear twice: in the address with which he opened the discussion, pages 278-282, and in the remarkable chapter entitled "What is the Value of the Religious Values of the non-Christian Religions?" Dr. Speer's contribution to this epoch-making meeting of the International Missionary Council was second to none. It culminated in the powerful sermon which he preached at the closing morning service on Easter Sunday, April 8, on "The Resurrection."

I have been rereading these chapters of the first and eighth volumes of the *Jerusalem Reports*—sent to them because I wanted the page references for these paragraphs, and then detained in them by sheer interest until I have reviewed them thoroughly. Let no one think or say that Robert E. Speer was simply a great missionary leader of the generation that is past; he was a prophet for the present day and for those that are to come. We cannot depart from the spirit of the Jerusalem Meeting with which he had so much to do, for that spirit is eternally true and ever new." [158]

Cyril Haas, M.D., who rendered many years of distinguished service as a medical missionary in Turkey with the American Board, has told of Robert Speer's aid and inspiration.

In his student days, Dr. Haas had heard Robert Speer speak at conferences and acquired a great admiration for him which he never lost. During Dr. Haas' medical school course in New York City he was sorely tempted in the work he was doing and in his surroundings. He knew that he would derive strength and help just from a glimpse of Robert Speer, and one day a week he would go to the entrance of the Presbyterian Foreign Board at 156 Fifth Avenue, take his position unobtrusively there and watch Robert Speer come to work. Dr. Speer did not know Dr. Haas, and he did not know that he was there, but Dr. Haas said that just the sight of Robert Speer's face as he came to his work gave him strength for his own service in the coming weeks. Another friend of Robert Speer's, Kenneth Latourette of Yale, records that Robert Speer had not known of Dr. Haas' habit and that when Dr. Latourette told him later, Robert Speer "looked embarrassed, said nothing, and changed the subject." [159]

Daniel A. Poling, world leader of the Society of Christian Endeavor, Editor of the *Christian Herald,* has written:

Robert E. Speer was one of the half dozen men who profoundly influenced my life toward full-time Christian service and whose influence continued and steadily increased through the years of my ministry until he went to his "coronation."

His little book, *The Deity of Jesus,* settled that vital matter for me! His biography of Hugh Beaver, the immortal Princetonian, lighted a torch that flamed over my college days. Robert E. Speer was inspiration. Quietly impressive, even shy and retiring, he was born to leadership. Inevitably he was a man out in front. With John R. Mott, he made up the greatest Christian team of the generations through which they moved—the inspired trumpeters of Christ's Crusade.

John is still with us and when Robert went on ahead there was a lonesome place against the sky.[160]

Clarence E. Macartney, pastor of the First Presbyterian Church of Pittsburgh, Pennsylvania, and a former Moderator, wrote:

I heard him first when I was a junior in the Seminary at Princeton. He was one of those able men, like John R. Mott, Bishop William F. McDowell, and others, who came to visit the colleges and seminaries and greatly stirred the young men, kindling worthy desires in their hearts and deepening their devotion to Christ. He came to the First Church of Paterson, where I began my ministry, to deliver one of his missionary addresses. He had just returned from a tour of South America. He told of being on the deck of a steamboat, on the Magdalena River, in Colombia, when a passenger or one of the crew fell overboard. As the steamboat rushed on down the rapidly flowing river, Dr. Speer heard out of the darkness behind the boat the pitiful cry of the unfortunate man calling for help. Then silence! "The night was dark; the river was swift; and he was gone!" This incident he used in a most impressive way to illustrate the darkness of those who live and die without God and without hope.[161]

John Timothy Stone, former pastor of the Fourth Presbyterian Church in Chicago, President of the Presbyterian Theological Seminary there, and former Moderator of the Church, has written of Robert Speer:

Robert E. Speer's influence over me began when I was a student at Amherst and he was at Princeton and his early writings influenced me much at that time. We became friends at Northfield in 1891 and 1892, but our more definite friendship began when I was pastor of the Brown Memorial Church in Baltimore, following Maltbie D. Babcock in the pastorate there. Dr. Speer preached for me several times in that church and it was through his influence and introduction that I first went to Camp Diamond in New Hampshire, at the invitation of Horace Coleman. We spent many summers with our

families at Camp Diamond and our cottages were near together, at Mr. Coleman's kind arrangement. There it was that
we grew into the close friendship which has lasted through
the years. There was scarcely a week in the intervening period between the summers when we did not correspond.
During my Moderatorship in 1913, we were in constant touch
with matters concerning the church at large.

Our days at Camp Diamond were "play days" and that
happy colony, Mr. Coleman included, were like one great
family. We gave ourselves largely to the children and to one
another. I remember, during those days when Mr. William
Moody and his wife were guests at the Camp, that Will said
to me once, "Stone, do everything in your power to make
Speer *play*. He needs that more than anything else, for he
works too hard all the rest of the time." During those days
we entered into the fun of the camp very generally. I remember his good nature and patience, especially in our games
with the children, in baseball and other pastimes. We had
frequent experiences together in what would have been
termed "foolishness" to many. We had mock trials, and
three of our boys, his son, Elliott, Carl Erdman, son of Rev.
Charles Erdman, of Princeton, Dr. John Strong's son, and
myself—formed a little organization called the "Four Brothers Circus" and in our procession, or parade, we even persuaded Robert Speer to stand on a platform on the back of
a work horse and parade with us in his wife's swimming suit,
adorned with fastidious ribbons and sash. He entered in
with all his heart.

I wish to speak especially of our fishing trips together. The
Camp Diamond lakes had an outlet called "The Dead Diamond," which flowed down some fifteen or twenty miles or
more into the "Swift Diamond" and then, about an equal
distance, into the "Magalloway"; (a stream made famous in
the early writings of the renowned fisherman, Dr. Prime).
We used to love to fish the "Dead Diamond," and, starting
out early in the morning, we would fish as far as we could
and still reserve time to get back to camp at night. We sometimes even went down to the farm, which was run by Owen

Crimmins, and sometimes stayed with Owen at his little cabin overnight. Robert Speer and I took many trips down the river and learned to know its banks and prize-fishing holes extremely well.

As we walked along in our heavy fishing boots through the woods and wading streams, he was quite prone to sing some of the old famous hymns; although he could not carry a tune, he loved the words and attempted the harmony. I can hear him now, far ahead of me on the stream, or behind me, his voice ringing out in the priceless words of such old hymns as "Jesus Saviour, Pilot Me," "I Love to Tell the Story," "Pass Me Not, Oh, Gentle Saviour," and "Sweet Hour of Prayer." He knew them all by heart and we did not mind his inaccuracy in the music. He had a merry laugh, when a good joke or story was told but the story was always clean and humorous if it provoked his merriment.

We had a rule that we would always clean our own fish and do so before retiring. He used to love the great stories of Owen Crimmins as we cleaned our fish around his cabin fire, sometimes very late at night.

He published a small, humorous life of Crimmins, in which he told several of those quaint and absurd yarns. The little book was illustrated by some photographs of his companions. It showed a side of him which no one would have realized, save his close fishing friends. I remember, after one of those long trips when we stayed with Owen overnight, we both were remarkably successful in fishing the West Branch of the "Dead Diamond." We were fishing for the whole camp and there were many guests there, otherwise we would not have been so extravagant in our catches. (There was no limit then in the law as to the number of fish to be taken, but simply as to their size. They must be over seven inches.) We seldom kept fish that were less than eight or nine inches. I remember when we filled the great milk pans with our fish that night; it was almost midnight, for we were lost in coming home, and an old, white birch on the bank which we both recalled in the moonlight told us where the trail was. We had not walked more than an hour when faithful Owen Crimmins, with his lantern, evidenced his coming to meet us, and also the shrill bark of his faithful dog. I remember that night when we counted our fish (believe it or not!), Speer had 202 and I had 199. Remember, we were fishing for the camp or we might have been termed "fish hogs," I am sure.

He was an excellent fly caster. In those days we used wet flies, with three flies on the cast. His favorite flies were "Montreal," "Royal Coachman," "Red Ant," and "Black Gnat." I myself was always partial to the "Royal Coachman" and "Silver Doctor." Frequently we caught two, and sometimes three, fish at a cast. We used as light rods as were made in those days and although in later years I have used a dry fly, I have never forgotten the thrill of wet fly fishing, especially when you had more than one fish on the line. We frequently stayed out in the open overnight with balsam boughs for our bed and a small piece of canvas for our roofing.

Another place we used to love to fish was Hell-Gate Camp on "Swift Diamond." The stream had its name from the danger which the river drivers encountered when driving the logs. It was over in that country that we met a camp watchman called Deacon Cahill. We stayed with him one night and became, afterwards, fast friends. Deacon was there to overcome a tendency to strong drink, and that friendship lasted the rest of his life, as far as Speer was concerned. I was never patient with him, as Speer was, in the recurrencies of his old habit, and although I corresponded with him for years, Speer did so longer and was more patient. He used to send us some of the letters he had from Deacon and it was through Speer's influence that he was won to Christ and became an earnest Christian.

Speer always cared for the ordinary man, and for the little fellows. And although he had intimate friendship with the great, his democratic spirit and devotion included the unknown and ordinary beings.

He never flaunted his piety, and his modesty and quiet

spirit controlled him at all times. You did not hear him ever in egotistic statement or self-praise. I think he was one of the most unselfish and selfless men I ever knew.

I remember that during those trips we once discussed briefly the organization of the Church. Little did I dream, at that time, that fifteen or twenty years later, it would fall to my lot to be Chairman of the Committee of Fifteen which was appointed by the General Assembly on Reorganization, on which Committee were many of the ablest men and wisest thinkers of the Church. We were able to effect a change which reduced the number to four Boards, and established the General Council. Dr. Speer always believed this should be done but felt it was an impossibility. However, no one was more pleased than he when this was accomplished.

He was always my friend and counselor. I suppose, more than any other man, he had the influence over me to advise me, or "suggest" is a better word, to accept the call from Baltimore to Chicago. I remember what he said when I went to his home in Englewood. "John, if you want to continue a great work in a lovely city, stay where you are in Baltimore. If you want a hard job, in a big, unfinished, uncouth city, with infinite problems and greater possibilities, go to Chicago—but it is for you and God to decide."

To know Robert Speer was to love him, to respect him, to honor him. Since his death, I have always felt I have lost an elder brother and a beloved chum. But as it has been said of other great men, his truth and character go marching on.[162]

The Honorable J. Leighton Stuart, a Presbyterian missionary in China from 1905 to 1946, a member of the faculty of Nanking Theological Seminary in Nanking from 1908 to 1919, President of Yenching University from 1919 to 1946, and American Ambassador to China from 1946 to 1952, has written of Robert Speer:

Reginald Wheeler has gleaned material from others for Dr. Speer's biography; therefore, I shall refer only to my personal reminiscences of this remarkable personality.

Dr. Robert E. Speer was first known to me as an inspiring

religious speaker. I heard him on several occasions in North-field, Massachusetts, and particularly in the great Student Volunteer Conventions, both at Detroit and Toronto. His addresses and those of Dr. John R. Mott were the high point of enthusiastic attention by the thousands of young people who heard them. Dr. Speer seemed to me at that time to be one of the great influences for depicting the marvelously strong and winsome personality of Jesus. He had also been one of the chief inspirations to many of my contemporaries.

In my Memoirs, *Fifty Years in China*, I have written of these student conferences and of Robert Speer:

"I found immense religious encouragement from the vital, practical, winsome concepts of religion presented and inspira-tion from the noble personalities who promoted, addressed or attended these very successful meetings. . . . Jesus Christ became an adored Master and the ideal object of a young man's enthusiastic devotion. . . . Like many other youth of the time, I owed most to Robert E. Speer for this fresh and fascinating appreciation of Jesus. This became then and still is the essence of my religious faith. It has remained undimmed and free from all disillusionment after all the experiences and altered theological views of these intervening years."

Later on I had the privilege of knowing Dr. Speer in other features which were more or less intimate, his devoted char-acter, his rare administrative ability and his literary gift, giv-ing him a distinguished position in human service.

Dr. Speer's daughter, Margaret, is a fine blend of the qualities of her father and mother. Yenching University has been fortunate in having her for many years as a teacher of English and then the Dean of its Women's College.[163]

Henry Smith Leiper, Secretary of the Missions Council of the Congregational Christian Churches, has written of Robert Speer:

My recollections of Robert E. Speer go back to 1908, when I first heard him at a meeting in Philadelphia called by the Laymen's Missionary Movement. That summer I was at Northfield and had a close contact with him at the Student

Conference, where he, Mott, and Eddy were the outstanding figures, along with Robert Wilder.

He made an indelible impression upon me, and stirred within me very strong resolves *not* to be persuaded to go into the work of the ministry or the missionary enterprise. I had been brought up in a home of a missionary of the Presbyterian Board of National Missions, but in my boyish mind I did not want to devote my life to that type of work. I wanted something with more fame, glory, and reward.

During my Freshman year at Amherst College, in 1909, Robert E. Speer came to preach and I recall telling him that I was astounded at the discovery that I had made in Amherst, that not a single man was preparing for the ministry, although the college was founded to prepare ministers. He said, "Henry, you can easily do something about that." I said, "What could I do, Dr. Speer? I am just a Freshman." He said very simply, "You can decide to be a minister and then there *will* be one." I had in my possession a Student Volunteer card that had been given to me by Ken Latourette but which I had not signed. Following the address which Dr. Speer gave at the Amherst College Chapel, I went home and signed the card.

From that time on until the end of his life I was fortunate in having many contacts with Dr. Speer, at his home in Englewood, at many conferences and in committees of the Foreign Mission Boards. During the period that I was Traveling Secretary of The Student Volunteer Movement I was in close consultation with him; and after my return from China, because of duties as a Secretary of the American Board, I was in many consultations and conferences where Dr. Speer was the leader. Through the years I read the books that came from his pen and tried to hear him every time he spoke.

His intense devotion, his profound faith, his knowledge of men and missions, his biographical writings and his personal friendliness always deeply appealed to me.

The author regrets that limitations of space do not permit the addition of the names of many other true friends and trusted co-workers of R. E. Speer.

In his home life and among his personal friends he was one of the most amusing men I have ever known. I always wondered why he brought so little humor into his public addresses, and noted with interest that toward the end of his life he was more inclined to let that side of his nature appear to his audience.

I remember the impression that Dr. Speer made on my son, who was later to be a missionary of the Presbyterian Board in China. When he was quite a small lad he heard Dr. Speer preach in our church. After the sermon, my son Hal said to Dr. Speer, taking his hand, "Gee, Dr. Speer, that was swell." I remember the grin with which the great preacher accepted this very genuine word of appreciation.

During the years when it fell to my lot to work with the Ecumenical Movement, Dr. Speer was a member of the committee that called me as Secretary in 1930, and attended and chaired in a crucial meeting which set up the program. He did not live to see the close association of the International Missionary Council with the World Council of Churches, but I am sure it will be true to say that the persons whom he most deeply influenced, at least in America, were among the individuals who had the greatest share in the development of the World Council and in bringing it into intimate relationship to the International Missionary Council.

The last great address that I heard Dr. Speer give was at the dinner held in New York in honor of Dr. Mott, after his return from Sweden, where he was awarded the Nobel Prize. In that address, Dr. Speer showed not only his serious side but his humor, as he recalled the long years of intimate association the two great stalwarts of the missionary movement had shared in this and other lands.

Dr. Speer and Dr. Mott were both laymen; both held positions of the highest ecclesiastical nature, each in his own way illustrating the priesthood of believers and the potentiality of the lay ministry.[164]

Emile Cailliet, of the faculty of Princeton Theological Seminary, wrote concerning Robert Speer:

When I was on the faculty of the graduate school of the University of Pennsylvania, I was invited every year to lecture at the Princeton Institute of Theology. Like every other visiting professor, I lived at the Princeton Inn. Every morning the activities of the day were opened at the Princeton Theological Seminary by a Bible Hour of which Dr. Speer was in charge. He would get up, have an early breakfast, and although my lecture came much later, I made it a point of getting up so as to sit at the breakfast table with him. If there ever was anyone who did not need to prepare, it was Dr. Speer; and yet I never saw anyone prepare more carefully. Even throughout the breakfast, after the usual kind word of welcome and friendly inquiries, he would remain silent. I respected his silence because I knew it was that of an active meditation on his coming Bible Hour. So you may ask why did I sit at the table with him at all. The answer is: just to be with him and look at him. He was a Presence. It was good to be there. After the Institute was over, I would come back to Philadelphia, and often my wife would exclaim, "Why there is light on your face!" And I would merely answer, "I spent a few days with Robert Speer."

When I published my larger treatment of Pascal (*Pascal, Genius in the Light of Scripture,* 1945) and reached the final pages of the book, it suddenly occurred to me that the ultimate faith of Pascal as I had finally come to understand it, had been most forcefully vindicated in our day by Robert Speer in his admirable book, *The Finality of Jesus Christ.* This I wanted to say, but knowing Robert Speer, I could not do so without his permission, which he generously granted.

I would add just one apparently insignificant note, yet one which provides a real insight into the man. When he published his so valuable *Five Minutes a Day,* I asked him to inscribe one copy for my wife. This he did, adding to the inscription, "with Dr. Cailliet's permission." Where is such refinement of the Christian gentleman found in our day?

It is hard for me to realize how much of my own life and thinking I owe to Robert Speer and especially to his book

The Finality of Jesus Christ. In my final Senior course at the Seminary, I always urge our future ministers to keep the book on their desks next to the Bible and a concordance.[165]

J. Christy Wilson, Professor of Foreign Missions at Princeton Theological Seminary, has written:

When Samuel M. Zwemer was eighty years old, among all the greetings which he received, the octogenarian and his family appreciated most deeply the affectionate note written in the distinctive hand of Robert E. Speer on Easter Day, 1947, not long before the call of this close friend to higher service. It said, in part:

"My dear Sam:
"So this week on Saturday you will be four score—and thank God it is not 'labor and sorrow' but 'work and joy.' Thankful you will be, and we who love you will be thankful with you for the way the Lord has led you, and for all that He has given to us and to the Church through you. . . . A four-score blessing! I can imagine God saying: 'This is my dear, true, powerful servant Sam.' He is one of my best and bravest. Angels, take special care of him! Let no harm come to him. Breathe his mind and heart full of power.' That is my prayer for you, dearest old friend.

Robert E. Speer" [166]

The tribute by Mrs. Charles Kingsley in her biography of her husband, expresses the love and admiration which those who best knew Robert Speer felt for him:

To the Beloved Memory
of
A Righteous Man

Who loved God and truth above all things—
A man of untarnished honor—
Loyal and chivalrous—gentle and strong—
Modest and humble—tender and true—

Pitiful to the weak—yearning after the erring—
Stern to all forms of wrong and oppression,
Yet most stern towards himself—
Who being angry, yet sinned not.
Whose highest virtues were known only
To his wife, his children, his servants, and the poor.
Who lived in the presence of God here,
And passing through the grave and gate of death
Now liveth unto God for ever more.[167]

XXI. His Books

ROBERT E. SPEER WROTE AND EDITED SIXTY-SEVEN BOOKS. THE subjects included studies of the Bible, expositions of foreign mission principles, history and problems; statements in defense of foreign missions, analyses of student problems and suggestions as to their solution, studies of the principles of the Christian faith, with supreme emphasis on the meaning and finality of Christ; seven biographies, and five volumes containing biographical sketches.

Robert Speer's books were not written in an ivory tower, in a secluded retreat, or out of the release of a six months' or a year's sabbatical; they were forged like iron in the heat of exacting administrative duties and forensic discussion and debate, incessant travel and constant public speaking of the kind in which often a promise or an engagement to speak twice on Sunday developed into five or more engagements, with Sunday school, Bible classes, and special groups added to the responsibility of two sermons.

A number of his books went into multiple editions; over 50,000 copies were printed of two of them, *Rethinking Missions Examined*, a defense of foreign missions and an analysis and criticism of "Rethinking Missions," the Laymen's Report published in 1933, and *Five Minutes a Day*, a devotional book originally prepared for Robert Speer's own personal use; 40,000 copies were printed of a biography, *One Girl's Influence*, the life of Louise Andrews. No Christian leader of Robert Speer's generation was more influential in his spoken word and through the products of his pen.

In the Appendix are listed his books, with titles, number of pages, date of publication and the publisher.

This chapter deals, in outline and in summary, with twelve selected volumes of special interest that bear his name. Characteristic quotations from some of these books are included.

The first of the twelve books described in this chapter, the third book written by Robert E. Speer, is *Studies of the Man Christ Jesus*, which appeared in 1896. The title comes from I Timothy, 2:5: "One mediator between God and man, the man Christ Jesus."

This volume grew out of Bible study with students. The author wrote:

These studies were undertaken for the use of the college students who gathered each summer at Northfield, and to whom the picture of Jesus presented there proved helpful, both strengthening faith in His real Deity and increasing admiration for His perfect and glorious humanity. Later these studies were reviewed with a group of British students at Keswick, and with little companies at Rutgers and Bryn Mawr colleges. They are published now, not so much for general reading as for the use of Bible classes, especially of college students, and for others who love to discover ever fresh angles from which, in their own study of the Gospels, they may view the sweet face of Jesus. . . .

Jesus was "the man Jesus" but He was "the man Christ Jesus"—the One anointed and sent, the Heaven-born. An understanding study of Him excludes Him from the class of natural phenomena. Whoso begins with the acknowledgment, "This was a righteous man," cannot stop short of the confession, "Surely this man was the Son of God." . . . Increasing knowledge of Jesus requires increasing imitation of Jesus. A study of His life is perilous to the insincere. For those who long to be like Him it is both duty and delight.

This was the Man Christ Jesus, God of God, Light of Light, Very God of Very God, Saviour, Redeemer, Lord and King. But whatever He was, He is meaningless to us save as we enter into our inheritance in Him. . . . For our sakes He lived a life of love and free of stain, leaving us an example that we should follow in His steps. But this is not all. "It must be affirmed that Christ is something more than His exalted ethical character."

Christ is far more. If He were only this, our faith were vain. Christ is the world's life. Passing centuries, however many their number, could not erect an exalted ethical character into Christ of today and forever, and the study of that Character is largely profitless save as it leads men and nations to hear the voice of Jesus as on the last day, the great day of the feast, He stood and cried, saying, "If any man thirst, let him come unto me and drink. He that believeth on me, as the Scripture hath said, out of the depths of his life shall pour torrents of living water." [168]

In this book, *The Man Christ Jesus*, a student of Robert E. Speer and his service can find the germ, the comparatively obscure seed, from which grew and flowered his prodigious and unique output in the spoken and printed word and in his far-flung, creative and world-wide service.

In 1933, thirty-seven years later, this early study of Christ was followed by a volume, *The Finality of Jesus Christ*, which contained the L. P. Stone Lectures, given at Princeton Theological Seminary, 1932-1933, and as the Gay Lectures at the Southern Baptist Theological Seminary in 1933.

John A. Mackay, President of Princeton Theological Seminary, has written of this volume:

This book, in a very real sense, is Dr. Speer's *magnum opus*. Here the two passions of his life were combined: a passion to explore the incomparable significance of Jesus Christ and a passion for the world-wide missionary movement. Here, too, appears the vast range of the author's interests and his unexcelled knowledge of church history, Christian biography, the missionary movement, and com-

parative religion. The book is a great apologetic for the
unique, absolute, final and cosmic character of Christ and of
the religion which He founded.[169]

A volume which appeared in 1902, *The Marks of a Man*,
which contained the Merrick Lectures delivered at Ohio
Wesleyan University that year, when Robert E. Speer was
thirty-five years of age, presented a challenging statement
and description of the active life and service that would follow and flow from the life in Christ, and the belief in Him.

In that book Robert E. Speer described the qualities he
believed to be admirable in a man, qualities which should be
cultivated by other men, especially young men. He listed six
"marks of a man": truth, purity, decision, service, progress,
and patience. In a smaller volume, published in the previous
year, in 1901, *Things That Make a Man*, Robert Speer had
given a briefer summary of these principles and qualities.

In the book, *The Marks of a Man*, Robert E. Speer describes a letter he had received from a man who related his
problems in unbelief and his unsuccessful search for happiness, and gives his reply:

I sent him in reply eight suggestions as to how a conscientious but unsatisfied man may find freedom and peace of
heart:

1. Think about Jesus Christ and not about yourself.
2. Do the sort of things for other people that you would
do if you loved them.
3. Do not ever talk of yourself or boast or seek praise or
pity. Remember the rules of Archbishop Benson: "Not to
call attention to crowded work or petty fatigues or trivial
experiences. To heal wounds which in times past my cruel
and careless hands have made. To seek no favor, no compassion; to deserve, not ask for, tenderness. Not to feel any
uneasiness when my advice or opinion is not asked, or is set
aside."
4. Do with absolute faithfulness every duty.

5. Rejoice at all the good you see in others and all the honors they achieve, and admire all that is admirable in all things.

6. Counteract all beginnings of evil, whether of thought or of act, by some positive thought or deed of good.

7. Do not do evil, thus avoiding remorse, and will to love, thus winning peace.

8. Do not be impatient. Go on coveting the best and highest, but remember that time is necessary for all things—to separate us from all past failure and shame, and to bring us to the goal, and remember that it will be unconsciously, probably, that we shall draw nearer to it.[170]

In the Merrick Lectures, delivered fifteen years later, entitled: *The Stuff of Manhood*, Robert Speer further developed this theme, "the stuff of manhood" included discipline and austerity, the conservation and release of moral resources, an unfrightened hope, the joy of the minority, and the life invisible.

Our purpose [he said] is to urge our keeping, if we have not lost them, and our regaining, if we feel them slipping from us, some of the elemental moral qualities and spiritual resources which are vital to the capacity for duty and to the living of a full and efficient life. . . .

The appeal of Christ was always addressed to the sacrificial and the heroic. In every call He issued to men there is this unmistakable note of austerity. He never smooths things over for the sake of pleasing people or of winning followers. . . . He was looking for men of iron and of austerity. "If any man will come after me, let him deny himself, and take up his cross and follow me." . . . When St. Paul comes to write of the Happy Warrior, we find him setting this in the foreground: "Endure hardship, as a good soldier of Jesus Christ." [171]

Robert E. Speer wrote twelve books describing the character and work of those whom he thought to be admirable and to be emulated. Five of these books were biographies; seven contained biographical sketches. The fullest and most detailed of these biographies was that of Sir James Ewing, a missionary in India for forty-six years, President of Ewing Christian College, who was knighted by the British Government for his service to India. This book appeared in 1928.

Robert Speer wrote a biography of a young girl named Louise Andrews, daughter of an intimate friend, who lived in Plainfield, N. J. She died before she was twenty years of age, but her brief span of life was characterized by a most beautiful influence and spirit. The book about her was entitled, *One Girl's Influence*; the biography was privately printed and over 40,000 copies were sold. A girls' camp bearing her name, The Louise Andrews Camp, has been established in New England.

Of the other ten biographical volumes, *Young Men Who Overcame*, published in 1905, containing biographical sketches of twelve young men, outstanding in their generation in character and service, was widely read. I remember reading this book when I was a student at Yale and feeling the stimulus and appeal of the challenging record of these fellow students and contemporaries in preparatory school and college.

Of the group described in this book, Hugh Beaver was a son of a governor of Pennsylvania, a dear friend of Robert E. Speer; "Manny" Holabird was an outstanding amateur golfer and a star athlete at The Hill School who died before entering college and left a shining name at his school and among a wide circle of friends; Horace Tracy Pitkin, a graduate of Yale, a missionary in China, who, with members of his family, was killed by the Boxers in China in 1899; Walter Lowrie was a member of the Pennsylvania State Legislature and Senate, a United States Senator, who was elected Secretary of the Senate, and resigned that position to become the first Secretary of the Presbyterian Foreign Board in 1837; three of his sons went to the foreign field as missionaries, one of them dying in China; another, forced to return from India, acted as an associate of his father as an assistant secretary of the Foreign Board, and became Secretary, serving until 1891. William Earl Dodge was a member of the Dodge family, which had large interests in the Phelps-Dodge corporation. Several of them served in Christian educational work in the Near East, Bayard Dodge being President of the American University at Beirut for a number of years. Courtland Van Rennselaer Hodge, a member of the Hodge family well known for its contribution in service and in theology in the Presbyterian Church, went as a missionary to China, where, with his wife and small children, he was killed by the Boxers in 1899.

In 1931 appeared a little book entitled, *Owen Crimmins: Tales from the Magalloway Country*, a biography and a record of the stories and anecdotes recounted by Owen Crimmins, the caretaker of a logging camp in the glorious country of New Hampshire and Maine near the Canadian border of the Province of Quebec, who became a guide and fishing companion of Robert Speer on the latter's fishing trips there. At the "Stunt Night" held during the Post-War Conference, at Princeton, N. J., in June, 1920, Dr. Speer regaled the members of the Conference with some of the tall tales of Owen Crimmins.

Mrs. Speer wrote of this book:

All the names of the streams and the hills speak of the beauty of forest and of the wilderness; Owen Crimmins' stories are full of the folk lore of the men of the North Woods; one hears them in innumerable forms. They were the repetition of old fables; but from year to year fresh incidents would be added with the dignity and confidence of the scrupulous and conscientious historian. One was the tale of the faithful dogfish, so beautiful and trustful that it followed Owen home over the trail, only to be drowned in the spring when it fell off a bridge! Another story was of the duck shot with a cherry stone and identified for years by the cherry tree growing from his neck. One winter the deer had crowded so tight into the meadow around the farm house that their breath froze two inches thick against the windows and Owen had to run over their packed backs to secure fish from the river.[172]

The concluding paragraph of this book reveals Robert Speer's love of fishing and of life in the open:

Alas, the dear, vanished and unreturning days! Owen is gone, and the fish are gone and the streams that we knew are gone. But the memories will never go; theirs and the friendships enshrined within them, one keeps forever, to be renewed in the good fishing country in Paradise, where the rivers of water run clear as crystal.[173]

In 1899, appeared one of Robert Speer's most effective volumes, *Remember Jesus Christ*, with the sub-title *And Other Talks About Christ and the Christian Life*. In the Preface appears the statement: "All the chapters of this little book were first spoken as addresses to the Summer Bible Conferences at Northfield, some to the young men, some to the young women. They are but simple talks to the heart and will of students. Our Lord and our Lord's desire for His disciple's life is their only theme. What other theme is worthy?"

In the initial chapter of this book Robert Speer gives his reasons for selecting the title:

There are doubtless reasons for clinging with loving preference to the King James Version of the Bible. There is a sweetness of phrase in it that will never be surpassed, and its familiar turns of expression are woven into the fiber of all our thought and feeling. But the reader of the Revised Version has these advantages: he knows that he is nearer to the exact meaning of what the Bible writers said and, though he does lose some of the melody of the older version, now and then he comes upon a change of language that brings out truth hidden before and flings a lane of glory across the page.

Since beginning the use of the Revised Version, seven or eight years ago, I have had many such experiences as this, and one which came in the spring of last year has meant so much to me that I wish to speak of it to you. We were going on a long inland journey, on a house boat, up a river in Southern China, and ordinary habits of Bible study were interrupted so that it was necessary to invent some method adapted to the new conditions. I thought of the simple plan of watching each evening, when we had our little gathering for family prayers, for the most meaningful phrase in the passage that we read together, and of making that phrase the subject for study, such study as was possible, the next morning. One evening the old medical missionary, who was the head of our little party, was reading in the King James Version the second chapter of the Second Epistle to Timothy, and I was following him in my pocket Revised Testament. There seemed to be no notable change until we came to the eighth verse, which he read, "Remember that Jesus Christ of the seed of David was raised from the dead, according to my Gospel." In the Revised Version I saw that the verse was altogether different. It read, "Remember Jesus Christ." It sent a thrill through me as though Heaven had been opened just a little. . . .

Where will you find a more *sufficient* rule of life than this —"Remember Jesus Christ"? A man to whom Christ is not as yet all that Christ wants to be said to me half hopelessly this morning as he turned away after we had been talking together, "I am all at sea." I told him that I hoped he would make port soon. I should like to give him these sailing orders: "Remember Jesus Christ." Dear fellows, if any of you feel all at sea, there is nothing that will be of so much help to you in making the port as these three words, "Remember Jesus Christ."

Here is a test as to whether or not the Holy Spirit is in our lives. Have our minds been full today of recollections of Jesus? If not, then the Holy Spirit has not been there doing

His supreme work of revealing Jesus; for that is what he came here to do—to hide Himself behind Jesus, and to make all men think of Jesus, and to fill the minds of men with the memories of Jesus Christ. "He shall bring to your remembrance me." Are you remembering Jesus Christ? There is nothing deeper than this, nor anything beyond this. The whole life of Christ's disciples is wrapped up in this—remembering Jesus Christ.

Dear fellows, let us begin it now. Tonight when you lie down to sleep, try to bring back some scene or word from Jesus' life, and think of Him; and if in the darkness you awake, remember Him; and tomorrow morning, when the sunrise softly comes, remember Him. Let us begin now—remembering Jesus Christ.[174]

In 1933 over 50,000 copies were printed of a booklet called "Rethinking Missions Examined." This little book criticized sharply the so-called "Laymen's Report on Foreign Missions," which had appeared some months before.

Robert Speer began with general recognition of the literary merits of the Report and its rich humanism. He wrote:

Perhaps the most satisfactory single chapter, although not without qualifications, is the chapter on "Women's Interests and Activities." This was the one place where the Commission allows itself to speak with "enthusiasm." Missionary women know well the weaknesses and inadequacies of their work, but we dare to say, with care and deliberation, that their work is the best work being done in the world today. . . . Christianity and Christian missions deserve a far larger measure of credit than is given, even here, for the change in the life and thought of women in India, China, and Japan.[175]

In the booklet Robert Speer made trenchant criticisms of the theological basis of the Report and the plan of administration which it recommended. The issues which were involved are described in Chapter XVI.

A book for devotional reading and prayer entitled *Five Minutes a Day* was published in 1943. In the preface Robert E. Speer wrote:

The material of this little book was prepared entirely for personal and private use, and not for publication. It is printed now because The Westminster Press learned of it and wanted to make it available for the help of other common Christian folk—lay people, men and women, in our Churches—in the pressure of our daily life and work. It has been cast in form suitable for individual use or for use in family worship, or in connection with grace at meals. The book does not contain homilies or meditations. It simply provides for each day Bible verses and a poem embodying one central thought and an appropriate prayer. . . . It is a simple, homely affair for busy people who can find, because they must, a little time at the beginning or ending of the day for a bit of quiet thought and prayer.[176]

The book has been widely used throughout the Church; it was a source of strength to a Presbyterian missionary who was held a prisoner for ten months by the Communists in China. His experience was a dramatic expression of the comfort, courage, and guidance which this little book brought to thousands of Christians in their daily work, problems, and trials.

The missionary, John D. Hayes, a member of the North China Mission of the Presbyterian Church, wrote:

During my first trial of forty days, the Communist Court had succeeded in thoroughly confusing my mind, "cracking it," one might say, by getting me to think as true incidents that had never happened. In the second court, a fortnight later, they set themselves the task of breaking my spirit. God has made us in His likeness, and the mind may go, but through His grace the spirit will hold—the spirit of loyalty to Him, to one's friends and to the truth as one sees it.

Some days after the second court had begun its series of questions with a view to having the prisoner reveal the reasons for the deeds he had done "against the people," I was asked to write on America. It was recognized that the United States had begun in a revolution aimed at meeting deep-felt needs of "the people." I was asked to trace present tendencies in their historical development and their future import. I knew what the court was aiming at—an elucidation of what it called "economic imperialism"—but I wanted to write truthfully. So I asked and received permission to have brought to me the two-volume *History of American Civilization* by Charles E. Beard. I looked forward to my first bit of real objective study after three and a half months of subjective analysis and its all but overpowering strain, so I described the books in such a way that the most illiterate would have no difficulty in identifying them.

You can imagine my surprise when the messenger came back in the evening with two books of quite different size and both much smaller than the volumes asked for. I will be frank to say that on my first sight of them, I was disappointed. They were Stanley Jones' *Christ and Human Suffering* and Dr. Speer's little book of daily devotions, *Five Minutes a Day*. As the messenger handed the books to me, he said, "The man in charge of your things does not understand English and just casually picked up these two books." Immediately his words took on for me a new significance. It was as if God were saying to me; "These are the books you need. I know the strain under which you are living. Open, read, and find strength in my Word."

I knew what it was to be spiritually thirsty. I drank deeply of that life-giving stream; Dr. Speer's little book, with its selections from the Scriptures and its remarkable collection of poems and prayers, was truly my mainstay during the most severe strain of the remaining days at court. I learned many of the poems by heart (a favorite was "Horizon," on page 340), and I had the joy of passing them on to others. May that book be for others what it has been for me—the evidence that, as my Master walked with others, He will with us.[177]

The reading on page 340 of *Five Minutes a Day* was:

HORIZONS

And we have the word of prophecy made more sure; whereunto ye do well that ye take heed, as unto a lamp shining in a dark place, until the day dawns, and the day-star arise in your hearts. 2nd Peter 1:19.

I am the light of the world; he that followeth me shall not walk in the darkness but shall have the light of life. John 8:12.

Thou art my hiding place. Ps. 32:7.

My heart gives thanks for yonder hill
That makes this valley safe and still,
That shuts from sight my onward way
And sets a limit to my day;
That keeps my thoughts so tired and weak
From seeking what they should not seek.
On that fair bound across the west
My eyes find pasturage and rest,
And of its dewy stillness drink
As do the stars upon its brink;
It shields me from the day to come
And makes the present hour my home. . . .

I thank Thee, Lord, that Thou dost lay
These near horizons on my way.
If I could all my journey see,
There were no charm or mystery,
No veiled grief, no changes sweet,
No restful sense of tasks complete.
I thank Thee for the hills, the night,
For every barrier to my sight,
For every turn that blinds my eyes
To coming pain or glad surprise.

For every bound Thou settest nigh
To make me look more near, more high;
For mysteries too great to know;
For everything Thou dost not show,

Upon Thy limits rests my
heart;
Its safe horizon, Lord, Thou
art.

Frances L. Bushnell

In a volume entitled *Christian Realities*, published in 1935,
Robert E. Speer included a revealing statement "What Jesus
Christ Is to Me and Does for Me."

Jesus shows me the possibility and duty of a man as to his
character and his service.

In the effort to attain this for myself, He does for me what
I know I cannot do for myself, and what I have never found
any friend, however dear, able to do for me.

He gives me a clearer moral vision and the courage to try
to live by that vision.

He gives me the desire to work in the world as intensely as
He worked.

He kindles me, when I grow sluggish or indifferent, to a
positive and aggressive antagonism to evil within and without.

He gives me confidence in the truth, and so helps me to
rest, no matter what happens in the world, because I know
that God and the truth must prevail.

He counterbalances, as I cannot, the variable circumstances
and unequal conditions of life, and takes care of the excesses
that are beyond me.

He gives me grace and strength to try, at least, things that
I know are impossible, and to attempt, first of all, the things
that are hardest to be done.

He helps me to refuse to do good when I know that something better can be done.

He helps me to keep on when I have to, even though I
know I cannot.

He saves me from the fret and killing of pride and vanity,
and helps me to cease to care for the things that make people
sick.

He helps me to keep the central things clear and not to be

fogged and broken down by the accessories and secondary things.

He gives me a new and inward living principle by His life and His resurrection.

He reveals as sin my difference from the God I see in Him; He forgives it and deals with it and all that it involves by His cross.

Lastly, I believe that He is Himself the principle of life and that there is another personality in me that would not be there if it had not been for Him and if it were not for Him today.[178]

XXII. Prayers of Robert E. Speer and Emma Bailey Speer

O Lord Jesus Christ, we thank Thee that Thy love is a love for the whole world of men and also for each single child of Thy Father's human family. Help us to love with like love to Thine, to see both human need and human needs and the very bodies of the needy, not altogether only but also one by one; to be moved both by human hunger and wrong and also by the hungers and wrongs of persons whom we can know and whom we can serve and in whom we can find Thee and minister to Thee according to Thy word: "Inasmuch as ye have done it unto these, ye have done it unto me."

(page 41) R.E.S.

Our Blessed Lord Jesus Christ, who for the love of man didst lay aside the glory which Thou hadst with the Father before the world was and didst humble Thyself to be born of a virgin and to take on Thee our human flesh and to live our human life, and to drink the cup of our human suffering and death, we thank Thee that by Thy humility Thou art exalted and art raised over death as the Prince of Life, and art yet to reign in power and glory over all things as Lord of lords and King of kings. Be pleased, we beseech Thee, to set Thine authority in our minds and hearts, that Thy Kingdom may begin in us. For us Thou didst humble Thyself. In us now, O blessed Saviour, be Thou exalted. Hear us, we pray Thee, as we bow before Thee and in joy and love confess that Thou art Lord, to the glory of God the Father.

(page 43)   R.E.S.

O Lord Jesus Christ, we thank Thee that we have besides the story of Thine earthly life and the experience of Thy constant presence, the blessed hope of Thy coming again, when we shall see Thee as Thou art, and when Thou wilt bring with Thee all whom we love who have left our mortal sight and are safe with Thee. Forbid that we should lose the joy and strength of the daily expectancy of Thy return. May our eyes be ever toward Thy coming, not in memory of the past alone, and not alone in common human experience or in the mystery of death, but in Thy visible, personal appearing, remembering Thy most sure word, "I will come again. Watch therefore, lest coming suddenly I find you sleeping."

(page 96)   R.E.S.

O Thou who art of purer eyes than to behold iniquity, who dost require of those who would truly worship Thee clean hands and a pure heart, what can we do, whom sin has stained, but cast ourselves upon Thy mercy and accept the purifying discipline of Thy burning love? We thank Thee for the fire that consumes our dross, for the blood of Jesus Christ Thy Son which cleanses us from all sin, for the pain that purifies, for the despairs of earth from which the sure hope of heaven is born, for the light out of darkness, and for the Everlasting Day beyond our mortal light.

(page 121)   R.E.S.

Our Heavenly Father, we thank Thee for the times and for the experiences when we feel the need of Thee most deeply. We know that the only true life is life that is aware of Thee and of its need of Thee. Forgive us that we have so often ceased to live by forgetting our absolute dependence upon Thee; and deliver us from the pride of our strength which is weakness and the folly of our self-confidence which is death. Give us the mind of Christ who did always the things that pleased Thee and who was one with Thee in all things, and make us also one with Thee in Him. Help us by Thy Holy Spirit to use memory and imagination, will and affection, to make Him and Thee our greatest reality, and by Thy power fulfill in us the sense of Thy Presence and the Purity and joy of Thy Life.

(page 152)   R.E.S.

Our Father, we thank Thee for the human life of Jesus; for the simple, natural boyhood; for His love of out-of-doors, of the mountains and the sky, of the flowers and the sheep, of the lake and the brooks and the garden; for His friendships; for His gentleness and His courage and His faithfulness; that He trod the full pathway of our human lot and bare our sins in His own body on the tree. We thank Thee that in the man Christ Jesus and in His human life Thou dost give Thyself to us, convincing us of Thy forgiveness and love, and issuing us into Thy redemption, the freedom of the souls that are in communion with Thee through Jesus Christ, Thy Son our Lord.

(page 157)   R.E.S.

O God our Father, deliver us from the foolishness of self-confidence, from all boasting and vanity, from pride of energy and false notions of success. Teach us that our springs are not in ourselves but in Thee, that so far from being able to do what we will, we can neither will nor do any good except by Thy grace and with Thy help, that it is when we are weak in ourselves that we are strong in Thee, that Thy power is made perfect in our conscious lack of power that compels us to lay our helplessness on Thy strength. Here may we find our rest and feel, pouring through all our impotence, the tides of Thy mighty Spirit, for Thine is the kingdom, the power and glory.

(page 280)   R.E.S.

O Thou who art the Way, the Truth and the Life, who didst come in the flesh of humanity that we who are of this flesh might have life abundantly in Thee, help us to accept Thee and Thy gift. Be Thou our life today. May the mind that was in Thee be in us, that every thought of ours this day may be in captivity to Thine obedience. May our wills conform in all things small and great to Thy will. May we walk in the light, as Thou art in the light, and, cleansed from all sin by Thy blood, may we have fellowship one with another in home and in work today, and fellowship above all and through all with Thee. As Thou didst invite Thy first disciples to come to Thee and to go with Thee, and to abide where Thou didst abide, so may we hear Thy call to us today and straightway rise up to follow Thee in all the moments of this day, that it may be filled with the holiness and peace and strength and joy of Thy presence.

(page 305)   R.E.S.

O God, our Father, we thank Thee that Thine only-begotten Son took our nature upon Him and was born of a Virgin, that He grew up under a mother's loving care and that on His cross He made sure of a home for her with His dearest friend. We thank Thee for His constant tenderness toward all women and for His first meeting on the Resurrection morning. We thank Thee for His influence through all the centuries in protecting women from wrong, in securing justice and equality, in opening the paths of service. And we thank Thee for the faith and devotion with which women in all ages and in all lands have answered Thy love in Him, and in fidelity and sacrifice fulfilled Thy will. Wherever they still suffer injustice and wrong we pray Thee to deliver them. Wherever their power is wasted on inferior ends, recall them to their great mission. Help them as they mold the future in the child life that is in their care to believe in the possibility of Thy Kingdom and to train for its citizenship that which Thou hast entrusted to them, in the Name of Thy Holy Child Jesus.

(page 324) R.E.S.

O God our Father, after whom the whole family in heaven and on earth is named, who hath made of one blood all the nations and hath appointed unto them the bounds of their habitation, forgive us that we have so shamefully marred our human unity and have made of the earth which Thou didst create for peace a field of conflict and war. Thou art a God of righteousness. Cleanse us from all evil and by Thy judgments overthrow all falsehood and wrong, purge away all hatreds and establish truth and peace among all men. O mighty and righteous and loving Father, do Thou intervene and do through us and for us what we have been found unable to do for ourselves. Make peace, O God, who madest man, make peace.

(page 374) R.E.S.

"O Lord, prepare my heart, I beseech Thee, to reverence Thee, to adore Thee, to love Thee; to hate, for love of Thee, all my sins, imperfections, shortcomings, whatever in me displeaseth Thee; and to love all which Thou lovest and whom Thou lovest, Give me, Lord fervor of love, shame for my unthankfulness, sorrow for my sins, longing for thy grace, and to be wholly united with Thee. Let my very coldness call for the glow of Thy love; let my emptiness and dryness, like a barren and thirsty land, thirst for Thee, call on Thee to come into my soul, who refreshest those who are weary. Let my heart ache to Thee and for Thee, who stillest the aching of the heart. Let my mute longings praise Thee, crave Thee, who satisfiest the empty soul, that waits on Thee."

(Y.W.C.A.)   E.B.S.

"Grant us, O God of peace and truth, the gracious help of Thy Spirit, that we may amid the things seen which are temporal have knowledge of the unseen things which are eternal. Especially we pray Thee to help us to find in the toil and tumult of life the rest of Christ, that we may know Him and the strength of His fellowship and the guidance of His love. Forgive us that we are so little like Him who perfectly stooped to be made in the likeness of men, and by Thy grace and the power of His resurrection lift us up, we beseech Thee, into His purity and goodness, His faithfulness and obedience, that we may walk even as He walked and work even as He worked who did always the things that pleased Thee and finished the work that Thou gavest Him to do. In His name."

(Y.W.C.A.)   E.B.S.

"O Lord in whose hands are all the issues of life, teach us how to use all that Thou hast given us. Show us how to live to the uttermost, so that we may truly know the meaning of work and love and prayer, of loyalty and of joy. Show us how to use every second of time, every ounce of strength, and every resource of energy. Forgive the wastage of the past, the indolence, the wrong attitudes, the darkness of self. Let us open all our heart and mind to Thee and receive from Thee the strength and the power, the wisdom and the joy that Thou hast promised and that Thou alone canst give. And these things that we need, O Father, we ask in ever fuller and deeper measure for those whom Thou hast given us. Thou wilt show us the path of life. In Thy presence is fullness of joy."

(page 279)   E.B.S.

XXIII. A Message to His Missionary Friends

On Robert E. Speer's birthday, September 10, 1948, one year after his death, Mrs. Speer sent a copy of his book of devotional readings, *Five Minutes a Day*, to the missionaries of the Presbyterian Foreign Board, with the following letter:

When he was a lad at school in Andover, Robert Speer, like other thoughtful boys, was confronted by the eternal question: "Who am I? Where did I come from? Where am I going? Who, and What is behind it all, and what is its meaning, this tangled, puzzling business of human life?" With a clear head, and the firm discipline of legal training, he studied the evidence, in nature, which he dearly loved, in history, where tragedy is so evident, and in the church and the Bible.

Before he went to college he had read the Bible through with great care, and in the Gospels he found the answer to his questions. He saw that God is real, the eternal, ever-present and all powerful Creator, and he saw that God, in His power, His majesty, His glory, and His perfect, selfless love had entered the human scene at a definite point in time and space, had in truth been born of a Virgin, thus lifting all womanhood from the level of a segment of the race to a place of highest privilege and responsibility: that in this human scene He had lived the life of a boy and man among men, as a member of a people prepared through centuries for His coming, and enduring now the limitations of a subject people. In this setting, and working as a carpenter and teacher, He met the full brunt of evil and sin, and died at the hands of men blind with hatred of His holiness. But He rose again from death to become in fullest truth the Redeemer of the world, very God of very God, conqueror of sin, disease, hatred and death, ever present among us as the eternal, ineffable, wholly real Spirit of all light and life and love, and always far more ready to help us than we are to receive His help. From this conviction he never faltered, though his apprehension of it grew ever greater and deeper, transforming him, as Paul was transformed, "in the inward man."

In this truth, central, cosmic and eternal, he saw the answer to all questions and all needs, and to share this truth with all men everywhere became for him henceforth the one business of life. This was "the pearl of great price," and honor, preferment, wealth and power, were not even temptations as compared with it.

The Bible, so easy to neglect and so often misunderstood, held this truth. The church, even with all its human imperfections, was its channel, and so the Student Volunteer Movement and the Board of Foreign Missions became the natural steps to his life work.

Prayer, of which he seldom spoke, was as natural to him as breathing, Bible study as necessary to him as his daily food, and "the practice of the Presence of God" was the very essence of his life.

Like the Scottish philosopher, Hogg of Madras, he understood that "God waits only on our obedience to release His omnipotence in the service of His love," so his one purpose was to bring every thought into captivity to Christ. His reading all centered on this, and for his own satisfaction he had collected out of his notebooks, the little *Five Minutes* that goes to you with this message. He knew the cost to you of your high calling, the perils, the loneliness, the frictions, the separations, the anxieties, the disciplines, but he knew, too, that the wealth of God is greater by far than all our human needs. He never began or ended the day without kneeling in prayer that we "might be—all of us—filled unto all the fullness of God."

With this hope and faith the little book goes to you. May the Spirit whom he so loved and trusted make us "always abounding in the life and joy of our Lord."

Yours in sincerest faith and gratitude,
Emma Bailey Speer

Rockledge
Lakeville, Connecticut
September 10, 1948

APPENDIX I. Honorary Degrees

Robert E. Speer graduated from Princeton University in June, 1889, receiving the B.A. degree. He was valedictorian of his class. In subsequent years he received eight honorary degrees: an M.A. from Yale in 1900; a D.D. from Edinburgh in 1910; the degree of LL.D. from Rutgers and from Wooster in 1916, and from Otterbein in 1926; the degree of Litt. D. from Juniata in 1920, from Washington and Jefferson in 1938, and from Princeton in 1939. The citations of three of these degrees, from Edinburgh in 1910, from Rutgers in 1916, and from Princeton in 1939, follow:

DOCTOR OF DIVINITY

University of Edinburgh:

Robert Elliott Speer, M.A., Secretary, American Presbyterian Board of Foreign Missions.

Mr. Speer is an alumnus of Princeton, where he graduated in 1889, and had not finished his theological curriculum when he was invited in 1891 to fill the position which he still holds. He has written a number of Biblical studies, beginning with *The Man Christ Jesus* in 1896, and, in particular, has published contributions to the literature of missions, including *Missionary Principles and Practice* in 1902, and *Missions and Modern History* in 1904. He held the appointment of Duff Lecturer in 1909-10, and chose for his subject, *Christianity and the Nations*, which has just been published. The roll of our honorary graduates in divinity contains the names of only two laymen; it is never likely to be a large one; but I regard it as a privilege to ask you to add to that list the name of one who, though not a preacher by calling, is recognized as a speaker of commanding power, as a great spiritual force in the Church to which he belongs, and who, by his speaking, his writings, and his administrative work, exercises an altogether unique influence on the religious life of the community.

June 15, 1910.

DOCTOR OF LAWS

The Trustees of Rutgers College have directed that the honorary degree of Doctor of Laws be conferred on Robert Elliott Speer, graduate of Princeton University, Secretary of the Presbyterian Board of Foreign Missions, speaker of rare spirit and power, writer on religion and missions, guide of leaders and workers in statesmanlike policy, servant of the Church and the world-wide Kingdom of God, an example in word and life to many friends, in recognition of his unswerving steadfastness in the faith once delivered, his unsparing devotion to the missionary cause, his gift of high incentive to young men in all our universities and colleges, his power in organizing great forces of the Church, and his executive position in a great denomination always sharing largely in the life of this college.

Rutgers College
October 14, 1916.

DOCTOR OF LETTERS

Robert Elliott Speer, valedictorian of the graduating class fifty years ago; as an undergraduate and later active in the Student Volunteer Movement for Foreign Missions; for nearly half a century Secretary of the Presbyterian Board of Foreign Missions; a Moderator of the General Assembly of the Presbyterian Church; a forceful supporter of interdenominational relationships, at one time president of the Federal Council of Churches of Christ in America, and during the World War chairman of its wartime commission; author of many books and articles dealing with missions, the Bible and the Christian faith.

A capable and inspiring administrator, a champion of the cause of missions, carrying the Gospel to the ends of the earth, a wise and faithful servant in the vineyard of the Lord.

Princeton University
June 20, 1939

APPENDIX II. Addresses at The Hill School

"Dr. Speer . . . has spoken from The Hill [School] pulpit every year since 1891"—*The Hill News*, October 5, 1939. Only once in these forty-eight years did he repeat a sermon or an address.

March 1, 1904	Mr. Speer assists in dedication of the Alumni Chapel.
December 6, 1904	Mr. Speer spoke at the Pottstown Y.M.C.A. meeting.
February 16, 1909	Editorial in *The Hill News:* "Probably there was not one of us who did not feel a stir of ambition as Mr. Speer gave his strong talk on Abraham Lincoln."
November 21, 1910	A Son of Light.
December 12, 1910	"Consider Him."
January 23, 1911	"This one thing I do."
April 24, 1911	"O my God, my soul is cast down within me."
November 6, 1912	Editorial in *The Hill News* praising Mr. Speer.
April 15, 1914	Easter Service: First chapter Romans, fourth verse.
November 18, 1914	Editorial in *The Hill News:* "Robert E. Speer on Race Problem."
February 17, 1915	"Christian Character."
April 14, 1915	"Hope."
February 2, 1916	Mr. Speer Reads Story by Kipling. "Conversation."
May 17, 1916	"The Meaning of Religion."

November 15, 1916	25th Anniversary of his first visit to The Hill. "Preparedness."
January 24, 1917	"Boundaries."
February 14, 1917	"Reconstruction of the World by Christianity."
April 25, 1917	"The Justifiability of War."
June 2, 1917	"For Each Man Shall Bear His Own Burden."
October 4, 1917	Pleads that every boy make a good beginning.
November 29, 1917	"Do Your Duty or Die First."
January 24, 1918	"How Can a Man Be Born Anew When He Is Old?"
February 28, 1918	"Christ's Simple Life, a Life for Everyone to Follow."
April 25, 1918	"Song of Deborah."
May 16, 1918	Urges moral courage in strong terms.
October 4, 1918	"What Hast Thou That Thou Hast Not Received?"
November 29, 1918	"Harder to Win a Peace than to Win a War."
December 29, 1918	Places truth and justice above life.
January 24, 1919	"The Lessons of the War."
February 22, 1919	"Liberty."
March 14, 1919	"Moral Uses of the Body."
April 25, 1919	Easter Sermon: "The Resurrection of Christ the Cornerstone of Christian Religion."
May 16, 1919	"The Goodness and Severity of God Needed by Men."
October 23, 1919	"Story of Jonathan and Absalom."
November 14, 1919	"Temptation."
April 22, 1920	"Consider Jesus."
May 20, 1920	"Changing Our World."
September 30, 1920	"Know Ye Not That I Must Be About My Father's Business?"
October 21, 1920	"Opportunity of Present Generation to Influence World's Future."
April 22, 1921	"Martin Luther's Three Principles of Life."

May 6, 1921	"Four Principles by Which to Live—Moral Revolt, Freedom, Power, Sacrifice."
October 5, 1922	"Purpose of Education."
December 2, 1922	"Children of the Light."
January 14, 1923	Reads Kipling's "Miracle of Puran Bhagat."
April 26, 1923	"Is Lying Justifiable?"
October 25, 1923	"St. Paul's Character."
October 16, 1924	"We are Trustees of Our Name, of Our School and of Our Country."
	Addresses first Mission Band—"Shortness of Distance between Points on Earth."
December 4, 1927	"Consider Jesus."
October 11, 1928	"Good Character."
October 11, 1929	"Friendship."
May 15, 1930	"Can a Man Be Made Over Again?"
December 12, 1930	"Two Attitudes of Life as Personified by Two Sons of David."
March 12, 1931	"If the foundations be destroyed, what can the righteous do?"
March 17, 1932	Memorial service for Dr. Joseph Cook.
October 13, 1932	"Christianity."
March 16, 1933	"Christ's Fellowship."
November 16, 1933	"Life of Major Gordon."
April 19, 1934	"A Venturesome Life."
October 25, 1935	"Brotherly Love."
April 26, 1935	Easter Sermon, "Victory Can Be Won Both After and Out of Defeat."
October 24, 1936	"Steadfastness."
November 11, 1937	"Environment, Heredity, Will the Main Factors in a Man's Career."
October 5, 1939	"The Fool's Prayer."
May 2, 1940	"The Modern World's Belief in Jesus Christ and Christianity."
November 15, 1940	"Invisible Movements of Thought."
May 1, 1942	"Judas Iscariot."
December 4, 1942	"The Qualities of the Future World."
January 28, 1944	"It's the Little People and Things in Life that Change the World."
May 24, 1946	"The Value of the Body as Compared to the Value of the Soul."
June —, 1947	"Co-operation not Conflict."

APPENDIX III. Books by Robert E. Speer

Title	Publisher	Number of Pages	Date of Publication
The Gospel of Luke	International Committee Y.M.C.A.	62	1892
Studies in the Book of Acts	International Committee Y.M.C.A.	159	1892
The Man Christ Jesus	Fleming H. Revell Company	248	1896
Report on Missions in Asia, Persia, China, Japan, Korea	Board of Foreign Missions of the Presbyterian Church in the U.S.A.	383	1897
Missions and Politics in Asia: Studies of the Spirit of the Eastern peoples, the Present Making of History in Asia, and the Part therein of Christian Missions	Fleming H. Revell Company	271	1898
A Memorial of a True Life; the Biography of Hugh Mc-Allister Beaver	Association Press	308	1898
Remember Jesus Christ	Fleming H. Revell Company	220	1899
Studies of the Man Paul	Fleming H. Revell Company	303	1900
Presbyterian Foreign Missions	The Board of Foreign Missions of the Presbyterian Church in the U.S.A.	296	1901
Christ and Life	Fleming H. Revell Company	232	1901
What Constitutes a Missionary Call	Student Volunteer Movement	30 —	1901 1901
Missionary Principles and Practice	Fleming H. Revell Company	552	1902

Title	Publisher	Number of Pages	Date of Publication
The Principles of Jesus	Fleming H. Revell Company	280	1902
A Young Man's Questions	Fleming H. Revell Company	223	1903
A Memorial of Howard Tracy Pitkin	Fleming H. Revell Company	310	1903
The Second Coming of Christ	Gospel Publishing House	47	1903
Missions and Modern History (Two Volumes)	Fleming Revell Company	714	1904
Young Men Who Overcame	Fleming H. Revell Company	229	1905
The Marks of a Man	Methodist Book Publishing Company	197	1907
The Master of the Heart	Fleming H. Revell Company	241	1908
The Value of Hardness	Robert Scott, London	45	1908
A Memorial of Alice Jackson	Fleming H. Revell Company	128	1908
"How to Speak Effectively Without Notes"	Fleming H. Revell Company	28	1909
Servants of the King	Young People's Missionary Movement of the U.S. and Canada	219	1909
Paul, the All-Round Man	Fleming H. Revell Company	127	1909
The Deity of Christ	Fleming H. Revell Company	64	1909
The Duff Lectures for 1910: Christianity and the Nations	Fleming H. Revell Company	399	1910
Missions in South America	The Board of Foreign Missions of the Presbyterian Church in the U.S.A.	179	1910
The Hakim Sahib, The Foreign Doctor, A Biography of Joseph Plumb Cochran, M.D., of Persia	Fleming H. Revell Company	384	1911
A Christian's Habits	The Westminster Press	114	1911
The Light of the World	The Central Committee of the United Study of Missions	372	1911

Title	Publisher	Number of Pages	Date of Publication
The Cole Lectures for 1911: *Some Great Leaders in the World Movement*	Fleming H. Revell Company	295	1911
South American Problems	The Student Volunteer Movement	270	1912
Men Who Were Found Faithful	Fleming H. Revell Company	187	1912
One Girl's Influence, the Life of Louise Andrews	Privately Printed	125	1914
The Smyth Lectures for 1913: *Studies of Missionary Leadership*	The Westminster Press	283	1914
John's Gospel, The Greatest Book in the World	Fleming H. Revell Company	208	1915
The Unity of the Americas	Missionary Education Movement of the United States and Canada	115	1915
Report on Siam, the Philippines, Japan, Chosen and China	Board of Foreign Missions of the Presbyterian Church in the U.S.A.	512	1916
The Stuff of Manhood:	Fleming H. Revell Company	184	1917
The Merritt Lectures for 1917: *The Christian Man, The Church and the War*	The Macmillan Company	105	1918
How to Speak Effectively without Notes	Fleming H. Revell Company	28	1918
The New Opportunity of the Church	The Macmillan Company	111	1919
The Gospel and the New World	Fleming H. Revell Company	313	1920
Report on India and Persia	Board of Foreign Missions of the Presbyterian Church in the U.S.A.	694	1922
A Missionary Pioneer in the Far East: A Memorial of D. B. McCartee	Fleming H. Revell Company	224	1922
Of One Blood: A Short Study of the Race Problem	Council of Women for Home Missions and Missionary Education		

Title	Publisher	Number of pages	Date of Publication
	Movement of U.S. and Canada	258	1924
Race and Race Relations	Fleming H. Revell Company	434	1924
Seeking the Mind of Christ	Fleming H. Revell Company	187	1926
The Unfinished Task of Foreign Missions: The James Sprunt Lectures	Fleming H. Revell Company	348	1926
The Church and Missions	George H. Doran Company	252	1926
Report on China and Japan	The Board of Foreign Missions of the Presbyterian Church in the U.S.A.	528	1927
Sir James Ewing	Fleming H. Revell Company	307	1928
Are Foreign Missions Done For?	The Board of Foreign Missions of the Presbyterian Church in the U.S.A.	152	1928
Some Living Issues	Fleming H. Revell Company	280	1930
Author, Chap. X, "What is the Value of the Religious Values of the non-Christian Religions?	International Missionary Council	424	1928
	International Missionary Council	22	1928
"Lu Taifu": Charles Lewis, M.D., A Pioneer Surgeon in China	The Board of Foreign Missions Presbyterian Church in the U.S.A.	216	1930
Owen Crimmins: Tales from the Magalloway Country	Fleming H. Revell Company	93	1931
"Rethinking Missions Examined: An Attempt at a Just Review of the Report of the Appraisal Committee of the Laymen's Mission Inquiry"	Fleming H. Revell Company	64	1933
The Finality of Jesus Christ	Fleming H. Revell Company	386	1933
Christian Realities	Fleming H. Revell Company	256	1935

Title	Publisher	Number of pages	Date of Publication
The Meaning of Christ to Me	Fleming H. Revell Company	192	1936
George Bowen of Bombay: A Memoir	Privately Printed	366	1938
John J. Eagan: A Memoir	Privately Printed	226	1939
When Christianity Was New	Fleming H. Revell Company	192	1939
Five Minutes a Day	Westminster Press	384	1943
Jesus and Our Human Problems	Fleming H. Revell Company	194	1946

APPENDIX IV. Footnotes

1 The facts that follow concerning Robert Speer's ancestry and family are taken from an unpublished Memorial which he wrote about his son Elliott after Elliott's death.

2 Robert E. Speer, writing for his own family and not for publication, describes his boyhood.

3 His mother's grave.

4 R. E. Speer, *Remember Jesus Christ*, pp. 53, 54.

5 R. E. Speer, *A Memorial of a True Life: A Biography of Hugh McAllister Beaver*, Fleming H. Revell Company, 1898; pp. 39, 40.

6 R. E. Speer to his brother William, Sept. 9, 1883.

7 Naseby, the battle fought June 14, 1645, near the village of that name in central England, where Cromwell defeated Charles I.

8 Written by R.E.S.

9 R. E. Speer's record for his children.

10 John Henry Strong to W. R. Wheeler.

11 C. F. P. Bancroft to R. E. Speer, July 29, 1885.

12 C. F. P. Bancroft to James McCoss, July 29, 1885.

13 Rev. Frederick Schweitzer to W. R. Wheeler, 1953.

14 V. Lansing Collins to Harry L. Bowlby, Nov. 27, 1933.

15 T. H. P. Sailer to W. R. Wheeler.

16 Austin Philip Guiles to Mrs. R. E. Speer.

17 Arthur Y. Meeker to W. R. Wheeler, Jan. 7, 1954.

18 William Harris to W. R. Wheeler, April 1953.

19 F. J. Tooker, M.D., to W. R. Wheeler, Feb. 6, 1952.

20 Fred G. Klerekoper to W. R. Wheeler, 1953.

21 James B. Hodgson to W. R. Wheeler, 1953.

22 William P. Shedd to his mother, Oct. 18, 1891.

23 Address by R. E. Speer, Student Volunteer Movement, Third International Convention, Feb. 1898.

97 R. E. Speer, *Some Living Issues,* 1930; Chap. IV, "The Virgin Birth."

98 R. E. Speer, *Some Living Issues,* 1930; Chap. XII, "The Equality of Women in the Church."

99 William M. Miller, Jr. to W. R. Wheeler, Sept. 29, 1953.

100 R. E. Speer, "How to Speak Effectively Without Notes."

101 R. E. Speer. Address.

102 Notes by W. R. Wheeler.

103 F. Ernest Johnson to W. R. Wheeler, April 6, 1953.

104 John H. Reisner to W. R. Wheeler.

105 Bishop Francis J. McConnell to W. R. Wheeler.

106 Walter W. Rankin to W. R. Wheeler.

107 Samuel McCrae Cavert, Address at Memorial Service at the First Presbyterian Church in New York, Dec. 15, 1947.

108 R. E. Speer, *Christian Realities.*

109 R. E. Speer, *Missions in South America,* p. 78.

110 John A. Mackay.

111 Samuel Guy Inman to W. R. Wheeler.

112 Samuel Guy Inman to W. R. Wheeler.

113 Samuel Guy Inman to W. R. Wheeler.

114 Fred C. Macmillan to W. R. Wheeler.

115 R. E. Speer, "A Sunday in Santiago," Chap. IX, in *Modern Missions in Chile and Brazil,* edited by W. R. Wheeler.

116 Stuart Nye Hutchison to W. R. Wheeler.

117 T. F. Smiley to W. R. Wheeler, July 22, 1953.

118 W. R. Hervey, M.D., to W. R. Wheeler, 1939.

119 Stanley A. Hunter to W. R. Wheeler.

120 R. E. Speer, "The Old, Ever New, Call of Christ," June 1, 1927.

121 Foreign Mission Board Manual, par. 1.

122 George T. Scott to W. R. Wheeler, Nov. 1953.

123 R. E. Speer to W. M. Hayes, July 8, 1921.

124 George T. Scott to W. R. Wheeler.

125 R. E. Speer to W. R. Wheeler.

126 John A. Mackay to W. R. Wheeler.

127 Archbishop William Temple to R. E. Speer.

128 Galen M. Fisher to W. R. Wheeler.

129 Action of Foreign Board concerning Laymen's Inquiry, Mar. 20, 1933.

130 R. E. Speer's Sermon in *The Christian Century.*

131 R. E. Speer, Memoir of Elliott Speer.

132   R. E. Speer to Cleland B. McAfee, Sept. 18, 1934.
133   R. E. Speer to W. M. Miller, Oct. 20, 1934.
134   R. E. Speer to Dr. and Mrs. W. M. Miller, Oct. 31, 1934.
135   Emma Bailey Speer to W. R. Wheeler, June 16, 1933.
136   W. R. Inge, *Personal Religion and the Life of Devotion.*
137   C. E. Scott to W. R. Wheeler.
138   R. E. Speer to C. E. Scott.
139   Howard L. Rubendall to W. R. Wheeler.
140   R. E. Speer. Address at Memorial Service for Elliott Speer, Nov. 11, 1934.
141   R. E. Speer to W. R. Wheeler, Nov. 10, 1945.
142   R. E. Speer, *The Crisis Decade,* Chap. 33.
143   Resolution of General Assembly, May 1937, Concerning Robert Speer's Service.
144   Letter of Appreciation of Robert Speer's Service by Syria Mission, 1937.
145   Robert E. Speer to editor of a missionary magazine concerning his retirement.
146   W. P. Schell to W. R. Wheeler.
147   Emma Bailey Speer to W. R. Wheeler, Mar. 30, 1954.
148   E. Fay Campbell to W. R. Wheeler.
149   Robert E. Speer to Lewis Mudge.
150   Willard C. Mellin to W. R. Wheeler, Aug. 6, 1953.
151   Eugene Carson Blake to W. R. Wheeler, June 1953.
152   From *John E. Williams of Nanking,* 1937, by W. R. Wheeler.
153   R. E. Speer to George H. Trull, Dec. 21, 1947.
154   Prayer of Thanksgiving for Robert E. Speer, Henry Sloane Coffin.
155   Christina Rossetti, "None Other Lamb."
156   W. H. Foulkes, *Facile Princeps.*
157   K. S. Latourette to W. R. Wheeler, Dec. 12, 1953.
158   Luther A. Weigle to W. R. Wheeler.
159   K. S. Latourette to W. R. Wheeler, Dec. 12, 1953.
160   Daniel A. Poling to W. R. Wheeler.
161   Clarence Macartney to W. R. Wheeler, June 10, 1953.
162   John Timothy Stone to W. R. Wheeler.
163   J. Leighton Stuart to W. R. Wheeler.
164   Henry S. Leiper to W. R. Wheeler, Mar. 19, 1953.
165   Emile Cailliet to W. R. Wheeler, Nov. 9, 1953.
166   J. Christy Wilson, *Apostle to Islam,* page 222.

167 *Charles Kingsley, His Letters, Memories of His Life*, by his wife, Chap. 21.
168 R. E. Speer, *Studies of the Man Christ Jesus*, pp. 7, 8, 244, 245.
169 John A. Mackay.
170 R. E. Speer, *The Marks of a Man*, pp. 169, 170.
171 R. E. Speer, *The Stuff of Manhood*, pp. 30, 31.
172 Emma Bailey Speer to W. R. Wheeler.
173 R. E. Speer, *Owen Crimmins*, p. 93.
174 R. E. Speer, *Remember Jesus Christ*, pp. 11, 13, 19, 33, 34.
175 "Rethinking Missions Examined," by R. E. Speer.
176 R. E. Speer, Preface, *Five Minutes a Day*.
177 John D. Hayes to Mrs. Robert E. Speer, July 26, 1953.
178 R. E. Speer, *Christian Realities*, pp. 34, 39.

Index

323

Description, in Introduction, by John A. Mackay, 9-11; description, in Preface, by W. R. Wheeler, 13-15; his attitude toward a biography, 15, 16; Mrs. Speer's opinion of a biography, 15, 16; action of the General Assembly concerning a biography, 16; choice of W. R. Wheeler as writer of the book, 16; his boyhood home, 21-23; death of his mother, 23; his great aunt comes to help in the home, 23; his first school, 23; his joy in hunting and fishing, 24; his physical health and illnesses, 24; his birth, September 10, 1867 in Huntingdon, Pa., 25; his ancestral background, 25; his great-, great-, great-, great-grandfather, Henry Carpenter, 25; his great-, great-, great-grandfather, Robert Elliott, 25; his great-, great-grandfather, Benjamin Elliott, 25; his great-, great-grandmother, Mary Carpenter, 25; Benjamin Elliott, first sheriff of Huntingdon County in 1787, and an associate judge, voted in the Pennsylvania Convention of 1787 for the ratification of the Federal Constitution, 24; Benjamin Elliott's daughter, Martha, marries David McMurtrie of Huntingdon, October 2, 1795, 26; William McMurtrie, son of David, grandfather of R. E. Speer, a successful merchant, iron master and land owner in Huntingdon, Pa., 26; William McMurtrie's daughter, Martha Ellen, marries R. E. Speer's father, Robert Milton Speer, 26; Robert Speer's grandfather, Robert Speer, comes to Huntingdon from County Antrim in 1822, 26; he begins business in one of